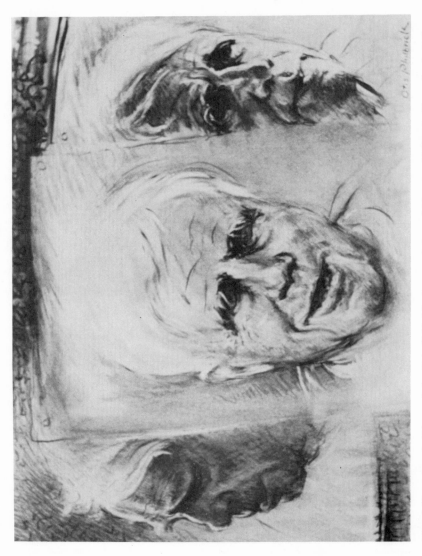

Sketch for triptych lithograph by Otis Philbrick, by permission of Margaret Philbrick, Westenhook Gallery, Sheffield, Massachusetts. By permission of the Jones Library, Inc.

ROBERT FROST

studies of the poetry

ROBERT FROST

studies of the poetry

Edited with an Introduction by
Kathryn Gibbs Harris

G.K.HALL &CO.

70 LINCOLN STREET, BOSTON, MASS.

Library of Congress Cataloging in Publication Data

Main entry under title:

Robert Frost: studies of the poetry.

   Includes index.
   1. Frost, Robert, 1874–1963–Criticism and interpre-
tation–Addresses, essays, lectures. I. Harris,
Kathryn Gibbs.
PS3511.R94Z9183   811'.5'2   79–19870
ISBN 0–8161–8397–X

This publication is printed on permanent/durable acid-free paper
MANUFACTURED IN THE UNITED STATES OF AMERICA

FOR

     . . . the elves
Although they are no less there.

Contents

Introduction

Judgment is the last business, if it is any business at all, of the serious literary scholar or critic. Judgment of whether a work of literature is bad or good is a poor habit which creeps into the real business of independent research, exploration, from the hasty magazine review or from the school book report wrongly taught. The studies in this collection represent not only a variety of separate views, but also the rich intellectual and life experience of the poetry and the poet we need to know more about. During the 1960s there were stirrings but during the 1970s there has been a real shift in the way students are reading Robert Frost's poems. Many of the old ways to understand Frost's poems anew which are set out here could not have been possible until the present time for reasons stated by the individual contributors. But one major advantage for current Frost scholars is the easier access we now have to early secondary material which can properly be documented; the most exciting development is that much more primary material has recently been made generally available and library and private holdings pointed up.

Robert Lee Frost died on January 29, 1963. The 100th anniversary of his birthdate was celebrated March 26, 1974, and these two dates are probably more significant to the present work in Frost studies than anything else. Early we loved the poems of Robert Frost in the editions for children, in the yellowing pocketbook editions we carried through junior high school. There we found the wisdom we had heard in the summers at the old farm: the resonances of bees in the apple blossoms—the woodland walks, the stars, and the Christmas snows. But while these things are in the poems, they are not the poems. Independent research into Frost's poems and their background is at the stage where, even now, we do not know how to state exactly what the poems are, and we may never be able to do that with precision. Indeed, Frost was against the idea of exactitude in either the arts or the sciences, but he did think it was possible to come close to a work of art or to a poet's sense. We are back to the long patience that comes before any sort of critical judgment.

The exciting, if often difficult, process of finding out about the poems' background and sense is the initial purpose of this book. The contributors to this volume hope that the research here published will help others to explore Frost's poems, to find first that delight and then that wisdom of which he spoke — and also to enjoy some of the various ways research takes.

Most of the early critical response to Frost's poems was printed in the form of reviews; Linda Wagner collects these in *Robert Frost: The Critical Reception* (Burt Franklin, 1977). Some of the major early essays (including work by Randall Jarrell, Lionel Trilling and Lawrance Thompson) were collected by James M. Cox in *Robert Frost: A Collection of Critical Essays* (Prentice-Hall, 1962). Critical books of the recent period began with Elizabeth Isaacs's *An Introduction to Robert Frost* (Alan Swallow, 1962) which reviewed then current background knowledge and suggested Frost might be read from an existential point of view. John Robert Doyle's *The Poetry of Robert Frost: An Analysis* (Hafner, 1962) gave a sophisticated structural analysis of the poems. Reuben Brower's *The Poetry of Robert Frost: Constellations of Intention* (Oxford University Press, 1963), which made the point that the poems had to be read as a whole canon in order to be understood fully, and Philip L. Gerber's *Robert Frost* (Twayne, 1966), which provided an overview of the career and the craftsmanship of the poems, were the only other book-length critical studies on Frost until Frank Lentricchia's *Robert Frost: Modern Poetics and the Landscape of the Self* (Duke University Press, 1975). Lentricchia's reading concentrated on two elements: the imagery in the poems and the relation of the poems to philosophers, several of whom Frost was known to have liked. (There was, in 1972, a critical book in Japanese by Shichinosuke Anzai, *Robert Frost no Shi,* published by the Taigenshobo Press, Tokyo which has not been translated into English.) Richard Poirier's long literary meditation *Robert Frost: The Way of Knowing* (Oxford University Press, 1977) compared Frost with a variety of poets past and contemporary, showing how the poems direct the reader to "things we cannot 'know' and whereof, as Wittengenstein suggested, we should not speak" (p. 295). But probably more helpful even than these major secondary sources were the primary materials to come out during this period, beginning with the scholarly edition of the poems edited by Edward Connery Lathem, *The Poetry of Robert Frost* (Holt, Rinehart and Winston, 1969).

Undoubtedly the letters, as Lawrance Thompson once advised me, are the chief helpful source for the scholar of Frost's poems. Those edited by Louis Untermeyer in 1963 were the first to appear — *The Letters of Robert Frost to Louis Untermeyer* (Holt, Rinehart, 1963) — and they reflected the poet's energetic literary wit. Thompson's scholarly, chronologically arranged, life-spanning collection, *Selected Letters of Robert Frost,* was published in 1964 by Holt, Rinehart. Some letters had been included by Margaret Bartlett Anderson in the volume *Robert Frost and John Bartlett: The Record of a Friendship* (Holt, Rinehart, 1963) which reflected friendship between the two families. Finally, in 1972, Arnold Grade edited *Family Letters of Robert and Elinor Frost* (Albany: SUNY Press). Each of these published collections of letters presented a somewhat different side of the poet's personality as he related to matters of family or business or friendship, literary and otherwise.

Also in the 1970s two books of largely primary materials were published. Elaine Barry's *Robert Frost on Writing* (Rutgers University Press, 1973) includes material (some previously unpublished) having to do with what the poet thought about writing and an introductory essay on Frost as a literary critic. In 1975 Reginald L. Cook brought out a book (*Robert Frost: A Living Voice* [University of Massachusetts Press]) of the tapes of readings and lectures by Frost at the Bread Loaf Writers' Conference which he edited and interspersed with chapters of explanation and reminiscence. But perhaps the single most helpful primary source of background of the poetry was Lesley Frost's *New Hampshire's Child: The Derry Journals of Lesley Frost* (Albany: SUNY Press, 1969). These journals, in facsimile, are those written by Frost's eldest daughter during the years at the Derry farm when she was between the ages of five and nine. They reflect the educational procedures of her parents and many situations which may have occasioned poems. Lesley Frost wrote the Introduction which, along with other essays and interviews she has done, have added to the understanding of the early period of the family. Lawrance Thompson and Arnold Grade did the editing and notation work for the volume.

Biography has recently become the focus of more attention. General interest and much anticipation awaited the three volumes of Robert Frost's official biography which came out haltingly. Lawrance Thompson (*Robert Frost* [Holt, Rinehart, 1966, 1970, and with R. H. Winnick, 1976]) waited a respectable time after the poet's death to publish, and died before completion of the third volume. Meantime, William A. Sutton noticed extensive biographical materials written by one of the very few independent researchers during Frost's early career which he brought to the attention of Lesley Frost. Much of the work of the late Robert S. Newdick was therefore published in *Newdick's Season of Frost: An Interrupted Biography of Robert Frost* (Albany: SUNY Press, 1976). Elizabeth Shepley Sergeant's *Robert Frost: The Trial by Existence* (Holt, Rinehart, 1960) and Jean Gould's *Robert Frost: The Aim Was Song* (Dodd, Meade, 1964) were superseded only because data were not available to them as was George W. Nitchie's semibiographical book, *Human Values in the Poetry of Robert Frost* (Duke University Press, 1960). In addition to these biographical studies we should note some of the many available memoirs and reminiscences that have been collected along with the critical work.

Primarily critical essays were compiled by Louis P. Simpson in his *Profile of Robert Frost* (Charles Merrill, 1971). Among the eight contributors were Frost specialists James M. Cox and William H. Pritchard and writers Alfred Kazin and Robert Penn Warren. Even a small press collection, *Gone Into If Not Explained* (Best Cellar, 1976), done by Greg Kuzma, included brief essays by younger poets and students. Richard Wilbur gave to it an appreciation of "The Gum Gatherer" and Maxine Kumin a delightful note on "Provide, Provide." The three-volume trilogy from the Universtiy Press of Mississippi, *Frost: Centennial Essays* (Vol. I, ed. Frost Centennial Committee, 1974; Vols. II and III, ed. Jac Tharpe, 1976, 1978) shows a feeling for the milieu during Frost's lifetime. To indicate some of the ore to be mined from these volumes by one example from Volume III, I cite the story told by N. Arthur Bleau, "Robert Frost's Favorite Poem" (pp. 174–177) with a note by Lesley Frost. When Bleau was a student, Frost, on a reading tour, told him the occasion of "Stopping By Woods On a Snowy Evening." Having gone to market to sell farm vegetables on December 22 and not having sold any, the poet and his horse cart came to a halt on the road home. The poet was saddened by the bleak weather and concerned about providing for his family with Christmas so near. Lesley Frost adds that when the same story was told to her, her father said he "bawled" — broke down and cried. This, he told her, meant that it was all right for men to cry. Compared with Frost's other versions of stories in the biographies and memoirs, this one stands on record as an instance of his use of story as parable (the variation to his daughter) and as an instance of his having spoken of the occasion of a poem twice with substantially the same story. The story becomes part of the background of the poem for the critic and may indeed have bearing upon the poet's original impetus and "truth of feeling." The critic will need to determine in what way Frost's own stories (primary material) and others' memory of them (secondary, but, in a sense, primary data) have meaning for the poems.

An *Atlantic Monthly* essay by Theodore Morrison (July 1967, pp. 77–79) probably initiated recognition of the complexity of Frost's personality, especially in his later years. Kathleen Johnston Morrison's *Robert Frost: A Pictorial Chronicle* (Holt, Rinehart, 1974) extended the view and added to biographical data. Other material, such as tapes and notes of reading and lectures, was generated by Frost's travels (particularly later in his life) and is today found unpublished in personal holdings and libraries. In 1964 Little, Brown did publish F. D. Reeve's account of *Robert Frost in Russia* but otherwise much of the travel material remains to be examined.

Textual scholarship of the primary materials is an untouched field for the critic. Principal textual scholar of the Frost material is Edward Connery Lathem who contributed a catalog of items circulated to major libraries during the anniversary year. Lathem's *Robert Frost 100* (David Godine, 1974) contains, to cite one important example, a description of a copy of *Collected Poems* (Henry Holt, 1930) owned by Genevieve Taggard in which Frost had penciled the dates of poems. She had, at his request, later erased most of them. The owner quotes Frost, in a note included with the book, as saying to her: "I didn't mind your having them, but someone else may get your copy and write an article" (Lathem, p. 56). In 1972 Lathem and Lawrance Thompson selected and edited *Robert Frost: Poetry and Prose* (Holt, Rinehart) which added a number of previously unpublished primary items including five groups of "Poems He Left Behind." Mr. Lathem has edited a new selected edition, *Robert Frost: North of Boston: Poems* (Dodd, Meade, 1977), containing some J. J. Lankes woodcuts that Frost liked. The original volume by that title is extended to include poems drawn from later books fitting, as the dust jacket explains, Frost's criterion of "scattered poems in a form suggested by the eclogues of Virgil." It is a timely edition because of the strong current interest in characterization in the poetry.

A useful listing of books from those which had belonged to the poet and were said to have been read to him was published in 1968 by Arnold Grade ("A Chronicle of Robert Frost's Early Reading," *Bulletin of the New York Public Library* 72, 611–28). Donald J. Greiner's book, *Robert Frost: The Poet and His Critics* (American Library Association, 1974), although highly selective, is annotated at length. In the same year Peter Van Egmond's *The Critical Reception of Robert Frost* (G. K. Hall) brought together briefly annotated reviews, interviews and talks, letters, news items, bibliographies and checklists, articles, anthologies, poems to or about Frost, dissertations, and foreign criticism. In 1976 Frank and Melissa Lentricchia compiled a listing which put together most of the earlier bibliographical work. Their appendices are newly helpful as well as their index of authors of secondary material, *Robert Frost: A Bibliography, 1913–1974* (Scarecrow, 1976).

Another source of stimulation of rereadings of Frost's poems has been the increase of papers read and sessions organized at scholarly and professional meetings. In fact, the occasion for this book and a nucleus of its contributors were drawn primarily from a series of three Frost seminar sessions of the Modern Language Association of America. At the Midwest MLA in St. Louis in November, 1976, in the seminar "New Approaches in Frost Scholarship," papers were read on Frost's literary sources remembered by ear, on psychological approaches to the poems, on biographical sources for the lyric voice, and on the realism-Romanticism paradox. That seminar petitioned MLA at the national level for the special session the following year, "The Intellectual Background of Robert Frost's Poems" (Chicago, 1977), at which papers were given on Swedenborg's philosophical influence on Frost and others, the Wordsworthian background, the religious attitudes in the poems, and Frost's Latin background. Another petition with more than 250 signatures requested a further session in New York, 1978 which was titled "The Biographical Background of the Poems" and included papers on problems of biography, Frost's life in New Hampshire, Frost's travels in the United States and his travels abroad, and Frost's relations with other poets he met.

For shape and balance in this volume, essays needed to be added to those already drawn from our meetings. For instance, a discussion of the poet's knowledge of Greek was sought to balance that of his Latin background while to complete the collection's treatment of scholarly methodology, which already included linguistic analysis of a single poem, we requested a general essay on Frost's sense of poetic form. Accordingly, the essays in the first section, *Form*, illustrate two approaches. Donald J. Greiner examines many facets of Frost's "old ways to be new," how Frost's intent to "make a difference" in American poetry was and was not understood. John A. Rea, whose essay was presented as a paper in the Division of Linguistics at MLA in 1977, gives a finely precise analysis, using textual methods as well as linguistic ones, of the poem "Nothing Gold Can Stay." Many of the hidden formal intricacies of this unusually rich poem are thus revealed. Both essays show the poet's intense concern with formal elements.

The second section, *Attitude,* presents two discussions of the general structure of the poems. Ronald Bieganowski ties the religious consciousness of the poems securely to Frost's sense of place. The metaphysical concept of his essay becomes easy to understand as it is explained in terms of Frost's attitude toward the world. Marjorie Cook, who organized a Frost session at MLA in 1974 on the topic of "Play in Frost's Poetry," concentrates on the attitude of detached irony as it comes into a possible clash with a sense of commitment.

Section three is titled *Problems.* Two essays, one by Philip L. Gerber and one by Clifford Lyons, attack the problem of the central paradox of freedom and necessity which so fascinated Robert Frost throughout his lifetime and which may be traced in his poems. These two well-known Frost authorities differ in their readings of the poems on this problem, both in assumptions made and in conclusions drawn. Both offer serious and consequential criticism. William A. Sutton, who edited the Newdick biographical materials noted earlier, contributes an essay on problems he has found facing both Newdick and Thompson in the biographical work, while Peter Van Egmond, whose bibliography is mentioned above, provides a note on current problems in bibliography, a modified version of his remarks at the MLA session in 1978.

The fourth section, *Background,* is necessarily the longest, containing seven papers. Sister Jeremy Finnegan uses her knowledge of Latin poetry and of an unusual variety of poems and other sources to show how Frost's auditory memory helped him in his work. Her essay is drawn from two papers, one read for MMLA in 1976, the other at MLA in Chicago in 1977. Robert Fleissner, with the ingenuity that characterizes his research, establishes a convincing connection between Wordsworth's Lucy poems and Frost's "The Road Not Taken" which sheds light not only on Frost's poem but also on his general life intention. The paper setting out this argument was delivered at MMLA in 1978. James K. Guimond analyzes, using biographical source material and reference to psychological mechanisms, Frost's *A Way Out,* the short play that has received almost no attention. He sees in the play a conflict between the "pastoral and urbane sides" of Frost's personality.

My own essay examines sources of the lyric impulse, first by itemizing the Frost poems that mention birds and noting their use and then, by using biographical reference, commenting on their "tone of meaning." The essay, an extension of one read at MMLA in 1976, also looks at the phenomenon of "hearing voices" as it relates to Frost's interest in Yeats. Nancy C. Joyner's essay, read as an MLA paper in 1974, makes a breakthrough in explaining Frost's use of biblical material. She examines especially his comedic use of scriptual references, showing how, even in the outrageously hilarious effects, the wit points up fresh and otherwise unavailable exegetical interpretation.

In one of the final two studies in the *Background* section, James F. Knapp concentrates on the Greek literature Frost liked the best and tells us why the poet was drawn to it. Engaging his own knowledge of the Greek language and literature, the author writes that Frost's "love for the early Greek world" allowed him to "sail in imagination to an age when tree and stone and brook were alive and sacred." This new reading is also informed by a knowledge of pre-Socratic philosophy which interested Frost. Mordecai Marcus's study of "Mending Wall" and other poems (which is based on a paper first presented at MMLA in 1976) tackles some psychoanalytic criticism of Frost by employing Erik Erikson's theory of developmental stages. The author questions whether the psychoanalytic critic can find a way to enhance the reading of poems for the general reader who has a "considerable sense of a wide range of human feelings." The author's analysis also shows the range of human feelings existing in the poems.

All of the work presented in this collection is newly researched and documented by Frost scholars. An effort has also been made to choose essays that reflect the extensiveness and variety of Frost's knowledge and interests. At the same time that the writers in this volume are in some way specialists, they have written essays that are lively and interesting and readable for a general audience. Sometimes, as in the discussion of the psychological approach to the poems, the writer has even made the general availability of his special approach the subject of part of his discussion. Therefore, although far-ranging areas of expertise have been brought together in this volume, it is hoped it will be helpful in a wide and general way, available in public as well as academic libraries, and of value even for the advanced high school student. This reference work attempts not to be exhaustive either about the background of the poems or about ways of reading them, but only to establish the considerable realms and ranges in Frost's literary accomplishment. The compiler is grateful to all of those who spent so many hours in bringing about their contributions to this volume, and to those who with vision and courtesy granted our efforts the right to be shared.

KATHRYN GIBBS HARRIS

Acknowledgments

Acknowledgment is made to Holt, Rinehart and Winston and to the Estate of Robert Lee Frost, Alfred C. Edwards, Executor and Sole Trustee, for permission to quote excerpts from books published by Holt, Rinehart and Winston which are both by and about Robert Frost. From *The Poetry of Robert Frost* edited by Edward Connery Lathem. Copyright 1916, 1923, 1928, 1930, 1934, 1939, 1947, 1949, © 1969 by Holt, Rinehart and Winston. Copyright 1936, 1942, 1944, 1945, 1947, 1951, © 1956, 1958, 1961, 1962 by Robert Frost. Copyright © 1964, 1967, 1970, 1973, 1975, 1977 by Lesley Frost Ballantine. Reprinted with permission of Holt, Rinehart and Winston, Publishers.

Acknowledgment is made to the Estate of Robert Lee Frost, Alfred C. Edwards, Exeuctor and Sole Trustee for permission to quote the contents of a draft typescript of Robert Frost's "Nothing Gold Can Stay" in the Amherst College Library which is quoted also by permission of the Trustees of Amherst College.

Acknowledgment is made to Margaret Philbrick for reproduction of the original drawing for a triptych lithograph by Otis Philbrick appearing as a frontispiece to this book, and to the Jones Library, Inc., Amherst for permission to print the drawing.

The editor wishes to thank all librarians who have been helpful to the e-search for this volume, particularly Edward Connery Lathem, formerly Dean of Libraries and Librarian of the College at Dartmouth; the research librarians of Texas A&M University Libraries, Irene B. Hoadley, Director; Winifred B. Sayers, formerly Curator at the Jones Library, Amherst; and the librarians of the Humanities Research Center, Austin. I thank the staff of G. K. Hall & Co., Publishers.

I FORM

The Difference Made for Prosody

Dead since January 29, 1963, Robert Frost would have to marvel today at the lingering presence of his public mask. Despite the unsettling revelations about his life and personality exposed in the many volumes of biographies and letters published since his death, the image of the grandfatherly, white-haired old bard of the nation remains intact for countless readers.[1] One point especially comforting to those who mistakenly persist in describing Frost as an undesigning author of witty asides and uncomplicated poems is that the poet stood firm in the face of criticism from peers and critics who insisted that modern poetry had to be different and difficult. One can envision these readers drawing the battle-lines: T. S. Eliot, Ezra Pound, and Wallace Stevens on one side; Robert Frost standing alone on the other.

Students of both Frost and modern American poetry know that such was not the case.[2] Although he refused to fashion a formal aesthetic or to publish many essays on theory and technique in an effort to educate an audience to the nuances of what was then called the "new poetry," Frost consciously assigned himself the task of changing outmoded ideas about prosody. Clearly not interested in or sympathetic with radical renovations of technique, he altered, never-the-less, many of the standard verse forms even as he insisted upon the need for traditional form in poetry. Reading through his letters, one can only admire his confidence that would "do something" to the state of American poetry. Three months after the publication in London of his first book, A Boy's Will, Frost wrote a letter (July 4, 1913) to his former student John Bartlett which is now well known to specialists. His faith in his ability to change traditional prosody is unmistakable:

> To be perfectly frank with you I am one of the most notable crafts-men of my time. That will transpire presently. I am possibly the only person going who works on any but a worn out theory (princi-ple I had better say) of versification. You see the great successes in recent poetry have been made on the assumption that the music of words was a matter of harmonised vowels and consonants. Both Swinburne and Tennyson arrived largely at effects in assonation. But

1

they were on the wrong track or at any rate on a short track. They
went the length of it. Any one else who goes that way must go after
them. And that's where most are going. I alone of English writers
have consciously set myself to make music out of what I may call
the sound of sense.[3]

If Frost and Bartlett understood what he was up to, other champions of the
new poetry did not. Many editors and reviewers were, in a word, bewildered by
Frost's poems. Accustomed to the militantly experimental forms in the poetry
of Eliot and Pound, today's readers may not realize that Frost's prosody generated controversy and puzzlement when his first books, *A Boy's Will* (1913) and
North of Boston (1914), were published in London. Although his poems "looked like poetry," whereas those of his more radically experimental peers often did
not, his achievement baffled many sensitive readers when it was read aloud. A
case in point is the anonymous two-sentence notice of *A Boy's Will* published
in the London *Times Literary Supplement* (April 10, 1913). Praising the "agree-
able individuality" which persuades the reader to "stop and think," the reviewer
argues nevertheless that some of the thoughts are so feebly expressed that
obscurity results. Frost's disappointment in this and other early notices is reflected in a letter (c. July 3, 1913) which his wife Elinor wrote to Margaret Bartlett:

Rob has been altogether discouraged at times, but I suppose we
ought to be satisfied for the present to get the book published and a
little notice taken of it. Yeats has said to a friend [Ezra Pound],
who repeated the remark to Robert, that it is the best poetry written
in America in a long time. If only he would say so publicly, but he
won't, he is too taken up with his own greatness."[4]

The passage of time between the initial notices of *A Boy's Will* and those of
North of Boston did not enlighten the bewildered. A year later the anonymous
reviewer for the *Times Literary Supplement* (July 2, 1914) mixed praise for the
"naked simplicity" of *North of Boston* with the complaint that the verse form
was monotonous.

Important not for their authorship or perspicacity but for their source, these
two short reviews illustrate the difficulty many readers faced when first examining Frost's poetry. The point is significant, for the sense of bafflement carried
over into even the substantial laudatory essays written by critics sympathetic to
Frost and to most of the new literature published between 1910 and 1925.
Note, for example, the combination of praise and puzzlement in Ford Madox
Hueffer's review in *Outlook* (June 27, 1914). Recommending *North of Boston*
to his readers as an extraordinary achievement, Hueffer resorts to the word
"queer" to describe Frost's prosody: "But Mr. Frost's verse is so queer, so harsh,
so unmusical that the most prosaic of readers need not on that account be
frightened away." Hueffer enthusiastically endorses Frost, ranking him higher
than Whitman, but it is clear that he does not understand Frost's breakthrough.

Quoting the first seven lines of the blank verse "Mending Wall," he says that they can hardly be called blank verse. His uncertainty is illustrated by his description of the line "Where they have left not one stone on stone" as a "truly bewildering achievement." Although he never urges Frost to write free verse, Hueffer wonders why he does not. Finally, he does not care what kind of prosody Frost uses as long as he continues to create: "He may use rhymed Alexandrines for all I care."

From today's persepctive, one can sympathize with Hueffer's observation about free verse. To the unprepared reader in 1914, "The Death of the Hired Man" and "Home Burial" *looked* more like free verse than blank verse, and thus it is not surprising that Frost was championed for a while as a new leader of the *vers libre* movement. Comparisons of his own prosody to free verse would later anger the more established Frost, but in 1914 he was in no position to quibble. He wrote to John Cournos (July 8, 1914):

> I have just read Hueffer's article and I like every word of it. What more could anyone ask for a while. My versification seems to bother people more than I should have expected — I suppose because I have been so long accustomed to thinking of it in my own private way. It is as simple as this: there are the very regular preestablished accent and the measure of blank verse; and there are the very irregular accent and measure of speaking intonation. I am never more pleased than when I can get these into strained relation. I like to drag and break the intonation across the meter as waves first comb and then break stumbling on the shingle.[5]

Lest the reader mistakenly believe that British critics made all of the unperceptive comments about Frost's versification, I call attention to statements by American reviewers Alice C. Henderson and Jessie B. Rittenhouse. Hueffer's confusion of "Mending Wall" with the free verse is bad enough, but Henderson insists in the *Dial* (October 1, 1914) that *North of Boston* is more a novel than a book of poems. Suggesting that Frost's rhythms are purposely monotonous, she writes: "Doubtless there will be many readers who will find Mr. Frost dull, and who will object to his verse structure. There is no denying that his insistent monosyllabic monotony is irritating, but it may be questioned whether any less drab monontony of rhythm would have been so successful in conveying the particular aspect of life presented." One wrongheaded notice of this sort would be hard enough to take, but Frost also had to endure a similar misunderstanding from the pen of Jessie B. Rittenhouse, who was at the time the secretary of the Poetry Society of America. Writing for the New York *Times Book Review* (May 16, 1915), she declares that Frost is not nearly as important as Whitman and that, besides, the short story would be a more appropriate form for his material.

The point is that Frost's prosody and verse forms, the very poetry which some readers today still refer to as a bastion of conservative technique which once served to balance the radical innovations of Eliot and Pound, were controversial nearly a decade before the publication of *The Wasteland* and "Hugh Selwyn Mauberley." Described as monotonous and dull, criticized as inept examples of iambic pentameter, and compared unfavorably to everything from free verse to the novel and the short story, his technique was so different that published praise was often tempered with bafflement.

Not every major review of *North of Boston* missed the mark. Writing with the advantage of many talks with Frost about prosody and sentence sounds, Lascelles Abercrombie tried to solve the puzzle for those willing to read his essay in the London *Nation* (June 13, 1914). Unlike Hueffer, Abercrombie notes immediately that "Mending Wall" and other poems in *North of Boston* are indeed blank verse: new and vigorous, perhaps; unfamiliar to both eye and ear, but blank verse nonetheless. Abercrombie explains that those looking for the kind of metrical modulation usually expected in poetry will be disappointed, for Frost's rhythms are not intended for aesthetic decoration. He was one of the first commentators to show how Frost's novel use of meter is designed "to reproduce in verse form the actual shape of the sound of whole sentences." One month later, Wilfred Gibson, another friend of Frost and thus privy to his ideas about prosody, explained the sophisticated artistry at work beneath the surface simplicity of the poems. Praising *North of Boston* as the most "challenging" new book of poetry in years, Gibson argues that the unexpected innovation of Frost's achievement "lies in its starkness, in its nakedness of all poetical fripperies" (*Bookman*, July, 1914).

Clearly, then, the first critical debates on Frost's poetry focused on matters of meter, rhythm, and accent. If, like Eliot and Pound, he had published essays explaining his ideas about poetic technique, some of the misunderstanding which greeted his first books might have been avoided. He chose, however, to confine his explanations to letters, interviews, short prefaces, and speeches.[6] One need only examine the difference between the letters written in 1894, when he published his first poem, [7] and those written in 1913 and 1914 following the appearance of his first two books to note his surge of confidence in the new technique. In a letter (March 28, 1894) to William Hayes Ward, editor of *The Independent*, Frost wrote, "Specifically speaking, the few rules I know in this art are my own afterthoughts, or else directly formulated from the masterpieces I reread."[8] Nothing in the letter suggests a breakthrough in terms of prosody. Nineteen years later, however, he wrote to John Bartlett (August) 6, 1913):

> I dont know whether I am a craftsman or not in your sense of the word. Some day I will take time to explain to you in what sense of the word I am one of the few artists writing. I am one of the few who have a theory of their own upon which all their work down to the least accent is done. I expect to do something to the present state of literature in America.[9]

What he "did" to American poetry was to insist that a poem must have definite form, be dramatic, and use voice tones to vary the "te tum" effect of traditional iambic meter. Although all three prescriptions reflect his belief that poetry should include the intonation of the speaking voice, his concern with form has philosophical implications as well. Frost writes about confusion, about the universal "cataract of death" that spins away to nothingness. Yet while he faces the chasm, he refuses to accede to its lure. Confusion is a universal state to be acknowledged as a kind of boundary against which man can act by creating form. No form is permanent, as Frost suggests in his famous phrase "a momentary stay against confusion," but man may delight in chaos because it provides the opportunity for form. Frost's letters are full of suggestions about the need to create form: "My object is true form — is was and always will be — form true to any chance bit of true life" (c. September 19, 1929). "The background is hugeness and confusion shading away from where we stand into black and utter chaos; and against the background any small man-made figure of order and concentration . . . To me any little form I assert upon it is velvet, as the saying is, and to be considered for how much more it is than nothing" (c. March 21, 1935). "I thank the Lord for crudity which is rawness, which is raw material, which is the part of life not yet worked up into form, or at least not worked all the way up . . . A real artist delights in roughness for what he can do to it" (c. March 7, 1938).[10]

When Frost applies his ideas about form to the art of poetry, he shifts his concern with universal chaos to the "wildness" of the creative impulse. The tension generated by the union of the untamed impulse and the countering restrictions of traditional meter and stanza forms reflects some of Frost's philosophical concerns as well as adds to the appeal of his poems.[11] To abandon poetic form is to court chaos. One can thus understand his aversion to free verse.

Frost also suggests that the absence of traditional form in poetry diminishes the dramatic element, a quality he prized. Calling on poets to show "a dramatic necessity" in their art, he explains that the intonations of the speaking voice are the best means for creating a sense of drama: "Everything written is as good as it is dramatic. It need not declare itself in form, but it is drama or nothing. A least lyric alone may have a hard time, but it can make a beginning, and lyric will be piled on lyric till all are easily heard as sung or spoken by a person in a scene — in character, in a setting."[12] Frost believes that sentences in poetry cannot hold the reader's attention unless they are dramatic and that only the entanglement of the "speaking tones of voice" in the words will supply drama.

His comments reflect his concern for what he calls "sentence sounds," his favorite topic when discussing prosody. Briefly, Frost tries to unite the free-ranging rhythms and tones of actual speech which do not necessarily have iambic pentameter and its variations.[13] This union was primarily responsible for the bewilderment experienced by the first reviewers of *North of Boston,* for while Frost seemed to be writing in traditional forms, his lines did not scan in the traditional way. Knowing that he had worked out something new, he accepted every opportunity to explain in letters and interviews his theories of versification. On September 18, 1915, he wrote to Walter Prichard Eaton: "I was grateful to both Howells and Garnett for making so little difficulty of my blank verse.[14] I have nothing in common with free verse people . . . I am only interesting to myself for having ventured to try to make poetry out of tones that if you can judge from the practice of other poets are not usually regarded as poetical . . . What bothers people in my blank verse is that I have tried to see what I could do with boasting tones and quizzical tones and shrugging tones (for there are such) and forty eleven other tones."[15] Similarly, he told William Stanley Braithwaite, ". . . a sentence is not interesting merely in conveying a meaning of words; it must do something more; it must convey a meaning by sound."[16]

In short, the three elements of form, drama, and sentence sounds gives Frost's poetry what Lawrance Thompson calls "a fresh vitality without recourse to the fads and limitations of modern experimental techniques."[17] Frost's scorn of radically experimental poetry is well known, but only specialists are aware of his 1935 essay in which he publicly denounces the innovations of his peers. In his "Introduction" to Edwin Arlington Robinson's *King Jasper,* he writes:

> It may come to the notice of posterity (and then again it may not) that this, our age, ran wild in the quest of new ways to be new . . . Poetry, for example, was tried without punctuation. It was tried without capital letters. It was tried without metric frame on which to measure the rhythm. It was tried without any images but those to the eye, and a loud general intoning had to be kept up to cover the total loss of specific images to the ear, those dramatic tones of voice which had hitherto constituted the better half of poetry. It was tried without content under the trade name of poesie pure. It was tried without phrase, epigram, coherence, logic and consistency. It was tried without ability.[18]

This statement amounts to a tirade. A careful reading of the paragraph suggests that while Frost indirectly criticizes E. E. Cummings (no capital letters), T. S. Eliot (no metric frame), Amy Lowell (eye images), and Vachel Lindsay (loud intoning), he turns an essay ostensibly in honor of the now dead Robinson into a confirmation of the value of his theory about dramatic tones of voice. From today's perspective, one can only note the irony of Frost's early position as a leader of the new poetry. In 1914–15, his versification was so startling that it baffled such seasoned analysts of modern literature as Jessie Rittenhouse and Ford Madox Hueffer. And yet while Frost was proud of his innovations with rhythm and the metric line, he lashed out at his colleagues who searched for *new* ways to be new.

Frost looked for *old* ways to be new. No matter how bewildering his blank verse appeared to the first readers of *North of Boston,* he always stressed the necessity for traditional form and coherent content. His variations with standard meter and rhyme were designed not to cast away the heritage of American poetry but to renew it. Frost showed how recognizable voice tones encourage natural departure from the iambic rhythm even though the predominate poetic foot of the entire poem remains iambic. In his best poems, like those which so puzzled Hueffer, he unites three levels of sound: the primary rhythm of the line, the pronunciation of words and phrases, and the sentence sounds communicated by inflections of tones of voice.[19] One problem facing the uninitiated reader is not to let his feeling for the predominately iambic rhythm violate the pronunciation of the words and phrases. The enduring vitality of "Mending Wall" and "The Death of the Hired Man" results from the tension between the opposite pulls of the freer voice tones and the stricter poetic meter all within the restrictions of traditional verse forms.

Lawrance Thompson calls attention to the following sentence from "Mending Wall":

> I could say "Elves" to him,
> But it's not elves exactly, and I'd rather
> He said it for himself.[20]

The reader who mutters "blank verse" upon scanning the first line may do a double take when looking at the second line with its eleven syllables and accent withheld until "not elves." A more impressive example of Frost's prosody is the first line from "The Death of the Hired Man": "Mary sat musing on the lamp-flame at the table . . ." Despite the efforts of early reviewers to read it as free verse, "The Death of the Hired Man" is a blank verse poem. The reader's sense of puzzlement results from the conversational tone, prosaic vocabulary, the trochee "Mary," the spondee "lamp-flame," the anapest "at the table," and the thirteen syllables instead of the traditional ten. Frost not only varies the sound from the "te tum" effect of standard blank verse, but he also links the unusual rhythm with theme. Realizing that a close proximity of trochee, spondee, anapest, and additional syllables forces a slow reading of the line, the reader turns to the next line and notes that the first word is "waiting": "Waiting for Warren. When she heard his step . . ." Although Frost again begins with a trochee, he assigns this line the ten syllables normally expected in blank verse. In addition to the opening trochee, he includes alliteration and a caesura which once more slow the reader to reenforce the sense of waiting before the rush of sound in "When she heard his step."

The reader who compares the virtuosity of these lines to the relatively color-less blank verse of "Waiting — Afield at Dusk," published just a year before "The Death of the Hired Man," will marvel at the confidence Frost shows in so much of his poetry after *A Boy's Will*. He learned to avoid the jerkiness and rigidity present in poems of five-stress lines which rely too much on metrical regularity and too many end-stopped lines. One is reminded of Ezra Pound's advice to avoid the metronome. After Frost realized the possibilities for uniting dramatic speech tones with traditional meter, he used run-on lines, feminine endings, and the variations of trochaic and anapestic feet to illustrate the old way to be new.[21] As if defining his understanding of himself as a poet, he wrote to John Bartlett (July 4, 1913) before the publication of *North of Boston*:

> But if one is to be a poet he must learn to get cadences by skillfully breaking the sounds of sense with all their irregularity of accent across the regular beat of the meter. Verse in which there is nothing but the beat of the meter furnished by the accents of the pollysyl-labic words we call doggerel. Verse is not that. Neither is it the sound of sense alone. It is a resultant from those two. There are only two or three meters that are worth anything. We depend for variety on the infinite play of accents in the sound of sense.[22]

The comment that there are only "two or three meters" worth anything is not an offhand remark. Twenty-six years after the 1913 letter to Bartlett, Frost wrote in "The Figure a Poem Makes" that the English language has "virtually" but two meters: "strict iambic and loose iambic."[23] When the meter is "strict" iambic, only one syllable appears between stresses. When it is "loose," two or more syllables are placed between stresses. Anapestic meter results when the meter is "strictly loose," when the poet consistently separates the accented syllables with two unaccented ones. Apparently the distinction between free verse and his own variations with traditional meter troubled Frost most of his life. As late as 1951 he returned to the problem in "How Hard It Is to Keep from Being King When It's in You and in the Situation," a poem collected in his final volume, *In the Clearing* (1962). A long explanatory passage concludes:

> Free verse, so called, is really cherished prose,
> Prose made of, given an air by church intoning.
> It is its beauty, only I don't write it.
>
> (p. 82, vv. 21–23)

While the reader grimaces at the poem's didactic doggerel, he notes the pains Frost continues to take even at age seventy-seven to insist upon the difference between "real" verse and free verse.

Frost's "real" verse, created by the "strain of rhythm/Upon a meter," is especially effective with dialogue. Manipulating the sentence sounds by using italics and dashes, he indicates pauses, spoken emphasis, and the general difficulties of communication. In "Home Burial," for example, two italicized words and six dashes in the final five lines suggest the anxiety and the strained relationship about to shatter a marraige. Heartsick over the death of her baby, Amy accuses her husband of forgetting the tragedy too soon. Her tone of despair and growing hysteria is fairly consistent throughout the poem, but the husband's changes. His tone is gentle at first as he tries to draw her out of her grief, to persuade her to talk about why she continues to cry. But when she persists in her accusation that he does not care enough, his gentle tone begins to give way to a mixture of frustration and anger. Listen as he pleads when she threatens to leave:

> "Amy! Don't go to someone else this time.
> Listen to me. I won't come down the stairs."
> He sat there and fixed his chin between his fists.
> "There's something I should like to ask you, dear."

The first line suggests that Amy has not always talked out her problems with her husband, that she has taken them to someone else. Since the dead child is a loss for both of them, he would like to comfort her this time. His plea is in vain. She interprets it as sneering, causing him to drown out his softly spoken "dear" with an angry, frustrated reply:

> "You make me angry. I'll come down to you.
> God, what a woman! And it's come to this,
> A man can't speak of his own child that's dead."

Although the husband is wronged, he compounds her despair when he implies that he cares more for appearances than for grief. Noticing someone approaching the house as Amy continues to cry, he asks her to be quiet until the person has passed. His callousness precipitates her angry accusation and his equally bitter reply, the poem's final fine lines:

> "*You* — oh, you think the talk is all. I must go —
> Somewhere out of this house. How can I make you —"
> "If — you — do!" She was opening the door wider.
> "Where do you mean to go? First tell me that.
> I'll follow and bring you back by force. I *will!* —"

Frost's canon has perhaps no better example of his skill in crossing the irregular rhythms of colloquial speech with the regularity of traditional meter. The persistent rhythm is iambic pentameter. The stresses are determined, however, not by the demands of standard verse but by the emphasis of speech. Each dash signals a pause, and each italicized word calls for heavy stress. Two of the five lines quoted are highly irregular, yet the basic iambic rhythm remains throughout the poem:

> "You—oh, you think the talk is all. I must go—
> "If—you do!" She was opening the door wider.

One can only wonder how Hueffer and Rittenhouse reacted to these lines of blank verse with anapests, spondees, more than five stresses, and more than ten syllables. Frost thought well of them indeed. On July 27, 1914 he wrote to John Cournos:

> I am not bothered by the question whether anyone will be able to hear or say those three words ("If—you—do!") as I mean them to be said or heard. I should say that they were sufficiently self expressive. Some doubt that such tones can long survive on paper. They'll probably last as long as the finer meanings of words.[24]

Dashes and italics ease the difficulty of determining the stressed syllables when reading a Frost poem aloud, but Frost does not offer these aids in every poem. Many of his difficult lines to scan are those which include a series or list of articles. In "Our Singing Strength" he writes, "Thrush, bluebird, blackbird, sparrow, and robin throng." The line reads smoothly because four of the five words in the series have two syllables. Depending upon whether or not the reader accents "throng," the line contains five or six stresses. One line in "The Self-Seeker" poses a more difficult problem, for it is composed largely of one syllable words: "Five hundred—five—five! One, two, three, four, five." This line contains the ten syllables traditionally associated with blank verse, but the number of stresses is not easily determined. The two dashes help, for they suggest that the reader accent the "five" that follows each. Yet the problem remains of what to do with the series of one through five. The solution is to stress six of the ten syllables: "Five hundred—five—five! One, two, three, four, five."

A similar difficulty exists in "Home Burial" with the lines

> "But the child's mound—"
> Don't, don't, don't, don't," she cried.

In a letter (July 27, 1914) to Cournos, Frost expresses his pleasure in these lines, but he does not specify how to read them: I also think well of those four 'don'ts' in Home Burial. They would be good in prose and they gain something from the way they are placed in the verse."[25] The clue, as Frost suggests, is the positioning of the four "don'ts." Normally when a single line of iambic pentameter is separated to make two lines of dialogue, the two parts are still read as one line with five stresses. For example, the following line from "Home Burial" separates in the middle, but both segments are read together as one line with five regular iambic feet:

> "You don't know how to ask it."
> "Help me, then."

With the puzzling series of "don'ts," however, the two halves of the line are best left apart. The dash following "mound" provides the clue. Assigning the first half of the line three stresses, Frost uses the dash to indicate the husband's incomplete statement and gradual lapse into silence. This division of the line permits Frost to accent each "don't" in the second half, just as the angry Amy probably does. The general five stress rhythm of the poem thus is reestablished:

"But the child's mound—"

"Don't, don't, don't, don't," she cried.

Frost's virtuoso command of prosody in "Home Burial" delighted many of those first readers of the poem in 1914 who thought it an example of the new free verse. The unsure reader who cannot determine the sentence sounds associated with each of the two speakers can look for guidance to an occasional mention of a character's name or to the alternating quotation marks. Frost sets himself an even greater challenge in a few of his longer blank verse dialogue poems when three or more characters talk. He is so sure of the unity of sentence sound and character that he omits the speaker's name as the poem progresses, leaving only the tone to differentiate the characters. In "Snow" the poem's first five lines set the scene, name the three characters, and describe the storm. The dramatic tension develops when Meserve stops at Cole's house to rest his horses before reentering the storm for the trek home. Although she does not like Meserve, Mrs. Cole wants him to wait until the storm subsides. Meserve speaks first, and Frost promptly establishes his two identifying sentence sounds. The first is his tendency to preach and to exaggerate the significance of every natural act. Describing the snow, he says:

> "You can just see it glancing off the roof
> Making a great scroll upward toward the sky,
> Long enough for recording all our names on.—"

Second, his extreme confidence borders on arrogance. Despite the storm's ferocity, he telephones his wife to scorn her fear for his safety:

> "My dear, I'm coming just the same. I didn't
> Call you to ask you to invite me home.—"

Meserve's "dear" is clearly sharper in tone than that of the husband in "Home Burial."

When Meserve goes to the barn to check his horses, Frost establishes the voice tone of Mrs. Cole, the second speaker. She detests his tendency to preach ("I hate his wretched little Racker Sect"), but she worries for his safety:

> "What is he doing out a night like this?
> Why can't he stay at home?"

Mr. Cole, the third speaker, reveals a gently mocking tone as he satirizes his wife's concern:

> "Don't let him go.
> Stick to him, Helen. Make him answer you."

Up to this point, Frost supplies the characters' names to establish contact with their respective sentence sounds. In the remainder of this long poem, however, the names are used sparingly, usually in descriptive, not dialogue passages. In sections like the following, the voice tones are the sole identification of the speakers.

> "... I'm going to call his wife again."
> "Wait and he may. Let's see what he will do.
> Let's see if he will think of her again.
> But then, I doubt he's thinking of himself.
> He doesn't look on it as anything."
> "He shan't go—there!"
> "It *is* a night, my dear."
> "One thing: he didn't drag God into it."
> "He don't consider it a case for God."

Listening to the sentence sounds, the reader can follow the exchange between Mr. and Mrs. Cole. She worries, and he continues to mock gently both his wife and Meserve. Frost, however, is too fine an artist to permit this long poem to degenerate into tonal monotony. Toward the end, he reverses the Coles's sentence sounds. Beginning to show concern, Mr. Cole wonders if his wife did enough to keep Meserve from reentering the storm. Although Mrs. Cole recognizes the reversal and rejects it, she, too, changes her tone. Criticizing the absent Meserve for disturbing her evening, she complains:

> "What did he come in for?—to talk and visit?
> Thought he'd just call to tell us it was snowing.
> If he thinks he is going to make our house
> A halfway coffee house 'twixt town and nowhere—"

Both changes in attitude are reflected in the respective voice tones with little use of names to identify the speakers.

"Snow" is a particularly intricate illustration of the sound of sense principle in a dialogue poem. Despite the predominately five-stress rhythm of the blank verse, Frost uses all of his skills to vary the lines: question marks, dashes, question marks followed by dashes in the middle of a line, and split lines. In an interview with Morris P. Tilley, he comments upon his technique. He does not name "Snow" as the poem referred to, but his description fits the poem. This interview was published in 1918, two years after "Snow" was collected in *Mountain Interval*:

> I have three characters speaking in one poem, and I was not satis-
> fied with what they said until I got them to speak so true to their

characters that no mistake could be made as to who was speaking. I would never put the names of the speakers in front of what they said. They would have to tell that by the truth to their character of what they said. It would be interesting to try to write a play with ten characters and not have any names before what they said.[26]

Not all of the dialogue poems succeed as well as "Snow" and "Home Burial." In "The Generations of Men" Frost depends again upon sentence sounds instead of names to pinpoint his speakers. The problem is, however, that the tones are not fully developed before he drops the identifying "he" and "she." Only by diligent notation of the alternating speakers can the reader keep track of the characters. "The Housekeeper" is another weak poem, as Frost admits in a letter (June 12, 1931) to Louis Untermeyer: "Even I know that not all my poems are equally good. Neither are they all equally bad. Some like The Housekeeper are very much worse than others. Don't ask me to go into the terrible details."[27] The usually astute Ezra Pound purchased this poem to publish in *The Egoist* (January 15, 1914), but "The Housekeeper" does not compare with the better poems of *North of Boston*. Although Frost never defined the causes of failure, several possibilities exist. First, the poem is one of his initial dramatic narratives. Published in 1914, "The Housekeeper" was written as much as a decade earlier when Frost was learning his art at the Derry (New Hampshire) farm.[28] The other reasons for the failure concern prosody and technique. Frost attepts to vary the blank verse line with anapests, split lines, and caesuras, but he fails to control the dramatic situation in the long monologue which describes Estelle's work load and John's refusal to sell the chickens. The central issue in "The Housekeeper" is Estelle's disenchantment with John and her decision to run away when he refuses to marry her, but this monologue nearly dwarfs it. The primary weakness is point of view. In "Snow" and "Home Burial" the characters involved in the dramatic situations participate in the dialogue. The immediacy gained by this technique is lost to "The Housekeeper" because someone other than a principal character narrates the action. Frost dilutes the potentially strong situation of Estelle's disillusionment with a common-law marraige of fifteen years because he does not let her speak for herself.

When Frost is at his lyrical best, the speech rhythms and variations determine even the position of rhymes. "After Apple-Picking" and "The Rabbit-Hunter," for example, are rhymed in spite of Frost's refusal to supply a traditional scheme to govern rhyme placement. The natural rhythm of the spoken phrases dictates both metrical variations and the unscheduled rhymes. At first reading, "After Apple-Picking" looks like free verse or even untraditional blank verse because of the surprising metrical irregularity which results in some lines of iambic dimeter. But when the poem is heard, the reader notes that it can be neither free verse nor blank verse because of the insistent sound of the iambic stresses and the gracefully placed rhymes.

Another essay could be written about the versification of these short poems.[29] In many of Frost's later lyrics, as opposed to the dramatic narratives, his genius with metrical variations and substitutions encourages the reader to ignore the central rhythmical pattern. Only by a deliberate notation of syllable count, poetic feet, and accent can the reader define the basic rhythm. Clearly, the more Frost wrote, the more confident and sophisticated he became with prosody. Even a lyric as short as the fifteen-line "November" has anapests, feminine endings to suggest uncertainty, unscheduled rhymes, and repetition of syntax. Yet the general cadence throughout is rhymed iambic trimeter.[30]

Frost continued to experiment with versification during his long career. How mistaken are those readers who even today insist that he was too conservative with technique to be honored with the great modern poets of his time. His successful innovations with the traditional forms and rhythms of poetry confirm his goal to discover old ways to be new. Nearly forty years old before he could find publication in book form, he nevertheless remained confident that he would "do something" to the dismal state of American Poetry at the turn of this century. Surely it is fair to say that Frost's experiments with prosody rejuvenated the traditional rhythms, meters, and patterns of rhyme which readers have always associated with poetry. Ford Madox Hueffer's initial confusion was understandable after all.

DONALD GREINER

University of South Carolina

Notes

1. The official biography by Lawrance Thompson is in the three volumes: *Robert Frost: The Early Years, 1874-1915* (New York: Holt, Rinehart and Winston, 1966); *Robert Frost: The Years of Triumph, 1915-1938* (New York: Holt, Rinehart and Winston, 1970); and, with R. H. Winnick, *Robert Frost: The Later Years, 1938-1963* (New York: Holt, Rinehart and Winston, 1976). Four volumes of letters are available: Margaret Bartlett Anderson, *Robert Frost and John Bartlett: The Record of a Friendship* (New York: Holt, Rinehart and Winston, 1963); *The Letters of Robert Frost to Louis Untermeyer,* ed. Louis Untermeyer (New York: Holt, Rinehart and Winston, 1963); *Selected Letters of Robert Frost,* ed. Lawrance Thompson (New York: Holt, Rinehart and Winston, 1964); *Family Letters of Robert Frost,* ed. Arnold Grade (Albany, New York: SUNY Press, 1972).

2. For the latest full-length discussions of Frost in the modern tradition, see Frank Lentricchia, *Robert Frost: Modern Poetics and the Landscapes of Self* (Durham, North Carolina: Duke Univ. Press, 1975), and Richard Poirier, *Robert Frost: The Work of Knowing* (New York: Oxford Univ. Press, 1977).

3. *Selected Letters,* p. 79.

4. *Selected Letters,* p. 78.

5. *Selected Letters,* p. 128.

6. See *Selected Prose of Robert Frost,* eds. Hyde Cox and Edward Connery Lathem (New York: Holt, Rinehart and Winston, 1966), and *Interviews with Robert Frost,* ed. Edward Connery Lathem (New York: Holt, Rinehart and Winston, 1966).

7. "My Butterfly: An Elegy," *The Independent,* 8 Nov. 1894.

8. *Selected Letters,* p. 19.

9. *Selected Letters,* p. 88.

10. *Selected Letters,* pp. 361, 418, 465.

11. For a comment on "wildness" and poetic form, see Frost's essay "The Figure a Poem Makes" in *Selected Prose.*

12. "Preface" to *A Way Out, Selected Prose,* p. 13.

13. For the best discussions of sentence sounds, see Robert S. Newdick, "Robert Frost and the Sound of Sense," *American Literature* (November 1937), 289-300; and Tom Vander Ven, "Robert Frost's Dramatic Principle of 'Oversound,'" *American Literature,* (1973), 238-51.

14. Frost refers to reviews by William Dean Howells, "Editor's Easy Chair," *Harper's,* Sept. 1914, pp. 634-37; and by Edward Garnett, "A New American Poet," *Atlantic Monthly,* Aug. 1915, pp. 214-21.

15. *Selected Letters,* p. 191.

16. William Stanley Braithwaite, "Robert Frost, New American Poet," Boston *Evening Transcript,* 8 May, 1915; rpt. in *Interviews,* pp. 3-8. See also Reginald L. Cook, "Robert Frost's Asides on His Poetry," *American Literature* (January 1948), 351-59; Robert S. Newdick, *Newdick's Season of Frost,* ed. William A. Sutton (Albany: SUNY Press, 1976), pp. 270, 363; Thompson, *Years of Triumph,* p. 669.

17. Lawrance Thompson, *Fire and Ice: The Art and Thought of Robert Frost* (New York: Henry Holt, 1942), p. 18.

18. *Selected Prose,* pp. 59-60.

19. For a close examination of the rhythm of specific lines of Frost's poetry, see Thompson, *Fire and Ice,* pp. 67-79.

20. All quotations from Frost's poetry will be from *The Poetry of Robert Frost,* ed. Edward Connery Lathem (New York: Holt, Rinehart and Winston, 1969) unless otherwise noted.

21. For an examination of the liberties which Frost takes with the traditionally rigid sonnet form, see Thompson, *Fire and Ice,* pp. 76-79; and especially Karen Lane Rood, "Robert Frost's 'Sentence Sounds': Wildness Opposing the Sonnet Form," in *Frost: Centennial Essays II,* ed. Jac Tharpe (Jackson: Univ. Press of Mississippi, 1976), pp. 196-210.

22. *Selected Letters,* pp. 80-81.

23. *Selected Prose,* pp. 17-18.

24. *Selected Letters,* p. 130.

25. *Selected Letters,* p. 130.

26. Morris P. Tilley, "Notes from Conversations with Robert Frost," *The Inlander,* Feb. 1918; rpt. in *Interviews,* pp. 22-26.

27. *Letters to Untermeyer,* p. 207.

28. See Thompson, *Early Years,* p. 553.

29. For an analysis of the shorter lyrics, see Eckhart Willige, "Formal Devices in Robert Frost's Shorter Poems," *Georgia Review* (Fall 1961), 324-30.

30. For other analyses of Frost's prosody and technique, see Elaine Barry, *Robert Frost on Writing* (New Brunswick, N. J. Rutgers Univ. Press, 1973); Reginald Cook, *Robert Frost: A Living Voice* (Amherst, Mass.: Univ. of Massachusetts Press, 1974); Herbert R. Coursen, "A Dramatic Necessity: The Poetry of Robert Frost," *Bucknell Review* (Dec. 1961), 138-47; Langdon Elsbree, "Frost and the Isolation of Man," *Claremont Quarterly*

(Summer 1960), 29–40; Donald J. Greiner, "Robert Frost's Dark Woods and the Function of Metaphor," in *Frost: Centennial Essays,* ed. Jac Tharpe (Jackson: Univ. of Mississippi Press, 1974), pp. 373–88; Herbert Howarth, "Frost in a Period Setting, *"Southern Review,* N. S. (October 1966), 789–99.

Language and Form in
"Nothing Gold Can Stay"

It would be hard to find a twentieth-century poet more insistent on langauge and on formal structure than Robert Frost. Lawrence Thompson claims that "form is the most important characteristic which Frost finds essential to poetry."[1] In fact, Frost "frequently ridiculed his free verse contemporaries by saying that he would no sooner give up the restrictions of meter and rhyme than he would play tennis with the net down."[2] This emphasis by the poet on formal matters, then, is *one* justification for concentrating on them in a detailed examination of his gem-like poem "Nothing Gold Can Stay."[3]

It is surprising that of well over two thousand items of Frost scholarship, only a handful have set out to treat formal matters despite the poet's own repeated comments on them. Thomspon, in *Fire and Ice*, devotes a routine chapter to examples of couplets, sonnets, iambic pentameter. Walton Beacham argues that Frost uses rhyme schemes and stanza form to establish irony. Keith Cox offers a four-page comparison of the syntax of two poems. Seymour Chatman analyzes pitch and stress patterns in "Mowing" according to Smith-Trager linquistic conventions. Eckhart Willige treats formal devices in four of Frost's poems, and Donald J. Lloyd and Harry R. Warfel contrast (in a paragraph) the phoneme types used by Frost in "Stopping by Woods on a Snowy Evening" with those of Ralph Hodgson's "Eve."[4]

"Nothing Gold Can Stay" has, of course, caught the notice of critics and been the object of several explications. For example, John David Sweeney and James Lindroth note that "Nothing Gold Can Stay" deals with the inexorable passing of beautiful things," and that "the theme of death and change is commonly used by poets." John Robert Doyle adds that "since the transitoriness of life is a fact . . . the significant thing is to accept the moment before it passes." Charles Anderson, in contrast, feels that "what remains after the gold vanishes is not so bad" and is only *"manqué* by comparison with the gold of newly minted creation," while John Lynen suggests that "the subject is not just the passing of a beautiful sight, but the corruption which seems to be a necessary part of maturing." Thompson stresses the epigrammatic quality of the poem and its ironic elements, claiming that the losses all lead to fulfillments. Alfred R. Ferguson goes further with this approach, explaining that Frost's metaphor of Eden and the Fall is that of the *felix culpa,* the paradox of the forunate fall.[5]

Thus critics have devoted themselves to meaning in this poem, to theme and to symbol, but with scarcely a mention of form or of language. Sweeney and Lindroth do observe that the poem has eight lines, and Doyle notes that it is one of the shortest of Frost's poems, "cleanly and directly written." Anderson points out that it consists of four "simple couplets embellished with meter and rhyme," and Ferguson points out that the lines are heavily end-stopped. But surely more attention should be paid to form in Frost's poetry, considering the poet's interest in it.

An examination of some of the formal linguistic elements in one of Frost's poems easily demonstrates that his concern with form is far from superficial, as some tools based on the perceptions of linguistic analysis will help make clear. Frost's "Nothing Gold Can Stay" is given below both in its final version and, in a fairly broad transcription using an essentially Trager-Smith symbolization based on a reading by the poet to help highlight some of its phonological structures in the poem.[6]

As Ferguson perceives, the eight lines of "Nothing Gold Can Stay" are heavily end-stopped. The undesirable result is that the poem will fall apart into eight fragments unless they can somehow be made to cohere both formally and thematically. One major function of the linguistic structures is thus to help organize the poem formally, and, in fact, to organize it in a number of ways simultaneously; this is a second reason for a close examination of its formal structure. Couplet rhyme helps to counteract slightly the end-stopped lines and contributes to the "epigrammatic" quality noted by Thompson, but with no further structure the poem then consists of four disconnected chunks rather than eight— not too much real gain.

Starting with consonantism, the most striking feature is the alliterative symmetry, based on the stressed syllables, which has been extracted below beside the final version of the poem.

Nature's first green is gold,	néjčərz fərst gríjn iz gówld
Her hardest hue to hold.	hər hárdəst hjúw tu hówld
Her early leaf's a flower;	hər árlij líjfs ə fláwr
But only so an hour.	bət ównlij sów ən áwr
Then leaf subsides to leaf.	ðen líjf səbsájdz tu líjf
So Eden sank to grief,	sow íjdən sǽjŋk tu gríjf
So dawn goes down to day.	sow dón gowz dáwn to déj
Nothing gold can stay.	nə́θiŋ gówld ken stéj

Notice first that only lines two and seven have all three stressed syllables in perfect alliteration within the line: *Hardest—Hue—Hold,* and *Dawn—Down—Day.* The symmetrical placement of these two lines helps bind the poem into a whole, as does the palindromic consonantism in lines four and five: *Only—So—Hour,* and *Leaf—Subsides—Leaf* (where we recall that any initial vowel [symbolized in the chart by O] will alliterate with any other initial stressed vowel).

N	G	G
H	H	H:
O	L	F
O	S	O
L	S	L
O	S	G
D	D	D
N	G	S

The arrangement down the center of the S-initial words is striking, as is the triangular placement of the L-initial ones. Only the first and last lines seem not to cohere alliteratively with the other lines, but this very lack of coherence, coupled with the lines' initial N and medial G, tends to unite them with each other (as does the recurrent word *Gold,* which appears only in these first and last lines and is, along with *Leaf,* the only recurrent stress-bearing word). Indeed, it is alliteration more than any other formal element that cements together Frost's eight end-stopped lines. The coherence of lines one and eight is further reinforced in that they are the only ones bearing initial stress (and so also the only lines not consisting of three perfect iambs), line one having an inverted first foot and line eight a truncated one. Willige claims that if there are "irregularities" of rhythm in a Frost poem, "they are likely to appear in the first line as if the poet had not yet caught its pace." This view of irregularity as a flaw is inadequate to capture its use here, as is clear from the climactic recurrence of the imperfect iamb in line eight. Alliteration also helps to associate thematically the key words *Green* and *Gold,*[7] not only with each other but both also with *Grief,* just as the rhyme scheme links *Leaf* and *Grief.*

Although less immediately apparent, the stressed vowel nuclei also contribute strongly to the structure of the poem. The back round diphthongs (underlying round vowels in the abstract vowel structure of Chomsky and Halle) at the ends of lines one through four bind those lines into a unit, as do the front rising diphthongs (underlying front vowels) at the ends of the second four lines. Philip Gerber suggests that at times Frost "concocts a pseudo-quatrain out of a pair of couplets," but he doesn't define the term "pseudo-couplet."[8] The basic bipartite division of the poem created by these contrastive diphthong types is enhanced by other formal devices to be mentioned below. Notice that the middle stress in lines one and three is on fronting diphthongs while that in two and four is on rounded ones, for an alternating A—B—A—B effect, whereas in the second half of the poem, the first two lines have fronting diphthongs in the center and the last two have rounding ones, in an A—A—B—B arrangement.

ej	ij	ow
a	uw	ow
ə	ij	aw
ow	ow	aw
ij	aj	ij
ij	æj	ij
ɔ	aw	ej
ə	ow	ej

The three rounded diphthongs in the fourth line make a striking contrast with the three front ones of line five and establish a clear border between the two halves. Indeed, the *ow–ow–aw* of line four recapitulates the final vowel nuclei of lines one through three. The first and the last stress of the poem are both on the nucleus *ej*. It may be significant that the last couplet of the poem is the only one where the lines do not end in a consonant, so that the open syllable yields an open ended finale, or trailing-off effect.

Turning now to the syntactic, and briefly thereafter to the semantic structure, one sees that in the first quatrain the first three lines all begin with Possessive + Adjective + Noun, with the fourth line contrastively different in its structure. This A–A–A–B pattern is matched also in the second quatrain where the first three lines all have the structure Adverb + Noun + Verb + Preposition + Noun, again with a contrasting fourth line. This pattern thereby not only unifies internally the first and the second four lines, but its repetitiveness also binds the two quatrains together, as did the alliterative devices discussed earlier.

Reinforcing the rhyme, the superlative ending *-st* joins line one with line two while the similarly placed adverbial ending *-ly* ties three and four (as do the indefinite noun phrases at the ends of those lines). But line one is like three with its copula while two and four (with deleted copulas) are the only lines lacking finite verbs, for an A–B–A–B pattern exactly matching that of the stressed vowel nuclei at the middle stress of those same lines. In the first quatrain the *Her* of lines two and three sets them against one and four, as in an "envelope quatrain," just as is the case with the initial *So* of lines six and seven in the second quatrain. In the first half of the poem, each *couplet* constitutes a complete clause (matching the rhyme structure and diminishing the end-stopped effect), but the second half contrasts with the first in that each *line* is a complete clause. Frost's reading supports this structure with his slight pitch rises (indicating nonfinality) at the ends of lines one and three, compared with terminal falling pitch at the ends of all other lines; that is, there is double bar juncture in one and three versus double cross in the rest of the Smith-Trager symbolization. Notice that only the odd-numbered lines of the poem have verbs marked with the third singular ending *-s* (although all words in rhyme are inflectionally bare).

Lines one and three of the first quatrain, containing the nearly synonymous *first* and *early,* are each affirmations eroded by he following lines. These same lines contain copulas that link contrastive terms (*green* with *gold, leaf* with *flower*), and in each instance a "pay-off" in the subsequent line concludes the necessary transience of these contradictory equivalences. But in the second quatrain three synonymous verbs of motion (*subside, sink, go down*) bind lines five, six, and seven together against the last line with its quasi-copula *stay.* And the "pay-off" of these "transient" verbs is the absolute of the final line, so reminiscent of the conclusion to a deductive argument in logic and containing the poem's only overt negative: *Nothing.*

No claim is made that the structural and meaningful uses of linguistic material in the poem are exhaustively accounted for here. The intent has rather been to exemplify Frost's use of such devices of phonology, syntax, and semantics for formal, structural purposes. And of course the analysis is acknowledgedly incomplete in the more serious sense that it has dealt *only* with these devices, for besides the mutability theme emphasized by most explications or the linguistic formalisms presented here, much remains to intrigue the observant and curious reader. Thus one is struck by the fact that the key words of the poem, the initial ones of the first and last lines, *Nature* and *Nothing,* are the very ones that G. B. Harrison, in what may be an appropriate simile for Frost's poem, says "ring throughout *King Lear* like the tolling of a knell."[9] What about the flower and the leaf, which recur as a topic in "In Hardwood Groves" and in "Leaves Compared with Flowers" and are so reminiscent of Chaucer?[10] What are the meanings to Californian Frost of the word *Gold,* which recurs more often in his poems than does *Green*? (This question might have been pondered [perhaps with a reading of "A Peck of Gold"] by Walter Sutton, Morris Weiz, and DeWitt Parker, who limit their discussions to this poem in its final form.)[11]

Explications of poems, of course, typically select a single aspect or, alternatively, exclude one or more aspects. Indeed, we have all noticed that critics go about reading a poem in quite divergent ways, with a variety of tools, each willing to suggest (with more or less tact) that any other way of going about reading the poem is not only iniquitous, but probably also inappropriate. However, since language is one of the primary resources available to the poet—as are human psychology, the social condition, and our literary heritage—one is tempted to agree with Roman Jakobson that "a linguist deaf to the poetic functions of language and a literary scholar indifferent to linguistics are equally flagrant anachronisms."[12]

Frost, in speaking of the reasons for his revision of "Stopping by Woods on a Snowy Evening," reminded Sylvester Baxter that "there should be two reasons, one of meaning and one of form."[13] It is in fact worth suggesting here that although very few scholars have done so, we might learn more about some of Frost's final versions of his poems by looking at his earlier ones.[14] In connection with "Nothing Gold Can Stay," it is striking to note that besides excising two-thirds of the original (and thriftily using it in "It Is Almost the Year Two Thousand"), Frost made a number of revisions which resulted in bringing about many of the formalisms examined above. The following is the poem in its original version:*

> Nature's first green is gold,
> Her hardest hue to hold.
> Her early leaves are flowers;
> But only so for hours.
> Then leaves subside to leaves.
> In Autumn she achieves
> A still more golden blaze.
> But nothing golden stays.
>
> Of white, blue, gold and green,
> The only colors seen
> An thought of in the vast,
> The gold is soonest past.
> A moment it appears
> At either end of years,
> At either end of days.
> But nothing golden stays.
>
> In gold as it began
> The world will end for man.
> And some belief avow
> The world is ending now:
> The final age of gold
> Is what we now behold.
> If so, we'd better gaze,
> For nothing golden stays.[15]

The poem developed through a number of successive states. It is therefore unlikely that effects can be dismissed as accidental when they result from many rewritings.

So Frost uses certain formal aspects of language to organize this fine poem in a variety of striking ways. Although we may be impressed by the complexities of the thing, in light of his frequent comments on form, we are not surprised. But

*By permission of the estate of Robert Frost and the trustees of Amherst College.

is there more to be said? in speaking of a poem by Browning, A. A. Hill once claimed, "It is form which gives meaning and not meaning which gives form."[16] Although this may be a strong assertion for most to accept (linguists included), it does lead us to ask whether form is meaningful to Frost as an embellishment or as a sort of scaffolding on which to hang his poems. Radcliffe Squires claims that for Frost form is separable from content, a source of amusement "having no other regard than itself."[17]

But Thompson makes clear that "for Frost the central problem of life was to find orderly ways of dealing with dangerous conflicts ... that might otherwise engulf and destroy him."[18] Frost himself insists that "A successful poem is a momentary stay against confusion," a way of imitating the original and divine creative act by fashioning order out of chaos.[19] Form, manmade form in fact, is to Robert Frost a major poetic theme, and this thematic importance is a *third* reason for examining his form in detail. Indeed, we can recognize easily this theme in the poet's concern with the formal activities of mowing and building and mending of walls, or, in addition to "Nothing Gold Can Stay," that striking little poem — "The Wood-Pile" — where Frost finds wood in a somewhat sinister forest "Cut and split ... / and measured, four by four by eight."[20] Poetic and linguistic form help Robert Frost impose order on the apparent chaos of the universe and of language by letting him find and arrange their underlying patterns into a bit of human neatness in the relentless wilderness. "After making a poem," he said, "you have no right to boast of anything but the form."[21]

JOHN A. REA

University of Kentucky

Notes

1. Lawrance Thompson, "Robert Frost's Theory of Poetry," in *Robert Frost: A Collection of Critical Essays,* ed. James M. Cox (Englewood Cliffs, N. J. Prentice-Hall, 1962), p. 19.

2. Lawrance Thompson, *Fire and Ice: The Art and Thought of Robert Frost* (1942; rpt. New York: Russell and Russell, 1961), p. 138.

3. Robert Frost, "Nothing Gold Can Stay," Yale Review, 13, (1923), No. 1, 31; and *The Poetry of Robert Frost,* ed. Edward Connery Lathem (New York: Holt, Rinehart and Winston, 1969), pp. 222-3.

4. Thompson, *Fire and Ice,* pp. 65-92; Beacham, "Technique and the Sense of Play in the Poetry of Robert Frost," in *Frost: Centennial Essays II,* ed. Jac Tharpe (Jackson: Univ. Press of Mississippi 1976), pp. 246-61; Cox, "A Syntactic Comparison of Robert Frost's '... Snowy Evening' and 'Desert Places,' " *Ball State University Forum,* 11 (1970), 25-8; Seymour Chatman, "Robert Frost's 'Mowing': An Inquiry into Prosodic Structure," *Kenyon Review,* 18 (1956), 421-38; Eckhart Willige, "Formal Devices in Robert Frost's Short Poems," *The Georgia Review,* 15 (1961), 324-30; Donald J. Lloyd and Harry R. Warfel, *American English in its Cultural Setting* (New York: Knopf, 1956), p. 327.

5. John David Sweeney and James Lindroth, *The Major Poems of Robert Frost* (New York: Monarch Press, 1965), p. 49; John Robert Doyle, Jr., *The Poetry of Robert Frost* (New York: Hafner, 1962), pp. 174–76; Charles R. Anderson, "Frost's 'Nothing Gold Can Stay,'" *Explicator,* 22 (1964), Item 8; John F. Lynen, *The Pastoral Art of Robert Frost* (New Haven: Yale Univ. Press, 1960), p. 154; Thompson, *Fire and Ice,* p. 169; Alfred R. Ferguson, "Frost and the Paradox of the Fortunate Fall," in *Frost: Centennial Essays* (Jackson: Univ. Press of Mississippi, 1974), pp. 436–39.

6. Robert Frost, "Nothing Gold Can Stay," *Robert Frost Reading His Poetry,* The National Council of Teachers of English, RCA Victor, 1944, side 2. I have departed from the commonly accepted Trager-Smith notation in using the symbol /j/ for the front rising glide in the place of their /y/, and in using /æj/ to represent the dipthong in Frost's pronunciation of "sank" which starts from a vowel position about like the /æ/ in "bad" and is clearly lower in its initial phase than is the /ej/ of his "day."

7. Frost stresses "green" in the first line, although it is equally possible to stress "first," as I did in my own first reading; but this yields some different details in the analysis both phonologically and semantically. I now prefer Frost's reading.

8. Philip Gerber, *Robert Frost* (New York: Twayne, 1966), p. 92.

9. *Shakespeare: The Complete Works,* ed. G. B. Harrison (New York: Harcourt, Brace, 1948), p. 1139.

10. Geoffrey Chaucer, *Legend of Good Women,* ed. F. N. Robinson (Boston: Houghton Mifflin, 1933), Prologue, lines 40 ff., and especially the notes to lines 40–65 and line 72, p. 955.

11. Walter Sutton, "The Contextualist Dilemma—or Fallacy?" *Journal of Aesthetics and Art Criticism,* 17 (1958–59), 224–26, discussing Morris Weitz's *Philosophy of the Arts* (Cambridge: Harvard Univ. Press, 1950), pp. 134–52 and Dewitt Parker, *The Principles of Aesthetics and Art Criticism* (New York: F. S. Crofts, 1946), p. 32.

12. Roman Jakobson, "Closing Statement: Linguistics and Poetics," in *Style in Language,* ed., Thomas A. Sebeok (Cambridge: MIT Press, 1960), p. 377.

13. Letter to Sylvester Baxter quoted in R. C. Townsend, "In Defense of Form: A Letter from Robert Frost to Sylvester Baxter, 1923," *The New England Quarterly,* 36 (1963), 243.

14. Such comparisons with early versions have been made by, e.g., Robert S. Newdick, "The Early Verse of Robert Frost and Some of his Revisions," *American Literature,* 7 (1935–36), 181–87; Walter Gierasch, "Frost's 'Brown's Descent,'" *Explicator,* 11 (1952–53), Item 60; David Hiatt, "Frost's 'In White' and 'Design,'" *Explicator,* 28 (1969–70), Item 41; R. Glenn Martin, "Two Versions of a Poem by Robert Frost," *Ball State University Forum,* 11 (1970), 65–68; Kenneth Rosen, "Visions and Revisions: An Early Version of Robert Frost's 'Our Doom to Bloom,'" in *Centennial Essays* (1974), pp. 369–72. A number of early versions also appear in such places as *The Letters of Robert Frost to Louis Untermeyer,* ed. Louis Untermeyer (New York: Holt, Rinehart and Winston, (1963), and especially in the endnotes of Lawrance Thompson's three-volume biography, *Robert Frost: The Early Years, 1874–1915* (New York: Holt, Rinehart and Winston, 1966); *The Years of Triumph, 1915–1938* (1970); and *The Later Years* (1976).

15. This version, now in the Amherst College Library, was sent to G. R. Elliott in late March or early April, 1920. Other versions of the poem between that here given and the final one from the Yale Review may be found in Lawrance R. Thompson, *Robert Frost: A Chronological Survey* (Middletown, Conn.: Olin Memorial Library, Wesleyan Univ., 1936), p. 30; a version identical except for punctuation is in Joan St. C. Crane, *Robert Frost: A Descriptive Catalogue of Books and Manuscripts in the Clifton Waller Barrett Library*

(Charlotte: Univ. Press of Virginia, 1974); The Library of Congress has three holograph versions; the earliest dated 1922, one undated, and a third dated 1924, the last being different only in punctuation from the printed version. Lawrance Thompson in *Robert Frost,* II, p. 565, note 14, mentions six known variant verions of "Nothing Gold Can Stay."

16. Archibald A. Hill, "Pippa's Song: Two Attempts at Structural Criticism," *University of Texas Studies in English,* 35 (1956), 56.

17. Radcliffe Squires, *The Major Themes of Robert Frost* (Ann Arbor: Univ. of Michigan Press, 1963), pp. 2, 3.

18. Thompson, *Early Years,* pp. xxii–iii.

19. Thompson, *Early Years,* p. xxii.

20. *The Poetry of Robert Frost,* pp. 101–02.

21. As quoted by Elizabeth Shepley Sergeant, *Robert Frost: The Trial by Existence* (New York: Holt, Rinehart and Winston, 1960), p. xviii.

II ATTITUDE

Sense of Place and
Religious Consciousness

In *Studies in Classic American Literature,* D. H. Lawrence senses a unique "spirit of place" as a fundamental characteristic of American literature. He insists that the new America has "its own great spirit of place. Every people is polarized in some particular locality, which is home, the homeland. Different places on the face of the earth have different vital effluence, different vibration, different chemical exhalation, different polarity with different stars: call it what you like. But the spirit of place is a great reality."[1] More specifically, Lawrence sees the spirit of place which inspires the young American literature as emerging from the new national experience. The escape from Europe, the beginning on unbroken ground, the submission to the virgin land, the confluence of cultures, and democracy give classic American literature its shape, its spirit, according to Lawrence.

Robert Frost often appears as an embodiment of the spirit of New England. His humor and wisdom, his wry wit, his stern endurance articulate something of the New England experience. The characters which populate his poems represent the spectrum of New England living and dying. But place, for Frost, characterizes his poetry and his religious awareness more completely than Lawrence's spirit would suggest. From as early as Lascelles Abercrombie's review of *North of Boston,* in which the critic pointed to Frost's link with classical pastoral poetry, Frost's allegiance to place has been noticed. John F. Lynen offers a full discussion of the continuity between Frost and the pastoral tradition while also identifying Frost's transformation of that tradition. Frost's pastoralism, he states, offers a "rural point of view" which characterizes his poetry.[2] Most recently, Richard Poirier senses Frost's reliance upon place in terms of Frost's "extravagance or extravagance," meaning both a physical or mental wandering and a verbal or rhetorical one.[3]

Beyond Frost's use of poetic tradition, his characteristic point of vantage, and his wandering, Frost's sense of place represents the workings of his spirit within his poetry. While the nation or a state, a farm with its terrain, or the ground itself shape his poetry and offer a perspective, place also locates his religious sense. The dimensions, limitations, specific qualities of a brook or

29

spring or pasture field become the means by which he learns of his spiritual life; such places test him with his doubts, fears, and affirmations of the self beyond inevitable death. For Frost, then, sense of place yields to the presence of his spirit, to spiritual realities which invite the poet to grow in his sense of self. Sense of place, as it reveals Frost's religious consciousness, offers a fresh, positive appreciation for his achievement and uncovers an aspect of his genius frequently overlooked. And yet, Frost's abiding instinct for the spirit has been consistently recognized by a number of critics as the most significant concern of his poetry.

Discussions of Frost's religious belief have considered the biblical materials present in his poetry, the metaphysical principles implicit in his poems, and the themes of faith, of immortality, and of the deity. The link between some poems and the Bible (the masques and "Directive" most especially) leads Sr. Catherine Theresa to outline Frost's knowledge of the scriptures, Marie Borroff to hear echoes of certain words and constructions from the Authorized Version of the Bible, William G. O'Donnell to discover that ideas in *A Masque of Mercy* are Christian, and Peter J. Stanlis to see Frost's treating man's relationship with God in the masques as "the culmination in form, technique, and theme of much that Frost has written."[4] The writings of David Hume, Henri Bergson, Emanuel Swedenborg, and William James help point to the philosophical principles of Frost's religious belief. Some of David Hume's ethical principles, according to Thomas K. Hearn, reveal the moral dimensions of Frost's characters. According to Dorothy Judd Hall, Frost learned from Bergson that the common bond between poetry and religion rests on "the concept of trust-without-experience." Kathryn Gibbs Harris points out that the Swedenborgians' appreciation for scientific knowledge gave the young Frost, who was baptized into the Swedenborgian church, "a holistic attitude toward science and religion." Lawrance Thompson throughout his biography traces the impact of William James on Frost's understanding of faith, and Thomas McClanhan sees Frost as a "philosophical poet who develops a theodicy which builds on that of William James."[5]

Themes of uncertainty and mystery in Frost's poetry have concerned other critics in their discussion of his religious beliefs. Frost's strongest religious poems come in the shadows of yearnings and doubt, according to Floyd C. Watkins. Laurence Perrine suggests that Frost found value both in uncertainty about a future life and in faith in it. For Anna K. Juhnke, Frost "plays" with religious matters as "a deliberate enactment of doubtful searching." Frost's "acceptance of mystery in existence" explains his hesitancy to speak of the supernatural for Marion Montgomery and suggests to Robert Peters that the experience of "Directive" is religious "in a broad, almost existential sense." On the notion of God, Carlos Baker finds "Frost is neither animistic enough to see God in Nature nor mystic enough to see Nature in God." Howard Mumford Jones concludes that "the God of Frost lies somewhere between the God of Job and the God of Voltaire."[6]

Frost's concern for matters of the spirit continued throughout his lifetime as the ultimate focus of his poetry; it attests to his seriousness.[7] The sense of place in his poetry embodies his religious consciousness in a way which insists upon the primary role of the spirit for Frost. Just as his reliance upon place continues from his first poems to the last ones, so does his spiritual life unfold from his first entering the pasture to his last clearing of the spring.

I

"The Pasture," used by Frost as introductory to his collected editions and to *Complete Poems* (1949), links his poetry to a sense of place. It suggests how the reader is to "come too," as spiritual companion, and it conveys the movement toward an inner life.

In "The Pasture," the poet declares his intention to go into the field where a calf totters against its mother, where a spring flows among the trees. This clearly defined area, this specific space, becomes the first of many places the poet enters and into which he invites the reader. He lives as a man of farms, of woods, of the New England states, of the earth itself. He crisscrosses the hills in walking a road or cutting a new path. He returns; comes home; reminisces; visits and revisits houses, wells, fields, and shores. The titles of his books catalogue different places: *North of Boston, Mountain Interval, New Hampshire, A Further Range,* and more. A peculiar locale characterizes "The Trial by Existence," "New Hampshire," "West-Running Brook," "Directive," and "Kitty-Hawk," among others. The poet identifies himself in relation to other people in terms of place; each person occupies "a place apart" which can reveal or conceal the self as in "Revelation." The dynamics of place put us in touch with his recurrent way of organizing experience; of structuring his poetry; and of perceiving himself, other persons, and the world about him.

The invitation in "The Pasture" clearly includes the reader: "You come too." The poet asks the reader not only to enter his poetic world, but also to accompany him in his return, to share his regeneration. Readers, then, come with a special relationship to the poet, as spiritual companions, which they must adopt to understand Frost. The reader can follow the poet as he recovers his origins in "The Trial by Existence," as he contemplates his sources through the topography of the West-Running Brook. In "Directive" the companionship reaches its fulfillment when the poet offers to the reader the goblet in order to "drink and be whole again beyond confusion," to share in the spiritual renewal of self.

"The Pasture" also directs our attention to the moral dimensions of Frost's poetry, to his religious consciousness. For such a questioning mind as that of Frost the term "religious consciousness" is to be understood in a comprehensive way. His religious sense can be defined according to William James, whose thinking Frost admired. For James, personal religion, not institutional, means "the feelings, acts, and experiences of individual men in their solitude, so far as they apprehend themselves to stand in relation to whatever they may consider divine." The whole concern of religion is "with our manner of acceptance of the universe."[8] Frost's kind of faith requires a broad view of religion such as Gordon W. Allport's description of it as an "habitual and intentional focusing of experience," or Michael Novak's view of it as a "unifying, meaning-giving drive."[9] Frost himself described his religious posture: "Now religion always seems to me to come round to something beyond wisdom. It's a straining of the spirit forward to a wisdom beyond wisdom."[10]

Frost's poems express his consciousness in the plain terms of everyday living as a balance between his restlessness and his attachment with the immediate world about him. His poetry reveals him as repeatedly anxious to "steal away," to "set forth for somewhere," while continually turning to "come by the highway home." His straining spirit tugs at his firmly planted feet in "The Sound of Trees." His heart aches to seek while his "feet question 'Whither?' " in "Reluctance." In "Away!" he obeys the urge of the song: "I'm—bound—away!" The song verbalizes his resolve to set forth. It also suggests a kind of obligation he feels to be off. While one place ties him down, other parts beckon to him. Determined to go, he feels constrained. To be bound away, to be moving from a place and yet feel bound to it, reveals his spirit as tending beyond himself. In one of his interviews Frost suggests the way he yokes his spirit to place: "I am not a regionalist. I am a realist. I write about realms of democracy and realms of spirit. The land is always in my bones."[11] That land, though limited here to a pasture, holds some clarity and tottering new life. As a native to the soil, he strains forward into the realm of the spirit. The natural world with its renewed life amid decay or its freshening hope gained from a return to origins prompts the poet toward awareness of meaning beyond his dissatisfactions and reluctances. He insists that the land is in his bones, that he lives as a native to the soil.

A deserted house, dark woods, decaying woodpile, or harvested orchard "temper" Frost's spirit. John S. Dunne provides a context helpful to understanding Frost's spiritual life when he speaks of a person's encounter with death, the quest of everlasting life, and the failure of the quest as stages in the tempering of the spirit:

> The things that come to an end in death are all the things that have their proper times and seasons in life. Spirit is not one of these things but is rather a man's relationship to each and all of them. Its tempered or untempered quality is the quality of the relationship he has to the things of his life.[12]

Frost encounters fear, loneliness, trust, and hope—"the end/Of a love or a season" in terms of places in his experience. He continually responds to these meetings with unknown, strange, and disturbing events by seeking to relate them to his life, to open himself by including them in his sense of self. According to

Dunne, to live with such awareness is to live as one "who cares more about his relationship to the things than about the things themselves and whose life therefore tends to be dominated by spirit."[13] Frost attends to his relationships as he strains within the confines of the land towards realms of wisdom and of the spirit.

Frost's poems reveal a religious consciousness as the poet repeatedly expresses himself as one who ties together his experiences. (The meaning of religion stems from the Latin *religare,* to bind, to tie.) He ties his life to the people and places around him; he attaches himself to the natural world. Paradoxically, in his bonds with the earth he finds endless inspirations for his spirit. As Poirier observes about "The Silken Tent," Frost establishes his poetry in this world with its countless ties while keeping his sights, much as the tent supports its central cedar pole, "heavenward."[14] A materialist for Frost "is the man who gets lost in his material without a gathering metaphor to throw it into shape and order. He is the lost soul."[15] Frost never gets lost in his material, never finds the world of matter, of things, satisfying. He gathers that world into a shape, ties it together. He thereby creates a new relationship with it for himself and so tempers his spirit.

Frost's poems offer a record of his spiritual history. This study will follow Frost in "The Trial by Existence," from his first volume *A Boy's Will,* through "West-Running Brook," to "Directive." Besides representing Frost over forty active years of writing and publishing, these poems mark three significant developments in the expression of his faith. He travels from heaven to earth with a youthful daring; he calmly meditates on the terrain of a contrary brook; with nostalgia he retreats to a farm no more a farm where he now can gain spiritual rebirth. The pattern of Frost's deepening sense of place represents his growing religious consciousness.

II

In "The Trial by Existence" Frost envisions earthly existence as a temporary absence from heaven for the sake of demonstrating one's valor. The bravest of souls who are slain on earth awaken in paradise to find a surprising reward. They

> Shall not dissemble their surprise
> On waking to find valor reign,
> Even as on earth, in paradise . . .

The soul wakes from death's sleep not to the quiet and passivity of "wide fields of asphodel" but to the challenge of daring earthly life once more. "To find that the utmost reward/Of daring should be still to dare."[16] The poem, with echoes of Plato's *Republic* and *Phaedrus,* has the soul leaving an existence of whole and white morning light to return to one "shattered into dyes," where colors and shadows paint the landscape.[17] The change from heaven to earth

Means the individual takes on a different identity by losing something from one's previous existence. Birth entails a "trial by existence" and "obscuration upon earth" for the spirit mystically linked to matter. Earthly life becomes a testing of the soul as existence in a material world shades and darkens what the soul knows before birth.

With the spirits before his throne, God tenderly describes "life's little dream." As a dream, life contrasts with the existence to which the souls wake after death. Heaven appears as life in full consciousness and in whole, white light; earth as a dream with its light shattered into many colors; and death as a sleep bridging the two worlds. But as God first speaks, "The tale of earth's unhonored things/ Sounds nobler there than 'neath the sun." Although standing up to the uttermost trials which earth might offer sounds heroic to the spirits who anticipate the challenge, God warns them that the perspective and understanding which they have in heaven will not console them while on earth. The fate of life

> "Admits no memory of choice,
> Or the woe were not earthly woe
> To which you give the assenting voice."

The distinctive trial of earthly existence is the complete forgetfulness of heaven and of the soul's choice to live on earth. In heaven the soul exists with clear and complete knowledge in the presence of God and in the company of other spirits. While on earth, the spirit lives inextricably bound to matter, ignorant of all that it once knew, unmindful of its original choice, without the consolation of God's presence, and lacking the comfort of companionship with other souls.

Heaven is the soul's origin, the place of perfection; the poem implies that each person longs to return to heaven, his native land. Earth is a foreign territory where the soul finds itself to be an alien, yearning for companionship. A person lives in the world as a voluntary exile, but an individual's status as a voluntary exile cannot be certified by explicit knowledge. Instinctive restlessness with the ways of earthly existence confirms the soul's longing for a whole and unlimited place to live. The poem presents a person existing either in clear awareness and in communion with God and others or in partial, incomplete knowledge and broken relationships which test a person's courage. The mystery of human existence arises from the opaqueness of the material world; creatures constantly seek to complete the fragmentary knowledge available on earth. For Frost, then, spiritual yearning for that unitive knowledge and for one's prenatal wholeness and for a community of spirits is inextricably bound with life on earth.

Frost's poem envisions an ordered, integrated universe: God watches over all as his plan works itself out. The poem presents the soul's choice to live on earth as part of God's plan. This fundamental orderliness may not be known immediately and clearly, but it does form the groundwork of existence. The soul travels the way of incarnation at its own choice; earthly life forms a stage in a journey which seeks a return to the soul's beginnings. The poet sees that souls on waking find themselves on earth, that humans are born out of a dream, as Eve was of Adam's. The poet suggests that we dream (choose) ourselves into being. It seems, too, that the poet will continually reenact that dreaming as he repeatedly dreams himself through poetry into a deeper being on earth. Using terms reminiscent of Wordsworth in his "Ode: Intimations of Immortality from Recollections of Early Childhood," Frost's poem speaks of earthly life as a temporary isolation from a soul's perfect state. Memories of its homeland prompt the soul in its deeply yearned-for return there. Within *A Boy's Will,* "The Trial by Existence" provides a context for the youthful poet's own journey. The youth's recollections of paradise contribute a tone of innocent idealism to the book and the hope for a sympathetic or Edenic world, as George W. Nitchie calls it.[18] As an exile on earth, the poet feels discontented with his environment while committed to his earthly existence which tests or tries the soul's worth. As a maturing poet he begins to gain self-knowledge by discovering in "The Trial by Existence" his own genesis.

This earthly world nourishes Frost's spiritual life because his sense of place embraces the inner, spiritual realm. As Frost himself suggests, "I write about realms of democracy and realms of the spirit. The land is always in my bones."[19] Though the poet feels his exile from heaven, he learns to overcome his feelings of dislocation by attending to the particular locale of the West-Running Brook. By uncovering the dimensions of this earthly realm which tie him to his sources and origins, he grows in his sense of self in that his life has continuity and significance beyond temporary dislocations.

In "West-Running Brook" Frost finds that nature's contraries of dissolution and resistant endurance define what "in nature we are from," what "is most us." By this deepening awareness of locale, Frost reveals the range of his own religious identity. In the poem's progress, Fred's and his wife's searching questions probe beneath the brook's topography. The poem begins with a geographical question, "Fred, where is north?" and establishes the terrain and the brook's direction. Fred's wife links them to the place and especially to the water:

> "As you and I are married to each other,
> "We'll both be married to the brook. We'll build
> Our bridge across it, and the bridge shall be
> Our arm thrown over it asleep beside it."
>
> (p. 258)

This vision of their presence alongside the brook transforms the dialogue between husband and wife and ties it to a discussion of the significance of their immediate surroundings. Man and woman become wedded to a place; locale unifies the human to the human as well as to nature: " 'We've said we two. Let's change that to we three.' " This dialogue, in seeming contradiction, will

be three-sided. Like the classical epithalamion, "West-Running Brook" concretizes the beginning of a union between man and woman as well as "the
beginning of beginnings."

The poem includes, besides the couple's perceptions of the brook, the interruptions of the narrator. Those interruptions substantiate that what is observed
actually exists in the scene. The narrator confirms the wife's naming of the
brook in the third line. What she and Fred say on this day will have lasting
significance for this land much as Eve's and Adam's naming creation in Eden:

> "West-Running Brook then call it."
> (West-Running Brook men call it to this day.)

The effects of this interruption and the later one about the sunken rock in the
black stream are to establish the natural world as the object of discussion and
to emphasize the subjectivity of Fred's and his wife's interpretations. The brook
is the locus of the conversation; it is the subject matter. The commentaries on
the brook appear highly personal and individualistic in contrast to the matter-of-
fact observations of the narrator. The poem channels these diverse perspectives
into an honest, significant conclusion.

The first observation about the stream is that it runs contrary to its surroundings, that it is unlike all of the other streams in the area. The brook's contrariness to its environment is one level of its significance and is the basis for the
couple's initial feeling of affinity with it. Perhaps the brook

> "Can trust itself to go by contraries
> The way I can with you—and you with me."
>   (p. 258)

Having established this identification, the poem focuses on the deeper contraries
of the brook with itself and on the specific responses to the brook by Fred's
wife and by Fred himself.

Fred's wife sees the water in a personal dimension:

> "Look, look, it's waving to us with a wave
> To let us know it hears me."

Fred objects to the personification because he feels that it can lead to a posses-
siveness. Her personification could isolate the meaning of the stream as well as
herself in "lady-land." The danger signalled here is the one of claiming nature as
personal property; so private an interpretation keeps the wife from significant
dialogue and from going beneath the rippling surface to the brook's underlying
meaning. With the interruption of the narrator the poem goes contrary to the
direction of the wife's subjective description.

The narrator's second interruption (a parenthetical one-sentence poem-
within-a poem) provides a description of what is in the stream which Fred and
his wife are observing. The white wave is like the white feathers of a bird strug-

gling against the undertow which, in losing the struggle, are "at last driven wrinkled/In a white scarf against the far-shore alders)" (p. 258). The white, rippling wave is what she saw as the brook's waving. She accepts Fred's objection to her observation as correct for himself, but she insists that her perception is real for herself. Fred offers to allow her interpretation to stand alone: "It is your brook! I have no more to say.' " Since they can trust themselves to go by contraries, she allows that he has more to say, and he does. And so the poem takes another direction.

What Fred sees in the flow of the stream is the action from which all existence originates, " 'the beginning of all beginnings.' " He says:

> "Speaking of contraries, see how the brook
> In that white wave runs counter to itself.
> It is from that in water we are from
> Long, long before we were from any creature."
>
> (p. 259)

This water and their present existence are part of " 'the stream of everything that runs away.' " Fred would define who they are not only by the brook's contrariness with its environment or even with itself, but also by the ultimate contrariness of existence itself, of which they and the stream partake. The flow and direction of existence is definite: to the abyss, ending in nothingness. It includes everything and everyone, as Fred realizes. Though this flow of existence is all-inclusive and destined for the void, resistance to the current offers hope. The flow is unresisted:

> "Save by some strange resistance in itself,
> Not just a swerving, but a throwing back,
> As if regret were in it and were sacred."
>
> (p. 259)

This strange vortex of regret and reluctance resists the flow of existence towards complete meaninglessness. Some positive result, some valuable residue comes from this resistance:

> "It has this throwing backward on itself
> So that the fall of most of it is always
> Raising a little, sending up a little.
>
> (p. 259)

This contrariness in life offers a small advance against the general downfall of matter. By "throwing backward on itself," nature overcomes ceaseless change, even death, with a continuum of life.

The image of matter as a universal flow meeting obstacles in its path has echoes in the writings of Henri Bergson, whom Frost read carefully and with intense interest, according to Lawrance Thompson.[20] In *Creative Evolution*

Bergson uses an image similar to Frost's stream with its "strange resistance." Bergson sees life as resisting the downward flow of matter: "Life as a whole, from the initial impulsion that thrust it into the world, will appear as a wave which rises, and which is opposed by the descending movement of matter."[21] The opposition to the descent of matter occurs in man for Bergson. In "West-Running Brook" it appears to be the same:

> "It is this backward motion toward the source,
> Against the stream, that most we see ourselves in,
> The tribute of the current to the source.
> It is from this in nature we are from.
> It is most us."
>
> (p. 260)

Alongside the stream, Fred points out to his wife that the stream signals more than its recognition of them; the stream and they are parts of one effort and movement in nature. For Fred the black stream represents the rhythm of his own life, of their marraige, of the natural world.

The poem concludes with a reconciliation of the different perspectives, with a meeting and marriage of what has been said. Fred and his wife agreed to be married to the brook, thus making themselves into "we three." There have been three descriptions of the brook: the wife's calling the brook "West-Running"; Fred's speaking of contraries; and the brook's waving which was according to the wife, "an annunciation." The poem flows toward a gathering of all the diversity. The landscape contains the streams which run in opposite directions; the brook keeps the counter motion within itself; Fred and his wife trust themselves to go by contraries. The poem concludes with the diversity of the sayings: "Today will be the day of what we both said."

In this dialogue of what "both said" the brook in its silence offers an annunciation. In his analysis of the poem, Robert H. Swennes concludes that "the meaning of 'West-Running Brook' hinges on the fact that there are three, not two, voices represented in the poem."[22] The brook's silent annunciation forms the third voice. Various annunciations in the Bible declare the special presence of God especially manifest in the promises of the births of Isaac, of Samuel, of the Messiah, and of Jesus. The West-Running Brook announces the presence of God within itself, within the couple, within nature. It declares that more fundamental and more powerful than the cataract of death is the source of life, is "time, strength, tone, light, life, and love." As the poem, in its way, verbalizes and externalizes what the couple see in the brook, so they announce their deep, interior union with one another and with nature. They share and contain the same spirit and movement, the tension of contrary forces.

The poem began with a question of direction: " 'Fred, where is north?' " The poem's energies move from questions about the surface to recognition of the forces within the stream. The poem turns from topography to the fundamental stratum of nature. By means of the place where the couple stand nature reveals itself as the origin of their being and the site of their existence. The moment alongside the stream is one backward motion, an island of resistance to the constant flow of life. In standing against the rush of matter, the couple strike a relationship with their own separate persons and a relationship between themselves. Both relationships rely on the inner life, on the spirit. Because they live on a level deeper than superficial contradiction, they can trust themselves to go by contraries. In that trust they celebrate their union with "the beginning of beginnings" which transcends the confusing flux of change. They recognize, as Fred says, that this river has waved "Ever since rivers . . . /Were made in heaven." In that recognition they discover the creative source of their selves, the transcendent genesis of their united spirit.

"West-Running Brook" forms a poetic locale which briefly holds back the general onrush. It is a momentary stay against confusion, containing in itself contrasting views. This poem exemplifies one kind of human resistance to the flux. Nina Baym sees Frost's poetic dynamic in this light: "Frost's poems are examples of the one kind of action, mind staying flux, which he recognizes as meaningfully asserting the human in a fundamentally nonhuman world."[23] This poem uncovers the balanced tension which underlies the natural phenomenon and the human responses, and, in celebrating a newfound spiritual oneness, the poem stems the initial confusion of a west-running brook.

The exile's restlessness with his trial by existence and the natural resistence discovered by the married couple in the contrary brook together prompt the poet in "Directive" to guide the reader back along the road to the almost forgotten spring of wholeness. In the natural setting of life, death, and renewed life, the poet finds the way to the original waters of spiritual rebirth. His journey back to the cold stream blazes the way to redemption because he returns to the decaying farm with its spring where he can "be whole again beyond confusion." The poem first shows the road's directions, then requires a testing under the guidance of the poet, finally allowing for salvific healing through nature's source and through poetry.

"Directive" begins by following a road back to an abandoned farmhouse. The directions are clear, the destination specific: withdrawal from the confusing "now" leads to an encounter with "a time made simple" in the dwindling farmyard. The poet's native restlessness and resistance from his nostalgic urge to return there:

> There is a house that is no more a house
> Upon a farm that is no more a farm
> And in a town that is no more a town.
> (p. 377)

The movement here is one physical action—walking along the deserted road—requiring two psychological exercises, retreating from the "too much" and entering the weathered graveyard where the loss of detail has simplified time. Here the poet reverses his previous direction and movement familiar in "Two Look at Two," "Stopping by Woods on a Snowy Evening," and "Come In." As James P. Doughterty points out, in the earlier poems the poet "turns back, withdrawing into human society." But in "Directive," Doughterty says, "directions are reversed; the guide turns 'back' into the woods, and recommends that the listener follow." The poet steps "across the deadline into a dark, inhuman nightmare."[24]

Unlike the escape of "Birches" or the frustration of "An Encounter," "Directive" provides a way out of the overwhelming complexity of the present moment. But the way out is the way in; the poem's escape takes the poet to a deeper involvement with his world by leading him to

> the height
> Of country where two village cultures faded
> Into each other. Both of them are lost.
>
> (p. 378)

When he allows his setting to work on him, he loses much of his confusion. In his meeting "the height of country," he finds his own personal source of identity.

The road in "Directive" connects the two locations specified in the opening lines; it links "this now too much" with "a time made simple." The poet again moves from surface detail to the enduring marble substance, from the "pretense of keeping covered" to the underlying reality of nature's constant flow of life. The change in location does not rupture the continuity of his life but strengthens it by returning him to the origins of nature itself. He backs away from the periphery of his life with its multiple engagements to his inner circle from the center of which springs his sense of self. He follows for himself the quarry road which the "enormous Glacier" chiseled from the monolithic substratum.

Besides taking the unfrequented road into the cool, scrutinizing woods, the poet looks for a special kind of companionship. While he does offer guidance to his partner, the relationship is more than that of pilgrim to guide. "Directive" calls for more involvement than does the simple invitation to companionship in "The Pasture." One can travel the road back to the abandoned house on a condition:

> The road there, if you'll let a guide direct you
> Who only has at heart your getting lost,
> May seem as if it should have been a quarry.
>
> (p. 377)

The indirectness and paradox understate the poet's appeal for trust. The poet-guide recognizes the other's reluctance. In line 36 the question is put more directly, but still in a conditional clause:

> And if you're lost enough to find yourself
> By now, pull in your ladder road behind you
> And put a sign up CLOSED to all but me.
>
> (p. 378)

The only other human being is to be the poet. When all sense of familiar, helpful landmarks disappear, one can turn to the poet. Though others become disoriented in "all this now too much," the poet is not lost; he knows where he is; he finds the way. After gaining his companion's trust, the poet shares the truth he has learned by revealing what he has hidden. While this retreat inward seems to imply a rejection of others, it requires the closest kind of exchange between the two travelers.

This dependence upon the poet is only one of several tests which the poem contains. The journey becomes a trial or "serial ordeal" while the poet retraces his steps over familiar terrain. The reader is tested from the start with the riddle of syntax and paradoxical statements, as Marie Borroff suggests.[25] This test begins on the verbal level and goes on to the physical, with the exercise and discomfort of the mountain's coolness and then to the personal, with examination by the unseen eyes in cellar holes and by the rustling trees. The poet himself proves to be a good guide by not only leading the way to the end but also by pointing out the features which make this an ordeal. His calm reassurance, "you must not mind . . . nor need you mind the serial ordeal," soothes anxieties while confirming his role as guide.

The field with its houses were the announced goal of this quest; they represent time made simple. When the poet and companion arrive at the field, their movement reverses the chronology of human development as they pass first "the children's house of make-believe," then the "house in earnest." They retrace the line of growth from adulthood to childhood back to infancy when the child is confined to the house and nursery. Their coming back to this field freshens their spirits much as in "The Pasture" where the newborn calf was found, where Frost introduced the freshening his poetry offers. In resisting the flow of their experience which adds detail upon detail, which "spends to nothingness" (as Fred observes in "West-Running Brook"), the poet with his companion take possession of themselves as they regain some of their spent energy.

"Directive," in the spirit of the West-Running Brook, seeks the beginning of all by going past the house to the stream at its headwaters:

> Your destination and your destiny's
> A brook that was the water of the house,
> Cold as a spring as yet so near it source,
> Too lofty and original to rage.
>
> (p. 378)

The stream itself runs fresh and cold because it is near its originating spring. The poet goes against the current. By making the trip he offers tribute to his source. Unlike the couple in "West-Running Brook" who saw themselves standing off from the bank resisting the flow, the two here make the backward motion. It is the effort itself of this moving backward from present to past, from valley of the raging flood to the mountain source, which makes them whole again. In contrast to the deteriorating house and shrinking field, this brook provides as constantly as ever pure, refreshing water. The brook remains unchanged, undiminished with the passage of time; it continues to be cold and vital while life and death, pine and lilac, mark the surrounding field and cellar hole. The guide's final action is to bring out the goblet from hiding; this last enigma becomes no obstacle with the guide's assistance. Identification with the persistent flow of life-giving waters amidst this scene of decaying houses, of broken dreams and myths, leads to salvation.

The act of drinking from the waters with the goblet is salvific because it puts the two companions in touch with their origin, that is, nature's wellspring of life. By reaching this destination they discover a completeness to their lives and come upon their destiny. The humble acceptance of their fragile lives as contained within the blurred world of change and death renews them. The contact with this source concretizes the poet's sense of wholeness. Frost is quoted by Theodore Morrison, a long-time friend, as singling out *source* as the key to "Directive":

> People miss the key to the poem: the key lines, if you want to know, are "cold as a spring as yet so near its source,/Too lofty and original to rage . . ." But the key word in the whole poem is source—whatever source it is.[26]

The poet reaches a special kind of source when he comes to the cold spring in "Directive." This stream flows with ground water which percolates to the earth's surface through sand, stone, or, here, the hard rock of the mountain. The water bubbles up fresh from below; the poet comes to where the water springs forth into the air. He drinks of water which is the rich overflow, the superabundance, of the earth itself. This kind of source has a unique tie with place; it represents the special fruitfulness of the natural world itself. At this spring the poet's exploration of place reaches a mature fulfillment in that he comes to his most intimate contact with the physical world; he comes closest to the source of life on earth at this origin of life-sustaining water; he comes nearest his own spiritual rebirth in the abandonment and death which he has had to undergo during this quest. At this moment alongside the water, the poet is graced with a sense of wholeness with himself, with nature. This wholeness becomes his holiness by redeeming him from his initial confusion, from the emptiness he had felt, from the "universal cataract of death" which he sees flowing past him among the "graveyard marble sculpture" of this farmyard.

Taking the goblet and drinking from it consecrates the relationship between the two companions. This Grail, though broken and minimized as a plaything, nonetheless allows them to drink of the healing waters. The poet promises wholeness here in the cool, uncertain world of nature which persistently refuses to be domesticated or mythologized. The woods and lilac and water continue to grow and flow as sturdily as ever. The poet has learned that when he can no longer identify where he is, when he is lost enough to find himself, he is then ready to allow the place to identify who he is. Instead of seeking clarity and understanding from any superficial and peripheral features, he looks to the unchanging, ever-changing substance of life in the natural world. In this environment where details have faded and essences remain, the poet finds the same process at work within himself. He withdraws from his outer edges to come to terms with his inner self. Frost refers to this impulse in an interview:

> I think a person has to be withdrawn into himself to gather inspiration so that he is somebody when he comes out again among folks ... He learns that he's got to be almost wastefully alone.[27]

Accompanying the poet requires a withdrawal to this place of the fecund minimum which does not decay into something meager or inadequate but rather bestows the fullness of life.

The quest itself offers form for the poet by providing a recognizable link between events in his life when marking the ground which has been covered. The walk and the tests along the way span the times and places which have passed since he had his beginning. In his "The Figure a Poem Makes," Frost uses the image of a road created in the act of walking for the creative process of writing a poem. For the poet the final recognition at the conclusion of writing is that

> like giants we are always hurling experience ahead of us to pave the future with against the day when we may want to strike a line of purpose across it for somewhere. The line will have the more charm for not being mechanically straight.[28]

Here in "Directive" the speaker with his partner go back over the line of develment. By walking the distance they can feel and internalize through sight, sound, and kinesthetic perception their interval of existence. The terrain offers a measure for them of the expanse of their lives. They can tie together many details and disparate experiences into a new bond which they did not have before their walk back.

To see "Directive" in its fullest dimensions is to consider it as a poetic quest. After the retreat back in time and the commitment to the guide and the search, after being at home with diminished things, after reaching the headwaters, the poem also offers itself as an emblem of the poetic process. The play with words in the opening lines, the paradoxes, and the reference to the riddle of parables all attract attention to the poem as a verbal endeavor. The role of guide is a thin disguise of the poet going through the terrain of language. The imagery and thrust of "Directive" resonate with Frost's descriptions of poetry as a point of departure, as a voyage of discovery, as a form holding back confusion.

Frost speaks of the word as a point of departure in his essay "The Romantic Chasm." The poet departs from safety and clarity when he is led by his spirit:

> In the beginning was the word, to be sure, very sure, and a solid basic comfort it remains in situ, but the fun only begins with the spirited when you treat the word as a point of many departures. There is risk in the play. But if some of the company get lost in the excitement, charge it up to proving the truth of chapter and verse in the Gospel according to Saint Mark.[29]

The word and the play with the word offer many directions, some of them dead ends, as Frost was aware: "These things are said in parables (that is, poetry, figure of speech), so the wrong people cannot understand them, and so get saved."[30] The readers, even the poet, must finally trust the poem to lead them to clarity and understanding. As Frost points out, "Every poem is a voyage of discovery. I go in to see if I can get out, like you go to the North Pole."[31] The poet, as an experienced traveler, will risk getting lost because he knows that he may discover renewed life.

As the turning back into nature with its wilderness offers a place with a perspective which can heal, so poetry can provide a comparable point of view. Frost suggests this dimension to poetry in an interview:

> Poetry is very, very rural—rustic. It stands as a reminder of rural life—as a resource, as a recourse. It might be taken as a symbol of man, taking its rise from individuality and seclusion—written first for the person that writes and then going out into its social appeal and use.[32]

Rural life suggests the open country and farming: *rural* people live on open land; *rustic* notes a clearer contrast with city living. "Poetry is very, very rural—rustic" as it takes us to open land, away from the crowding together in buildings paved against the earth. It offers a stance, a direction toward other people and toward one's self. Poetry demonstrates the need of being versed in country things if we are to face fear, loneliness, even death. As a resource, poetry represents the spiritual vision which can include strange, threatening experience into a whole life. Poetry requires an imagination open to birth and death, to a pattern of growth, fruitfulness, decay, and rebirth. As the poet here deepens his sense of place, specifically of rural place, he expands his religious consciousness through poetry. He journeys to the country, then through the verbal terrain of his poetry to spiritual realms.

Finally, the sense of form within a poem appears to be the same kind of understanding gained from journeying back to one's sources. As a sense of order arises from bridging the gap between the present and one's origin, so coherence emerges from the run of a successful poem:

> The figure a poem makes . . . It beings in delight, it inclines to impulse, it assumes direction with the first line laid down, it runs a course of lucky events, and ends in a clarification of life . . . in a momentary stay against confusion. It has denouement. It has an outcome that though unforeseen was predestined from the first image of the original mood—and indeed from the very mood.[33]

"Directive" runs a course of lucky events which ends in a momentary stay against confusion. The poem's directive points to poetry itself, and the poet guides the way. He holds out the goblet as "a metaphor for poetry," according to S. P. C. Duvall. The drinking cup becomes "a metaphor for metaphor: the form and container of the perennial and limitless source."[34] In its metaphors "Directive" represents the poet's religious consciousness as arising from his sense of place. Through metaphor he enunciates a relationship with the world about him. He firmly connects himself to nature, to its mystery of life with death; in so doing he defines himself as a person related to nature, as one with a spiritual identity continuous with nature's pattern and yet distinct from nature. Through the poetic journey here the poet backs out of the present moment with its overwhelming detail, gains a perspective, and backs into a world where the simple origin of life in nature refreshes his spirit. The poet allows the enduring natural world to reveal himself to himself. The confusing fragmentations of his experience grows into a unity which gives him a new, perfected awareness of the singularity of his life, an awareness of the lasting vitality of the world, and a responsibility to guide others.

III

Each particular locality holds its own vital effluence for D. H. Lawrance. For Frost a sense of place emerges from the world he inhabits and inspires him to life of the spirit. While Frost surveys the land and people of New England, his sense of place matures into a religious consciousness. His spirit lives with the courage which the trial of new life requires; he lives with a vision which prompts him to resist the flow of existence, thereby redeeming himself from the inevitable flux; he rests peacefully at the quiet, regenerative source of the natural world. The poems discussed here represent major landmarks on his spiritual journey. Each volume of his poetry adds a chapter to the story of his religious consciousness.[35] The reader learns of Frost's spiritual history only by coming too as pilgrim, as companion, to his poetry. What place offers to Frost his poetry offers to the reader: realms of the spirit.

RONALD BIEGANOWSKI

Marquette University

Notes

1. D. H. Lawrence, *Studies in Classic American Literature* (New York: Viking, 1964), pp. 5-6.

2. John F. Lynen, *The Pastoral Art of Robert Frost* (New Haven: Yale Univ. Press, 1960), p. 7.

3. Richard Poirier, *Robert Frost: The Work of Knowing* (New York: Oxford Univ. Press, 1977), p. 89.

4. Sister Catherine Theresa, "New Testament Interpretations of Robert Frost's Poems," *Ball State University Forum,* 11 (1970), 50-54; Marie Borroff, "Robert Frost's New Testament: Language and the Poem," *Modern Philology,* 69 (1971), 35-56; William G. O'Donnell, "Parable in Poetry," *Virginia Quarterly Review,* 25 (1949), 269-82; Peter J. Stanlis, "Robert Frost's Masques and the Classic American Tradition," *Frost: Centennial Essays,* ed. Jac Tharpe (Jackson: Univ. Press of Mississippi, 1974), p. 465.

5. Thomas K. Hearn, Jr., "Making Sweetbreads Do: Robert Frost and Moral Empiricism," *New England Quarterly,* 49 (1976), 65-81; Dorothy Judd Hall, "The Height of Feeling Free: Frost and Bergson," *Texas Quarterly,* 19 (Spring 1976), 128-43; Kathryn Gibbs Harris, "Robert Frost's Early Education in Science," *South Carolina Review,* 7 (Nov. 1974), 13-33; Lawrance Thompson and R. H. Winnick, *Robert Frost: The Later Years, 1938-1963,* especially pp. 397-400; Thomas McClanahan, "Frost's Theodicy: 'Word I Had No One Left But God,' " *Frost: Centennial Essays* II, ed. Jac Tharpe (Jackson: Univ. Press of Mississippi, 1976), p. 112.

6. Floyd C. Watkins, "Going and Coming Back: Robert Frost's Religious Poetry," *South Atlantic Quarterly,* 73 (1974), 445-59; Laurence Perrine, "Robert Frost and the Idea of Immortality," *Frost: Centennial Essays* II, pp. 85-98; Anna K. Juhnke, "Religion in Robert Frost's Poetry: The Play for Self-Possession," *American Literature,* 36 (1964), 152-64; Marion Montgomery, "Robert Frost and His Use of Barriers: Man vs. Nature Toward God," *South Atlantic Quarterly,* 57 (1958), 339-53; Robert Peters, "The Truth of Frost's 'Directive,' " *Modern Language Notes,* 75 (1960), 29-32; Carlos Baker, "Frost on the Pumpkin," *Georgia Review,* 11 (1957), 128; Howard Mumford Jones, "The Cosmic Loneliness of Robert Frost," *Belief and Disbelief in American Literature* (Chicago: Univ. of Chicago Press, 1967), p. 137.

7. Jac Tharpe, "Religion," in *Frost: Centennial Essays,* p. 413.

8. William James, *The Varieties of Religious Experience* (New York: Modern Library, 1902), pp. 31-32, 41.

9. Gordon W. Allport, *The Individual and his Religion* (New York: Macmillan, 1950), p. 4; Michael Novak, *Ascent of the Mountain, Flight of the Dove* (New York: Harper & Row, 1971), p. 3.

10. Robert Frost, A Sermon, Rockdale Temple, Cincinnati, Ohio, 10 Oct. 1946, as quoted by Victor E. Reichert, "The Faith of Robert Frost," in *Frost: Centennial Essays,* p. 420.

11. *Interviews with Robert Frost,* ed. Edward Connery Lathem (New York: Holt, Rinehart and Winston, 1966), p. 124.

12. John S. Dunne, *Time and Myth* (Garden City, N. Y.: Doubleday, 1973), p. 13.

13. Dunne, p. 91.

14. Poirier, p. xv.

15. "Education by Poetry," in *Selected Prose by Robert Frost,* ed. Hyde Cox and Edward Connery Lathem (New York: Collier Books, 1968), p. 41.

16. Robert Frost, *The Poetry of Robert Frost*, ed. Edward Connery Lathem (New York: Holt, Rinehart and Winston, 1969), p. 19. All further references to this work appear in the text.

17. Lawrence Thompson, *Robert Frost: The Early Years, 1874-1915* (New York: Holt, Rinehart and Winston, 1966), pp. 294, 555.

18. George W. Nitchie, *Human Values in the Poetry of Robert Frost* (Durham, N.C.: Duke Univ. Press, 1960), pp. 78–91.

19. *Interviews*, p. 124.

20. Thompson, *Early Years*, pp. 381–82.

21. Henri Bergson, *Creative Evolution* (New York: Modern Library, 1944), p. 293.

22. Robert H. Swennes, "Man and Wife: The Dialogue of Contraries in Robert Frost's Poetry," *American Literature*, 42 (1970), 369.

23. Nina Baym, "An Approach to Robert Frost's Nature Poetry," *American Quarterly*, 17 (1964), 723.

24. James P. Dougherty, "Robert Frost's 'Directive' to the Wilderness," *American Quarterly*, 18 (1966), 212.

25. Borroff, p. 50.

26. Theodore Morrison, "The Agitated Heart," *Atlantic Monthly*, (July 1967), p. 79.

27. *Interviews*, p. 76.

28. *Selected Prose*, p. 19.

29. *Selected Prose*, p. 78.

30. *Interviews*, p. 162.

31. *Interviews*, p. 188.

32. *Interviews*, pp. 75–76.

33. *Selected Prose*, p. 18.

34. S. P. C. Duvall, "Robert Frost's 'Directive' out of *Walden*," *American Literature*, 31 (1960), 487.

35. Ronald Bieganowski, "Realms of the Spirit: An Inquiry Into Robert Frost's Sense of Place," Diss. Fordham 1977.

Detachment, Irony, and Commitment

Frost's notorious authorial detachment sometimes creates problems in interpreting his meanings. The very subtle tones may seem enigmatic, and even irony may be difficult to discern. Much of the difficulty stems from the poet's extraordinary subtlety, even detachment, that produces an objectivity which the reader interprets subjectively according to his own attitudes, as I shall be doing here. To what extent is the poet detached? Is that detachment part of a constant ironic stance, precluding significant commitments?

I propose Frost operates in three major ways. He objectively presents what he considers an ambiguity inherent to the human situation. But at times he finds ironic contrasts between the expected and the actual event so severe that he can make no commitment. And at other times he moves beyond the detachment in objectivity and irony to a commitment that incorporates and transcends the essential ambiguity. A study of Frost's ironic vision suggests that to Frost detachment and commitment are related, and even necessary, to each other.

Given an inherent ambiguity, many philosophical questions have no clear answers. Detachment is a reasonable approach to this ambiguity rooted in man's limited knowledge, but the reasonableness is also the limitation of this approach, as we will see. In his detachment Frost is willing to ask, if not answer, the difficult questions, always wondering how much is too much. The poet's detachment can seem to foster a glib acceptance of whatever is. But detachment in technique seems to some readers to enhance a philosophical detachment, a fatalistic acceptance. Within the group of poems on this question of acceptance, the approach varies: "Acceptance" falls between the light tones of "A Peck of Gold," and the ominous tones of "Once by the Pacific" and is followed by "Lodged," in which man, like the flowers, clearly must take what comes—and survive if possible. "Acceptance," presented with more detachment than these other poems, seems more difficult to interpret, and the poet's attitude here toward essential ambiguity has been interpreted in several ways; that is, is there sympathy or ironic ridicule for the birds' acceptance?

The situation itself is clear: the birds accept the coming of night, which may suggest impending disaster, with "Let what will be, be."[1] Melodramatic touches, such as the poor waif's finding his perch just in the nick of time, indicate the poet is tongue-in-cheek, but to what extent? The birds accept "the change to darkness in the sky." The tone of that phrase is not for me ironic as the birds' acceptance is not discounted; the phenomenon is simply directly expressed. Without reassurance the sun will reappear, the birds still do not "cry aloud" at this "change to darkness in the sky"; the birds simply accept what has to be accepted. Both people and birds had better plan ahead for what they know will happen—in other words, find a safe perch when necessary. Such acceptance is the height of common sense and the beginning of serenity:

> Murmuring something quiet in her breast,
> One bird begins to close a faded eye.
>
> (p. 249)

But while man is like the birds in being unable to see into the future, he does not have to be fatalistic. Nor does the poem show such a fatalism; it shows the creatures saving themselves by accepting what must be. Some readers do find the poem ironic: since the bird is merely following its instincts, man should neither take literally nor adopt that philosophy of acceptance. However, the reader may be reading himself into the poem. In a dramatic—that is, objective—presentation, some such mirror effect may be inevitable. But *acceptance* may be a *positive* term in Frost's work. Even retreat may be strategically essential so that one can strike "yet another blow" (p. 470).

Frost can, when he wishes, divest language even more completely of the poet's attitude and simply present the dramatic situation, particularly when portraying the inherent ambiguity. In "The Draft Horse," for example, as a couple rides in the dark ("The most unquestioning pair/That ever accepted fate" [pp. 443–44]), violence occurs. What happens is clear enough; the couple move through the pathless dark, unable to see more than the man appearing to kill their horse, forcing them "to get down and walk the rest of the way." The characters, action, and scene are symbolic of the human condition: the stark, general details; the significance of the little drama; and the humanizing "frail" are all clues to the symbolic interpretation. What is not clear is whether the poet supports the attitude of that "most unquestioning pair." Their being "the least disposed to ascribe/Any more than [they] had to hate" seems like an admirable trait.

The implication of this ambiguity may be that we must act in just such a world despite the difficulty of not fully knowing causes or consequences and must recognize that our own attitudes may be our worst decision. Some critics feel that if an artist dramatizes the ambiguity and remains detached, he has somehow failed.

In "Bereft" the presentation is sufficiently objective that only the subtle use of tone and rhyme can finally hint that the speaker does not simply depend on God, accepting fate. The last line, "Word I had no one left but God," may be read in conflicting ways, each casting a different light on other details in the poem. Powerful, threatening forces in nature seem to the speaker even malevolent. The man is in a frightening situation, and his opening question calls attention to his sense of insecurity: "Where had I heard this wind before/Change like this is to a deeper roar?" (p. 251) Both the tight form and the succinct description intensify through understatement. The irregular rhyme scheme gives immediately a sense of relentless building with five repetitions of the same sound. The relentlessness and ominousness are enhanced by the low *o* sound in the first five rhymes and in the last six, with the hissing sounds of double *s*'s in the other rhymes. The snake imagery ("Leaves got up in a coil and hissed") reminds the reader of man's Fall, his inheriting a world in which he can be bereft. The situation seems beyond relief so that the reader is not likely to find much consolation in God's presence. Still, some may, and there is little in the poem to deny such a reading. On the other hand, the line "Blindly struck at my knee and missed" may be taken ironically, implying that God does not exist; for one to have "no one left but God" may be an emphatic way of saying just how isolated man is. The only slant rhyme in the poem is *abroad/God. God* turns out to be a jarring note, without reinforcements which could justify His helpfulness here. The wind knows the speaker has "no one left but God," but its tone is still "sinister": it is unimpressed. That God may not exist heightens both the sense of isolation and the threat of impending doom. The ironic reading is probably more appealing to most modern readers because it sharpens the contrast: the same Force which has bereft man and left him isolated is now called to comfort him. Still, much theology exists to explain that paradox.

Frost seems objectively to present situations of essential ambiguity; the reader may see discrepances that are to him ironic. A reader with his own strongly contrasting attitudes would probably override the subtle weightings in the poem. These difficulties of interpretation stemming from the poet's objectivity and detachment are complicated further when one looks at the poet's detachment from his speakers. Not only may the reader draw his own conclusions from an objective presentation of ambiguity, but he also may be given only few and subtle clues to the poet's attitude in a dramatic presentation of character. With excellent negative capability Frost is able to detail characters in their own words and deeds, a technique that at times exposes their limitations and more clearly reveals the poet's distance from them. Frost likes the challenge of characterizing a speaker through his own expressions and carefully details his speakers in diction and gesture. What Frost can do with characters he can do with narrators, even his poetic "I." Clearer understanding of Frost's poems has come with the recognition that his speakers are not necessarily his spokesmen. But then the reader must question the extent to which the narrator is reliable, that is, supported by the poet. Moreover, especially though a narrator, Frost may seem to take a position that in fact he is undermining, effecting an often subtle irony and exposing the narrator. The use of a persona is not necessarily an evasive technique; the poet may still inform the poem's tone. But Frost does not always choose to do so. When the presentation is sufficiently subtle and dramatic, the reader may not be sure whether the narrator is intentionally being exposed; perhaps the poet himself does not see these discrepancies. In "Trespass" the narrator seems reliable; in "The Road Not Taken," unreliable; in "For Once, Then, Something," questionable.

One could read "Trespass" superficially as a rigid insistence upon property rights. But the speaker in "Trespass" begins with an admission of the complications in his situation:

> No, I had set no prohibiting sign,
> And yes, my land was hardly fenced.
> Nevertheless the land was mine.
> I was being trespassed on and against.
>   (p. 364)

The trespasser has given the speaker a "strangely restless day" although the speaker knows he has little property right to the fossils in the area. Human and geological time units are contrasted and clearly structured by reference to clocks and fossils in the poem. Thus, the poet emphasizes the irony of "property rights" in the light of geological time, juxtaposing nature's endurance against man's transcience, but it is not altogether clear whether the narrator understands that ironic implication. He does, however, have a perspective on his somewhat ridiculous stance of clockwatching. Still, he insists there are necessary human courtesies in society:

> He asked for a drink at the kitchen door,
> An errand he may have had to invent,
> But it made by property mine once more.
>   (p. 364)

He knows he is overly concerned about being trespassed against, but he is finally at ease only when his property rights have been acknowledged. From his play with two prepositions ("trespassed on and against") in the first stanza to his awareness in the last stanza that the "errrand" may have had to be "invented," the speaker shows his perspective on his own situation. Because he seems reliable, his insistence on human courtesies seems more clearly supported by the poem, which is also to say, by the poet behind the poem. The poet informs the poem, perhaps to some extent beyond the speaker's understanding of himself, with the significance of boundaries, identities, and courtesies. I do not find the poet attacking property rights, nor do I find the poet portraying an entirely unwitting speaker who is exposing his limited vision.

The poet's detachment from the speaker's vision is evident in "The Road Not Taken," though many readers identify with the speaker and miss the poet's clues. The speaker adheres to the nostalgic regret, right down to the last line, but the poet has, it seems to me, structured within the poem an ironic interpretation of that vision—the Byronic pose; the contradiction in the speaker's calling the paths equally untraveled, then choosing to think he had taken "the one less traveled"; the wrenched rhyme; and the exaggerated nostalgia of the last stanza:

> I shall be telling this with a sigh
> Somewhere ages and ages hence:
> Two roads diverged in a wood, and I—
> I took the one less traveled by,
> And that has made all the difference.
>
> (p. 105)

The writer depends on us to use these clues to see the discrepancy between the speaker's attitude and the general knowledge that although one regrets his inability to travel both roads at once, railing against such givens shows immaturity. Of course, one may regret such forced options without necessarily railing against the human condition. That Frost understood such an attitude may explain in part why the speaker is drawn so objectively and realistically that many readers easily identify with him and find in the poem a note of sympathetic understanding for the nostalgic speaker.

"For Once, Then, Something" seems more problematic, both in the speaker's reliability and in the poet's attitude toward the subject of ambiguity. The narrator thinks himself superior because he knows that visions may be more solipsistic than mystical, and thus ridicules the ridicule leveled at him by his critic. He details, exposing as exaggeration, the portrait of himself seeking truth, "kneeling," "wrong to the light," "trying with chin against a well-curb." All he can see is the reflection of himself as cherubic and even godlike, looking out from a "wreath of fern and cloud puffs" in the slick superficiality of "shining surface picture." "Rebuke" and "lo!" suggest the exaggerated solemnity of his search and its inevitable failure; in the nature of things man cannot and should not know the Truth: "Water came to rebuke the too clear water." The obvious cliches and ridiculousness suggest that an ironic reading is intended. Indeed, the obvious irony makes the anticlimax seem sophomoric. His assertion that once he really did see something—and might have some truth—turns out to be the cliche that truth is not clear: "What was that whiteness?/Truth? A pebble of quartz? For once, then, something" (p. 225). The narrator's tone seems insufferably smug, even though we may accept the principle of an essential ambiguity. All the cliches about the search for truth are found here; the poet is surely aware of them, though the narrator may not be. The narrator too much enjoys bringing off what is an anticlimax. We cannot say whether the poet intends us to see the *narrator's* attitude as ultimately limited. To what extent is "For Once" poorly structured because the poet's stance is not so clearly evident as in "Trespass" or even "The Road Not Taken"? That I am not sure how the poet views the narrator is disconcerting because the poem does not simply present ambiguity in itself but suggests in the narrator an attitude toward it that can be acceptable in part and unacceptable in part. The *poet's* reticence here seems less objective and more evasive. Certainly, if the author, in trying to present all sides of a situation, presents finally a confused and contradictory tone within the poem, the experience is frustrating for the reader.

Is the poet avoiding commitment with this emphasis on ambiguity *and* objectivity? This question has often been raised, and to consider it, we must first consider the extent to which Frost the poet believes commitment is valuable and possible. Frost does explore the potential for irony in detachment; his speakers are almost always aware of possible reversals of man's expectations. A familiar criticism of Frost, made most recently by Marion Montgomery, is that because he realizes the constant possiblity for irony, he refuses to make commitments.[2] Frost is sometimes considered a whimsical escapist, a kind of General Ironist, one who knows both man's needs for rational certainty and his certain inability to achieve it.[3] In such a philosophy of total rational prudence, commitment is irrational and unwise. Considering man's inability to know and control much in his world and even in himself, considering his vulnerability to tragedy, and considering his given responsibility of life and death, he *can* view the whole of human existence ironically, always finding the absurd because neither the world nor man functions always rationally. This rational bias and a recognition of the essential ambiguity produce the General Ironist. Because the ironist wants a rational certainty, he constantly exposes the lack of such certainty in all attempts to esablish truth. Knowledge is fragmentary, and reality is never clear through appearances.

Is Frost such a General Ironist, at least in the genetle versions of spiritual drifter? One of his major themes is man's limited knowledge, and Frost does explore the potential for irony in the essential ambiguity.[4] With necessary ironic detachment he delights in exposing the glibness in much "thinking," particularly in much idealism. Wherever possible, he will frustrate superficial expectations: he reminds us, for instance, that peace is made possible only by war or the threat of war.[5] We cannot achieve the good except in relation to the necessary evil. Furthermore, he understands the truth in the General Ironist's stance: there is no rational certainty but instead a multiplicity of relative goods and realities. He plays, aware of the absurdities, with limited knowledge against a silent omniscience—his famous "The Secret Sits." Commitments or beliefs in such circumstances make man extremely vulnerable, and the General Ironist, even as spiritual drifter, will not risk a faith.

In *A Masque of Reason* Frost explores the problem of faith and acceptance: he has the principals in the mythic drama of ambiguity, Job and God, debate the old question again from both man's and God's points of view. In the myth of Job the essential ambiguity of man's situation has been created by Job's "freeing" God from the Deuteronomist's laws, which had limited God to rewarding virtue and punishing wickedness. With Job's trials a new principle is established:

> There's no connection man can reason out
> Between his just deserts and what he gets.
>
> (p. 475)

God explains to Thyatira that Job had to learn to submit to "unreason" (p. 481). From God's point of view, the result is freedom for God to be God. Even though God promises that He will do anything for Job "in reason" (p. 486), the meaning of "in reason" is still God's arbitrary definition. Job elaborates on man's need for reason which he equates with "design" (p. 482), and since he is talking with God, who is free to be God, Job questions the value of ambiguity inherent in the human condition:

> The obscurity's a fraud to cover nothing.
> I've come to think no so-called hidden value's
> Worth going after.
>
> (p. 483)

Job does finally get a reason: "I was just showing off to the Devil, Job,/As is set forth in chapters One and Two" (pp. 484–85). But that is not a reason Job can quite understand, and he relents: "Let's leave it as it stood./The point was it was none of my concern" (p. 485). The poem ends with a conditional "if". The Devil, "God's best inspiration" (p. 487), has been summoned, and as Job's wife is taking a picture of the three actors in the drama, she comments: "Now if you three have settled anything/You'd as well smile as frown on the occasion" (p. 490).

In "The Lovely Shall be Choosers" the poet dramatizes General Irony as a terrible irony of fate. The power of the Universe again insists on unreason:

> There is no connection man can reason out
> Between his just deserts and what he gets.
>
> (p. 475)

An actor in this drama of the potential of irony in essential ambiguity is a woman who has disregarded probable fate and thus roused the Supreme Ironist, here a disembodied Voice. Always man must act without knowing the consequences, and therein lies the opportunity for the Supreme Ironist, who delivers her to his henchmen, the Voices:

> "She would refuse love safe with wealth and honor!
> The lovely shall be choosers, shall they?
> Then let them choose! . . ."
>
> (p. 256)

The woman achieves nobility by accepting the consequences; she maintains her pride by not asking for sympathy. The Supreme Ironist foretells succinctly, objectively, her future and concludes:

> "You know them—seven ["joys"] in all."
> "Trust us," the Voices said.
>
> (p.257)

All the positive meanings of "trust us" intensify the bitter irony that her fate will be meticulously, relentlessly, impersonally carried out over the long years to come. That the fate is still to occur in the woman's life makes these omniscient Powers seem even more cruel.

Frost shows how man may come to terms with General Irony in *A Masque of Mercy*. At the end Keeper's insight reminds us of "The Lovely Shall be Choosers":

> And I can see that the uncertainty
> In which we act is a severity,
> A cruelty, amounting to an injustice . . .
>
> (p. 520)

Because of such uncertainty, Keeper concludes:

> Courage is what it takes and takes the more of
> Because the deeper fear is so eternal . . .
> Nothing can make injustice just but mercy.
>
> (p. 521)

Jesse Bel earlier has pronounced, "The saddest thing in life/Is that the best thing in it should be courage" (p. 49).

Although Frost does emphasize objectivity and essential abiguity, he knows not only the risk but also the existential necessity of commitment, as the General Ironist, in his extreme position, does not. The potential for irony stems from the discrepancy between appearance and reality, the essential ambiguity (not altogether a liability) in turn stemming from the inevitability of change and from man's limited knowledge of future changes and of the meanings of present, even past, appearances. Ironies teach man this limited nature of his knowledge and understanding. The General Ironist attempts to protect himself from the risks incurred from limited knowledge by not making any commitments; he attempts complete disinterestedness, or at least extreme detachment. In "I Could Give All to Time" personified Time has the General Ironist's perspective. He feels neither joy nor grief at the cosmic changes he effects; his detachment is supremely impersonal and objective, though his being "grave—contemplative and grave" perhaps suggests some concern but no active commitment. One can, at least in theory, have values without commitments, but one cannot have commitments without risks. One should not, however, always have to announce his commitments. In fact, in "I Could Give All to Time" the speaker can keep his commitments because he does not "declare" them:

> But why declare
> The things forbidden that while the Customs slept
> I have crossed to Safety with?
>
> (pp. 334-35)

The speaker is committed to various "forbidden" items. (Perhaps it is the commitment itself which seems forbidden.) He incurred some risk: he might, at the least, have had to declare those items and paid a tax, if not have had them confiscated. Despite Time's changes and (with a slight shift in metaphor) Customs's regulations, humans will make and will keep what commitments they can. Time may eventually alter all commitments, but at least for the present this speaker has managed to "escape" with these forbidden items. The five-line stanza pattern of the poem seems an extension beyond the usual limits of the more traditional four-line stanza. The speaker, though he relishes having outwitted the usually unchallengeable powers, is not superficially coy. In a spirit of challenge the speaker seems glad to have outwitted, for the present, the Supreme Ironist, and why shouldn't he take advantage of Customs's sleeping on the job? He is still playing the game by Customs's rules, which usually put him at a great disadvantage. The forces with which he must deal have power over the planet itself, leveling "peaks of snow" with the "running wave," changes that he understates as "a planetary change of style." Nor is Time limited by any littleness of spirit himself. He is simply impersonal and overwhelming. Though the speaker can grasp that perspective, he prefers to have his commitments if he can. With a solemnity that indicates his forbidden items are not mere baubles, he says he has crossed to "Safety" in this version of the "game played for mortal stakes." The repetition of *grave* in line five emphasizes its double meaning and contributes to the high seriousness achieved.

Frost and many of his speakers enjoy putting their skill, shrewdness, courage, wisdom, and luck to the test. Even knowing the potential for tragedy, Frost values the right to fail and the right to suffer, but he does not tolerate (at least for long) a martyr's complex. Frost does not finally have the ironist's rational bias: the ironist attacks any attempt at rational certainty precisely because he both idealizes it and knows it to be impossible. Rationally, he can be infallibly right, and that is precisely the trouble: the limits of reason are also the limits of irony. Usually Frost's speaker is not defeated or embittered, thinking himself a rational man thrown into a world neither clearly rational nor clearly irrational. He can even "escape" with having made commitments. Irony does not win all the battles in the war. Man knows enough with which to get ahead; he can create structures for meaning. Even a General Ironist is committed to structures, form.

While the General Ironist is not committed to a specific content because he believes nothing is rationally certain and worth one's commitment, he is indeed committed to his own structure of seeing discrepancies where relationships are said to exist. The ironist may insist that because truth cannot be known, he creates form simply for itelf, and an artist who is committed only to form takes essentially an ironic stance. To a General Ironist only the performance matters, not the content. Frost can seem more concerned about his successful stage presentation than about his substance. A much quoted text is Frost's letter to Kimball Flaccus, a young poet who Frost believed needed more form in his poetry, which may in part explain Frost's emphasis on form in this passage:

> I'm a mere selfish artist most of the time. I have no quarrel with the material. The grief will be simply if I can't transmute it into poems . . . . Let it hold its position while I do it in art. My whole anxiety is for myself as a performer. Am I any good? That's what I'd like to know and all I need to know.[6]

Frost may be an artist creating form for the sake of forming. As he says, "Any little form I assert upon this black and utter chaos is velvet, as the saying is, and to be considered for how much more it is than nothing."[7]

Frost speaks of poetic form specifically as commitments, as a series of commitments containing the risk that they will not be able to be kept throughout the poem:

> Every single poem written regular is a symbol small or great of the way the will has to pitch into commitments deeper and deeper to a rounded conclusion and then be judged for whether any original intention it had has been strongly spent or weakly lost; be it in art, politics, school, church, business, love, or marriage—in a piece of work or in a career. Strongly spent is synonymous with kept. (*SP*, p. 24)

These conscious commitments make the different between the wind and the singer in "The Aim Was Song," a poem that contrasts nature's undisciplined attempt with man's disciplined song. The wind is unrestrained and undirected: "[It] did its loudest day and night / In any rough place where it caught / . . . It hadn't found the place to blow; / It blew too hard . . ." (pp. 223-34). Man the singer shapes his material: "By measure . . . A little through the lips and throat. / The aim was song—the wind could see" (p. 224).

The poem is more than wind; it is also artistic "note." Through his form the poet has created a melody with a fairly regular iambic tetrameter moving smoothly and lightly with sufficient variation in pauses and turns to avoid monotony. The heavy accents come when expected and are thus emphasized for a strong sense of form in rhythm and meter. The quatrains rhyme A–B–A–B; the last sound in each line has its close echo in a single strong syllable. More euphony is added in plays with repeated words ("The wind the wind was meant to be") and nicely balanced grammatical units ("The aim was song—the wind could see"). In this carefully structured poem the first two stanzas describe the wind's noise and the last two, man's song; the title phrase is repeated twice, marking the beginning, middle, and end of the poem.

For Frost form enhances faith. Whereas the General Ironist emphasizes form as perhaps man's only certainty and only value worthy in itself, Frost counters, "I think [form] must stroke faith the right way" (*SP*, p. 106). To him the creation of form is itself a commitment beyond irony, to

> ... believe the poem into existence ... No one who has ever come close to the arts has failed to see the difference between things written with cunning and device, and the kind that are believed into existence, that begin in something more felt than known. (*SP*, pp. 44-45).

Writing a poem demands a faith beyond reason. In that commitment itself, we find his justification for a commitment not only to structure but also to belief: "Making little poems encourages a man to see that there is a shapeliness in the world."[8] Moreover, he wrote to Untermeyer, "Belief is better than anything else, and it is best when rapt, above paying its respects to anybody's doubt whatsoever. At bottom the world isn't a joke" (*SL*, p. 300). Frost's playfulness inlcudes this shrewdness about playfulness. He sees the irony of the ironic stance; he knows that belief is best.

Probably no one can accept irony as the only valid perspective. Man must live beyond irony; he must make commitments though he cannot know absolute values nor a certain future. As Frost frequently acknowledges, there is something beyond the rational—a gift outright, a leap of faith—in every significant commitment. It was necessary for the colonists to make such a commitment to the land before it was theirs, and themselves not England's'.

> Something we were withholding made us weak
> Until we found out that it was ourselves
> We were withholding from our land of living.
>
> (p. 348)

He says elsewhere, "It is important to be lost to something that gives you direction—direction is the great thing," a commitment that holds him rather than he it.[9] As the speaker of "The Gift Outright" reminds us, this is what we would die for.

There is, then, a realm beyond irony in which man, knowing the risks, makes commitments to those ambiguous appearances and relative truths. The vision of irony gives him a corrective skepticism of truth-as-dogma. Moreover, irony shows tht the struggles for knowledge and for faith are real; only if the struggle is real can commitment be real. Thus, the ironic perspective also enables him to transcend the ironist's stance. Transcending the ironist's stance, one can affirm the process itself, difficult as it is, as not only necessary but also valuable. Indeed, through the ironic perspective, the chaos of flux and relativity becomes the positiveness of possibility, of challenge. Aware of the concomitant possibilities of tragedy and defeat, Frost still affirms commitment.

Frost characteristically portrays a special commitment that incorporates his emphasis on objectivity and ambiguity—a commitment made by one who knows both the validity and the limitation of the ironist's stance, by one who agrees to be "loosely held." For instance, the speaker in "Not Quite Social" has done something against the social norms, but nothing so drastic that a law forbidding it exists. He sees it as

> ... merely giving you once more gentle proof
> That the city's hold on a man is no more tight
> Than when its walls rose higher than any roof.
> (p. 306)

He will let others be "not quite social" as well, but, as with himself, not cruelly antisocial: "I shall will to the common stock of air my breath / And pay a death tax of fairly polite repentance" (p. 307). He too is part of human society which shares the air and which finally gets its comeuppance in death. He will be held but loosely to social norms: "You may taunt me with not being able to flee the earth. / You have me there, but loosely, as I would be held" (p. 306). The speaker says he does not rebel against forms and norms, but neither will he have them too strict. The poet's playing within this iambic meter further illustrates his being "loosely held" to forms as nearly every line has at least two anapests, some have three or even four. Frost's being loosely held to the form is the detachment that gives perspective to commitment; it is the individual talent refreshing tradition.

In a more familiar poem, the woman in "The Silken Tent" is "loosely bound" to the world around through relationships. The poet compares her to a silken tent supported by a central cedar pole and guy ropes so that it seems to float free from the earth; it "Seems to owe naught to any single cord" (p. 332). Silk, with its great tensile strength, indicates the ties are strong; but the emphasis is on commitment rather than on restraint. The bondage is a positive one of love and thought.

The danger in being too tightly bound is not only a loss of reasonable human freedom (for instance, one should not have to report how he spent every penny, says the speaker in "The Hardship of Accounting"), but also a loss of proper perspective. In *A Masque of Reason* Frost describes the rigid commitment of one who lacks sufficient detachment, a commitment delightfully portrayed as a "Satanic tendency." When Job's wife sees Satan slipping away and becoming unavailable for the picture she wants to take, she says:

> Oh, yes, that tendency! O, do come off it.
> Don't let it carry you away. I hate
> A tendency.
> (p. 489)

Detachment and commitment are not mutually exclusive but are two sides of the same coin. Frost expresses this as a need for both seriousness and humor: if outer seriousness, then inner humor, and if outer humor, then inner seriousness (*SP,* p. 65). Eliot expresses the same need as a prayer in "Ash Wednesday": "Teach us to care and not to care. / Teach us to sit still." Such detachment gives the perspective essential for sanity—and also essential for realistic commitment.

Can commitment with detachment be total commitment? That is the debate between Dick the college boy and old Pike the weathered farmhand in "From Plane to Plane" as they both hoe corn and discuss a man's keeping his extrication when they see the village doctor going slowly, seemingly nonchalantly, to his next case. Pike, who "wouldn't hoe both ways [down and back on a row] for anybody" (p. 405), says:

> "A man has got to keep his extrication.
> The important thing is not to get bogged down
> In what he has to do to earn a living."
> (p. 406)

Moreover, he is sure that by this method he accomplishes more work than he would without detachment. Dick sees a similar detachment in the sun's work during the brief New England summers:

> "He bestows summer on us and escapes
> Before our realizing what we have
> To thank him for. He doesn't want our thanks."

As commitment is essential for individual direction, detachment is essential for perspective and balance in a pluralistic world where respect and communication are needed "from plane to plane." The detachment inherent in the ironic perspective is essential to maintain this working balance among conflicting pressures. Without detachment one can easily take oneself too seriously with no sense of the other or the outer, but with perspective one can live a life in which, knowing the risks, one willingly commits himself to goals he judges worthwhile. While one should not believe in judgments as absolute, neither should one refuse to make them. One sees both the difficulty of constructing an order than can be believed in—and the necessity for doing so. Irony and humor—both forms of detachment—may exist without nullifying belief. It is possible for one to live in relativity with a firm center of conviction. Frost understands belief in what he knows are necessarily and necessary as-if constructions. "The relationship we enter into with God to believe the future in—to believe the hereafter in" is one of the "four beliefs I know more about from having lived with poetry" (*SP,* p. 46).

Where then is the poet? His detachment is unusually different from the General Ironist's detachment. It is what has been called the aesthetic distance. His ironic perspective allows him to move beyond irony to balance idealism and despair. He knows the irony of irony as an absolute. He may be objective, ambiguous, even ironic—and still committed, both to form and to the mystery of belief. In his aesthetics as well as his clarifying vision Frost exemplifies the necessary confrontation with ambiguity, the values and limitations of ironic vision, the commitment and detachment of serious wit.

MARJORIE COOK

Miami University, Ohio

Notes

1. *The Poetry of Robert Frost,* ed. Edward Connery Latham (New York: Holt, Rinehart and Winston, 1969), p. 249. All subsequent references to this work are in the text.

2. Marion Montgomery, "Robert Frost: One Who Shrewdly Pretends" in *Frost: Centennial Essays* II, ed. Jac Tharpe (Jackson: Univ. Press of Mississippi, 1976), 213–22.

3. The term *General Ironist* is D. C. Muecke's. For a more complete discussion, see his book, *The Compass of Irony* (London: Methuen, 1969), and Wayne C. Booth, *The Rhetoric of Irony* (Chicago: Univ. of Chicago Press, 1974).

4. See such poems as "Love and a Question," "The Star-Splitter," "The Bear," "The Strong Are Saying Nothing," "Too Anxious for Rivers," "Neither Out Far Nor In Deep," "Design," "There are Roughly Zones," "The Lesson for Today," and "Forgive, O Lord."

5. See, for instance, the film *A Lover's Quarrel,* (New York: Holt, Rinehart and Winston, 1963).

6. *Selected Letters of Robert Frost,* ed. Lawrance Thompson (New York: Holt, Rinehart and Winston, 1964), p. 369. All subsequent references to this work are in the text, prefaced by *SL.*

7. *Selected Prose of Robert Frost,* ed. Hyde Cox and Edward Connery Lathem (New York: Holt, Rinehart and Winston, 1966), p. 107. All subsequent references to this work are in the text, prefaced by *SP.*

8. Quoted by John Ciardi, "Robert Frost: Master Conversationalist," *Saturday Review of Literature,* 21 March, 1959, p. 20.

9. Quoted by Daniel W. Smythe, *Robert Frost Speaks* (New York: Twayne, 1964), p. 28.

III PROBLEMS

Bound Away—And Back Again

To note an artist's limitation is but to define his genius.

WILLA CATHER

Even we who admire Robert Frost's poems "this side idolatry," perhaps we above all remain aware of at least one dimension in which the satisfaction they provide is incomplete. Whenever the things of this world are his aim, Frost moves easily from one superb performance to another. Responding to the query *Where are we now?* Frost is adept a offering crystalline images packed with answers. But facing the greater query *Wither are we going?* he is all promises. He leads his readers toward a misty precipice, halts, then turns back toward earth, as bewildered as before. His efforts to burst those barriers which inhibit significant contact with the ultimate riddle too often bear disappointing fruits.[1]

Symptoms of limitation mark Frost's first book. The poem "Into My Own" introduces his metaphor of dark trees, voices his desire that their mystery might guide him "unto the edge of doom," and offers his prayer for fulfillment:

> I should not be withheld but that some day
> Into their vastness I shall steal away . . .[2]

Some day! The metaphysical leap into his trees and beyond is not taken. Rather, the poem dissolves into a musing and speculative *what if?* "A Late Walk" offers a second approach to the metaphysical. His idle stroll inches Frost toward the prospect of ultimate encounter. Again he falters, stopping "not far from" his starting point, where he pauses to pick "the faded blue of the last remaining aster flower" to carry back as a momento of his effort.[3] He returns diminished; the transient "faded blue" of the flower must substitute for the cerulean might-

65

have-been blue of insight. The star dwindles into the terrestrial aster. In "The Vantage Point" Frost positions himself upon a lofty eminence, but to consider nothing which transcends the man-nature conjunction. Weary of scanning his trees, unsuccessful at peering beyond death ("The graves of men on an opposing hill"), he readjusts his focus to scrutinize an earthly ant hill.[4] "The Demiurge's Laugh" begins expansively. Frost, "running with joy on the Demon's trail," has actually entered his woods.[5] But promise diminishes rapidly; a coy drapery obscures what might have been witnessed among those trees. No revelation here. Above all other verses in A Boy's Will, the aptly titled "Reluctance" discloses Frost in a quandary. A promising journey through the woods, beyond all walls, up the promontory, only to turn in the inevitable retreat—this is the archetypal Frost attempt—"I have climbed the hills of view and looked at the world, and descended . . ."[6] He has come home to earth, his quest ended; the heart may ache to pursue, "but the feet question 'Wither?' "[7] Frost would have fifty more years of work but never would complete his pilgrimage. He is stopped at the border by—what? And we stop with him.

Ought we to expect any more of a poet who has given so much of value? Of a major poet, yes. And surely we are right to expect much of a poet whose ambition is to stand for the ages, as Frost implies through his consistent preference for universals over topicalities in the effort to achieve the "utmost ambition," which he nicely understates as lodging "a few poems where they will be hard to get rid of."[8] Comparisons with Shakespeare, Milton, Dante are not odious here, but instructive. If an alignment with the greatest seems prejudicial, then we might recall Frost's own rejection of the "downward comparisons" which prove delusory and counterfeit.[9] What is the obligation of the poet if not somehow, anyhow, to blast us off the crust of planet earth, to project us beyond the confinement of atmosphere, to shake off the weight of gravity and render us airborne?

What are man's legitimate expectations of the great? Neither Emerson nor Whitman need be established as a final arbiter in order for us to profit from recalling their efforts to clarify legitimate criteria. In "The Poet" Emerson, in taking as his theme the ultimate Sayer, therefore can speak of the poet as "the complete man," "the man without impediment."[10] The eye of that liberating god pierces every dark glass of existence; he answers not only *what* and *how* but *why* and thereby strikes off our shackles:

> There is a good reason why we should prize this liberation. The fate of the poor shepherd who, blinded and lost in the snowstorm, perishes in a drift within a few feet of his cottage door, is an emblem of the state of man. On the brink of the waters of life and truth, we are miserably dying . . . Therefore we love the poet . . . he unlocks our chains and admits us to a new scene.[11]

The greatest poet knows the life of the universe and pronounces its secret with a voice of thunder. He possesses the world, "a temple whose walls are covered with emblems, pictures and commandments of the Deity," and speaks intimately of every use of nature, most tellingly of the loftiest, "*ascension,* or the passage of the soul into higher forms."[12] This is the true poet, a furlong beyond the man of poetical talent. Seers such as Blake and Wordsworth leap into the mind.

Whitman, receiving his cue from Emerson, transforms his mentor's dicta into his own. In his 1855 "Preface" he declares the themes of earth (which Frost handles with vision and adeptness) "not small themes."[13] (Is he implying they are not large enough?) People expect more of The Poet, *they expect him to indicate the path between reality and their souls* (italics mine). This challenge Whitman repeats in those lines of *Leaves of Grass* which picture the human race as lost upon a frigid planet suitable only for graves:

> Wandering, yearning, curious, with restless explorations,
> With questionings, baffled, formless, feverish, with
> never-happy hearts,
> With that sad incessant refrain, *Wherefore unsatisfied soul?*
> and *Wither O mocking life?*
>
> Ah, who shall soothe these feverish children?
> Who justify these restless explorations?
> Who speak the secret of impassive earth?[14]

In casting the poet worthy that name in the role of light-bringer to man, Whitman exalts him as the true son of God. At long last, through the greatest poet and his songs "the secret shall be told."[15] As fully as he is able, Whitman inaugurates direct dialogue with death and its implications. In "Out of the Cradle Endlessly Rocking" and "When Lilacs Last in the Dooryard Bloom'd" his success is notable; it becomes spectacular in "Passage to India," with that poem's assurance, bolstered by the lyricism of the verse itself, that "the whole earth, this cold, impassive, voiceless earth, shall be completely justified."

It is in the rarified context of such accomplishments, it seems to me, that Frost falters (in company of course with an army of others: "I look in vain for the poet I have described," admits Emerson).[16] Frost attempts to enlist his verse in facing ultimate questions only to see these efforts abort as the pattern sketched out in "Reluctance" persists, then becomes prophetic. Frost gives every appearance of sailing forth bravely in quest of the transcendent, arrives at his characteristic point of bafflement, halts, and turns back. His reversal jells into mannerism and can be anticipated. He does not arrive where Whitman managed to arrive, even though in a poem such as "Directive" he comes very close to doing so. Set against the vision of Yeats and Eliot, his achievement pales.

Whitman's triumph rests upon his clear vision of existence as a circle in which life leads to death leads to life. Endlessly reiterative, autogenerative, this faith allows him to declare (with demonstrated reason) the beauty and grandeur of our passage from this world into the next, most lyrically stated, perhaps, in the thrush-hymn of "Lilacs." Whitman's universe admits no endings, only new beginnings, and all human passages share in the resplendent. In Robert Frost's verse the notion of the circulatory is present, of course, pervasively so. He is masterly in utilizing the ready-made circles fashioned by annual and diurnal movement. The counterparting play of seasons and the evolution of dawn into day and eventually into dusk quickly became basic to his method. But too often he allows these cycles no greater utility than to point up his mutability theme or to furnish a rich environment in which other concerns blossom. Everywhere, however, the circle is present, even if only partially, and even if buried until its effect is largely subliminal.

All too typically Frost's circles remain incomplete or are deliberately broken off before their arcs reach their natural point of closure. They do not weld into the solid rings of universal continuity which characterize Whitman's best verses. Typical are the circumstances of "The Wood-Pile," in which Frost, out for his stroll away from things of this world, away from life into the winter death of a swampy forest, happens upon an anonymous woodcutter's neatly stacked product burning with the smokeless fire of decay. Earlier, Frost has experienced an impulse to retreat but has resisted it, has pursued his goal this far. Now, however, he chooses to disregard the decomposing logs whose collapse into compost is the very metaphor which might project his thought beyond the brink, onward past winter toward spring, and complete the cycle. Rather than pursue implications which cry for attention, Frost turns away and back, content to understand that "only / Someone who lived in turning to fresh tasks / Could so forget his handiwork."17 As in "Out, Out—' " where onlookers turn away from death toward their round of earthly duties, the call of the familiar and the temporal proves to be compelling.

In declining to complete his circles, Frost adopts diversionary tactics which are brilliant in themselves yet serve mainly to waylay the attention. From the death theme and its potential for becoming a springboard into deeper waters Frost veers our eyes toward themes of secondary concern, however intensely felt. Both "The Death of the Hired Man" and "Home Burial" are cases in point. The former submerges the demise of Silas in a debate on man's responsibility to man. The latter diverts with a vivid dramatization of incipient madness; rather than speculate upon philosophical possibilities for consolation. Frost occupies himself in the pit of grief from which philosophy must spring. In both poems the significance of the death itself is left unprobed. Both poems manage pointedly to avoid tackling very much beyond the temporal. What the poems accomplish is important; what they do not accomplish is crucial.

"After Apple-Picking," one of Frost's half-dozen best lyrics, draws the circle again, doubly this time—dawn to dusk, spring to winter—and drives forward in an arc fleet and true as an arrow until the poet approaches the solid point toward which the poem apparently has driven since its first line. Here, on the edge of greatness, the verse dissolves into whimsical speculation upon the nature of the sleep: many questions, few answers. "Birches" describes a repetitive circle which rises from a magnificent metaphor encompassing the tree-swinger's pattern of repeated ascensions and descents, but it closes on a similarly whimsical note without ever revealing what is to be found by the ultimate climb heavenward through "black branches up a snow-white trunk."[18] The circumstances described in "Out, Out—'" invite thoughts which might explore deeply into man's transient passage, his frequently violent encounter with existence. When the onlookers to the slaughter of youth turn away to their own engrossing affairs, however, so do we; and whatever position might be established through considering Macbeth's dying tirade remain dormant in Frost's borrowed title. "The Star-Splitter" approaches mockery as it appraises man's drive "To satisfy a life-long curiosity / About our place among the infinities."[19] Brad McLaughlin has sacrificed his house in order to purchase his telescope, an instrument which does nothing to expand horizons but merely "split / A star in two or three the way you split / A globule of quicksilver in your hand."[20] Once again, Frost's brinksmanship turns us back at the border without insight into those infinities or our place among them.

That elusive quicksilver quality that handicaps any search into infinite explanations is only one of the several clues which for me betray Frost's personal confusion regarding the puzzle of eternity. Clearly apprehensive concerning man's fate, he resists all the conventional answers while obstinately holding back from any appearance of allying himself with those writers of naturalistic bent who rose to prominence during his young adulthood. Yet, historically at least, Frost belongs in the company of writers who matured within the same post-Darwinian context, and from the very first his poems share more than a little of the naturalistic worldview. An unmistakable note of pessimistic determinism haunts his poems. His people tend to remain earthbound, confined, acted upon, and extremely limited in their potential for vision or control. Many of Frost's people, in fact, might serve to populate the stories of Dreiser, Norris, or Stephen Crane, all of whose births occurred within four years of his own. Frost's circumstances are unique—he wrote verse. Yet Crane also experimented in verse—but with a difference:

> A man said to the universe:
> "Sir, I exist!"

"However," replied the universe,
"The fact has not created in me
A sense of obligation."[21]

Robert Frost remains always a good deal less explicit. What some might see as timidity in his stance, he, I suppose, would attribute to prudence, his wariness of propagandizing for easy solutions. Yet, in the ends to which he brings human creatures, he seldom implies much greater optimism than Crane does that mortals might ever come to understand their plight or seriously affect the lonely star on which they find themselves stranded. What restrains him from the stronger, more straightforward pronouncements he seems always on the verge of making?

Images of isolation and communication failure are prominent enough in Frost's first volumes so that an early admirer, Amy Lowell, could label *North of Boston* "a very sad book" whose major effect was of drab lives "twisted and tortured" by the disease of New England.[22] In the years after 1917 that negative strain is diluted considerably by Frost's retreat from the character poem and his corresponding emphasis upon music and richness of texture. Yet the dark view persists in making itself felt, often in symbolic fashion.

Frost's most characteristic metphor of restriction is the wall. The individual who attempts to break out from his confining cell of personality experiences difficulties which approach the insurmountable. Lafe Fairbanks and Doctor Magoon spar in "A Hundred Collars" without chancing upon any common meeting ground. An impregnable barrier of apprehension isolates the one from the other as effectively as the stone fence-under-repair in "Mending Wall" separates its two builders, isolated by tradition and habitual thought. Walls planted where there are no reasonable explanations for walls to exist remain walls nonetheless, and walls—mental, physical, psychological—seem to stand wherever one looks in Frost. The emotional/pragmatic barriers active in "Home Burial" and "The Death of the Hired Man" confirm this ubiquity.Frost's walls create boundaries to our oneness as a species and restrict our ability ever to reach out very far beyond our assigned territories, a fact which Frost recognizes in acknowledging that our lives are determined, "roughly," as he says, by "zones whose laws must be obeyed."[23] "Triple Bronze" enumerates successive layers of wall which jail us in—our hides, our homes, our national borders—but Frost stops short of adding the planet itself, the "quadruple bronze," as it were, which seals us off from what might await us after life is done.

What can man do in the face of bafflement? "Acceptance" opens with an image of the "spent sun," intrinisically a mutability image similar to Frost's bonfires, lamps, and stars. Strongly implied if not stated is a hint of Robinson Jeffers' open-eyed anticipation of that day of reckoning when the brave sun which lights our world shall "Die blind and blacken to the heart." Frost takes his message from the stoics: " 'Let the night be too dark for me to see / Into the future. Let what will be, be.' "[24] Ours, finally, is not to question or to perceive, he tells us in "On Looking Up by Chance at the Constellations," but rather to understand when we have reached he brink of the Unknowable: "We may as well go patiently on with our lives, / And look elsewhere than to stars and moon and sun."[25]

Rebuffed in his attempts to peer into the blackness beyond life, Frost does look elsewhere. Chiefly, his efforts go toward polishing his depiction of man's firm hold on the planet. His man-nature synthesis, a major glory of his verse from start to finish, underlies many of the gems upon which his fame justly rests. Various security symbols are utilized. A tuft of flowers serves emblematically to break the communication barriers and link mower with grass-turner; something of the same creates a numbus around the telephone which connects house with house during the frozen, isolating blizzard of "Snow." Anxieties are reduced as man and nature act to comfort each other, but who or what provides consolation for both as the end nears?

As if by instinct, and because the need is intense, Frost perceives the most that might be made, in his universe, of illumination symbols. Inner and outer dark is punctuated by lights, though many of these, like the shattered star drawn to earth by the telescope, prove of small aid to our seeing far out or in deep. Other stars serve little greater purpose, providing neither knowledge nor guidance. A quality of chill remoteness hangs about them. Stars in Frost's poems, in fact, are most prominent as ironic devices to remind us of the blank and fearful deserts making up space. The most meaningful star in all of Frost is that which has plunged to earth faded and icy, devoid of any message from whence it fell.[26] Cast into a stoneboat and hauled off by the farmer who finds it, this dead star is fit only for building up a wall of another sort than either night or space.

Lights of other types appear frequently without becoming beacons by which one might peer into any black cranny. The street lights beyond whose diminishing pools of radiance the lone walker strides away from the city of man in "Acquainted with the Night" are of this kind. Outer darkness beckons; the glowing moon sits in its sky blank faced, a clock that elects not to divulge the time. Street lights, jewel steady, are looked to as shields by the girl who flees homeward in "The Fear of Man," but these lamps fail to dispel her horror of the night. These are no blazing emblems turning midnight into noon; instead, they stand as momentary stays against confusion, like Frost's own poems in his most telling criticism of his efforts.[27] For lack of something more efficacious, Frost clutches such talismans, pale and meager as they may be: a bonfire roaring up a hillside (Not to see by but to scare ourselves with); the rim of light cast by the lamp beside which Mary waits for Warren; a feeble night light consuming itself beside an attic bed ("Five Nocturnes") but provoking only bad dreams and broken sleep.

It may appear always to be winter in Frost's landscape, piled snow blanking out any landmark or guidepost, as in "Desert Places" or by another manner of whiteness in "Design." Yet it is spring to which Frost most happily gravitates. He leans upon this promise in much the same manner and for the same reassurance that he enjoys being lured by even the dimmest of lights. Spring's presence may remain unhelpfully implicit, as in "The Wood-Pile," or when explicit be made to stand by itself, insufficiently examined. It is a rare poem in which spring provides any substantial inkling of belief. Frost remains enigmatic, like his moon-clock, declining to tell whether the time is right or wrong.

Even so, Frost's images of spring always manage to bear some pale promise of rekindled life (new light emerging from winter dark). His typical poem in this vein is "Putting in the Seed," with its delight in the apple tree's soft petals and its sense of triumphant regeneration as the dark soil allows a sturdy seedling to shoulder its way through the crust of earth. Just as he averts his eyes from human death, Frost's urge is to turn from winter back to the source and emblem of whatever fragmented security exists in his world. His archetypal moment becomes that miraculous instant when winter's frozen shell shatters upon impact with the insistent warm blade of spring. He most exults in directing us to that "day the sun lets go / Ten million silver lizards out of snow!" or that night of "The Onset" which sees January drifts sink, hiss, and rush downhill in "water of a slender April rill."[28] Newly created water both amazes and reassures, water formed by natural alchemy out of wintery void. Helpful as it might be, however, Frost's April moment has no power to buck the overwhelming weight of approaching darkness and serves only to impel us toward the big question mark which always remains unexplored, unanswered. In this manner the function of spring is paradoxical. Figuratively it prompts thoughts of regeneration which raise expectations without any means for satisfying them, and its eventual effect is palliative only. Confusion remains.

Water and light merge in the finest of that handful of verses which pledge to look Frost's highest theme squarely in the eye rather than to give it the customary sidelong glance: "For Once, The, Something." Sunlight slanting on a deep well creates a mirror (ingeniously, the wall once again) that shuts the speaker off from whatever white vision might be discerned in the depths beyond its reflective surface. And then, by miraculous chance, a drop of water falls from a fern, rippling the glass surface, obscuring what had been glimpsed, blotting it out: "What was that whiteness? / Truth? A pebble of quartz? For once, then, something."[29] We are required to be grateful, with Frost, for small favors.

From our failures emerge our triumphs. If restricted in coming to grips with Void, Frost never gives up the attempt, something like a bulldog with fangs clamped tight upon a trouser leg. At times he is able to achieve verses which, if not of the very highest order, still do what they do as well or better than anything else in the modern era. Of these efforts, "Stopping by Woods on a Snowy

Evening"—despite reservations I have stated elsewhere—seems beyond any doubt the most successful.[30]

"Stopping by Woods" brings into play nearly the full range of figurative elements which Frost developed for approaching his theme: the leisurely journey away from routine, mundane concerns. Darkness coming on fast. Snow lying far as eye can see, raising the question of blank. The urban-rural dichotomy. Contemplation of these dark woods, mysterious, inviting, fearful and alluring by turn, replete with Secret. Impulse, urge, the great step almost taken. Then the retreat—a moment of crisis reached, the country visitor shakes his horse's reins and heads back toward town, responding to a command of earthly duties, earthly promises. For most readers the rationale is convincing. In reality, these promises-to-be-kept constitute a variant image of the wall which impedes communication or movement. The circle completed in the poem does little, if anything, to decipher the secret of impassive earth; rather, it describes once again a brave sallying forth, a fruitless return.

The dazzling texture of "Stopping by Woods" employs Frost's most dexterous sleight-of-hand. Ambiguity is rife. Any ten readers of the poem can provide ten plausible analyses, all different. The circumstances of the poem must be such, or so. The poem implies this, or that, or something else. How adroitly Frost lures us into questions which cloud our eyes. Who can this lone traveler be? Where had he been? Where is he going? Whose woods? God's? Is the poem an autobiographical statement, concerning Frost and his career? Is it (like "The Death of the Hired Man") finally about human responsibilities? Its many sparkling facets attract, distract, and become at once an explanation for the poem's wealth and a symptom of its failure.

Above all, Frost in this poem betrays himself with prosody. What a simple— and fateful—matter it is to lose ourselves in the daring of its structure and music. It is one of the few verses Frost mentions outright in his essays; he expresses a justifiable pride in what he has produced, calling special attention to the "unnecessary commitment" he makes to form. His satisfaction is identical to the pleasure he takes in the rhyme-set of his "Reluctance," and in both cases the intricacy of form is a red herring which subtly shifts our attention away from the larger commitment to theme, which has been avoided. In the end, the journey of "Stopping by Woods" carries us no further than we were taken by "Reluctance."

The final significance of "Stopping by Woods" may be its service as a medium through which Frost figuratively confesses his inability to see beyond the dark brink. If so, that statement finds confirmation in his later and final work, where patterns of thought initiated in his early poems are restated. One comes upon Frost, for instance, in "The Sound of Trees," enticed by the mesmerizing sway of his woods seen from within the earthbound security of his home. He dreams of setting forth, determined to "make the reckless choice / Some day." When that day might arrive remains mystery. "In Winter in the Woods Alone," appropriately gathered within the "Quandary" section of *In the Clearing*, has him entering the forest, but only to hew a single tree and return with it. In "Away!" he does desert the world for the outer darkness. "I'm—bound—away!" he shouts —just prior to turning whimsical again with his resolution to return should he not find something to his liking beyond the border. As always, we wait in vain for the essential intimation of "what it by / 'Twere blessed to have seen—."[31]

How are we to unfold the riddle of Frost's too-frequent inability wholly to sweep us off our feet and into the ether of those heights suggested by Emerson? Can the answer lie in our own failure properly to decode his metaphors? We are accustomed to hearing Frost speak deliberately through symbolic meaning; that direction is pointed out for us wherever he invokes the poet's prerogative of saying one thing while meaning another.[32] "I trust my meaning is not too hidden," he wrote Louis Untermeyer as he burst into fame; "I can't help my way of coming at things."[33] But if Frost's expression of ultimate goals does rest among his figures, it is hidden too cunningly for most of us to discern, concealed, as it were, behind the stones of some private wall he was unable to scale. A conscious artist if ever there were one, Frost must have been aware how fitting it was that he should employ a confectionary tone in composing his late and most direct admission of what eluded him. His humorous couplet "The Secret Sits" is clear enough: while the race of man dances helplessly in its circle, hypothesizing, the Secret perches at the hub of the wheel, complacent and even smug in its supreme knowledge, but divulging nothing.[34]

PHILIP L. GERBER

State University of New York, Brockport

Notes

1. Philip L. Gerber, "Robert Frost—2074 A.D.," in *Frost: Centennial Essays*, ed. Jac Tharpe (Jackson: Univ. Press of Mississippi, 1974), pp. 31-41.

2. *The Poetry of Robert Frost*, ed. Edward Connery Lathem (New York: Holt, Rinehart and Winston, 1969), p. 5.

3. *The Poetry*, p. 8.

4. *The Poetry*, p. 17.

5. *The Poetry*, p. 24.

6. *The Poetry*, p. 30.

7. *The Poetry*, p. 30.

8. *Selected Prose of Robert Frost*, eds. Hyde Cox and Edward Connery Lathem (New York: Collier Books, 1968), p. 63.

9. *The Poetry*, p. 279.

10. Ralph Waldo Emerson, "The Poet," in *Major Writers of America*, ed. Perry Miller (New York: Harcourt, Brace, 1962), I, p. 531.

11. Emerson, p. 538.

12. Emerson, pp. 533, 535.

13. Walt Whitman, "Preface 1855," in *Leaves of Grass,* eds. Scully Bradley and Harold W. Blodgett (New York: W. W. Norton, 1965), p. 719.

14. Whitman, *Leaves of Grass,* p. 415.

15. Whitman, *Leaves of Grass,* p. 415.

16. Emerson, p. 538.

17. *The Poetry,* p. 102.

18. *The Poetry,* p. 122.

19. *The Poetry,* p. 177.

20. *The Poetry,* p. 179.

21. *The Complete Poems of Stephen Crane,* ed. Joseph Katz (Ithaca: Cornell Univ. Press, 1972), p. 102.

22. Amy Lowell, *Tendencies in Modern American Poetry* (New York: Macmillan, 1917), p. 105.

23. *The Poetry,* p. 305.

24. *The Poetry,* p. 249.

25. *The Poetry,* p. 268.

26. *The Poetry,* pp. 172–73.

27. *Selected Prose* (1968), p. 18.

28. *The Poetry,* pp. 237, 226.

29. *The Poetry,* p. 225.

30. Gerber, "Robert Frost—2074 A.D."

31. Emily Dickinson, "I've Seen a Dying Eye," in *The Complete Poems of Emily Dickinson,* ed. Thomas A. Johnson (Boston: Little, Brown, 1960), p. 266.

32. *Selected Prose* (1968), p. 24.

33. *The Letters of Robert Frost to Louis Untermeyer,* ed. Louis Untermeyer (New York: Holt, Rinehart and Winston, 1963), p. 14.

34. *The Poetry,* p. 362.

"Not Unbounded"

Such words as boundaries, bounds, bonds, walls, limits may suggest to us forbidding thoughts of grim restraints, dark bondage, oppressive law, order, discipline, or hostilities and unfriendliness—any or all of which may seem to threaten our more congenial leanings toward light and freedom, adventure, initiative, originality, and democratic friendliness. A reading of Robert Frost, however, shows that there may be other and wiser ways to think of walls and bonds, both literal and figurative, and may make clear that free attainment and bounds are not necessarily contradictory.

"Beech" is the first poem in *A Witness Tree*, 1942. There can be little reasonable doubt that Frost is there speaking in his own person. The tree is witness and proof that he is "not unbounded." Not only does the tree witness the presence of a corner stake helping to mark the boundaries of his farm; it stands also as a sign of inner as well as outer bounds, relating we may say to what the speaker thinks, feels, does, aspires to. An affirmation such as "Beech" has wide-ranging implications. We may know some of them in other Frost poems and through what he has said in lectures, letters, conversations. There are a few short poems on themes of boundaries, walls, bonds. "Trespass" is amusingly forthright about oversteppers of property lines. While there was not anything necessarily sinister in the trespasser's presence—he might be a geologist looking for specimens "in which there was little property right"—he was ignoring "what was whose." But at last the trespasser acknowledges the property owner:

> He asked for a drink at the kitchen door,
> An errand he may have had to invent,
> But it made my property mine once more.[1]

We may smile because we recognize such little anxieties in ourselves, anxieties, however, which are more serious if we find intruders wandering about the house. Some may not smile, feeling that poetry and property do not or should not mix, even though the boundary lines of their own lots are, as they should be, accurately recorded at the courthouse and they keep their doors locked. Reading here of the speaker's concern about "my woods," we may question the contrast some draw in discussing "Stopping by Woods on a Snowy Evening," a supposed contrast between the man stopping to gaze and the insensitive owner of the farm, fortunately too far away in the village to be troubled: "Whose woods these are I think I know."

The rhythm and rhymes of "Triple Bronze" give the substance a lilting incisiveness. This poem has more scope than "Trespass," and although the manner is playful, the poem seems to speak with conviction. The stanzas move readily from one wall to another. The first ("For inner defense my hide") may remind us of the words of Shakespeare's Richard II—"this flesh which walls about our life." The nearest most of us can come to the second wall ("I make . . . / Of wood or granite or lime / A wall too hard for crime") is with dead-bolt locks. There is clear approval in the poem of national boundaries, the third wall.

"Bond and Free" strikes a deeper note in tone and substance. The first stanza introduces the theme of the adventuring mind and the bonds of the heart:

> Love has earth to which she clings
> With hills and circling arms about—
> Wall within wall to shut fear out.
> But Thought has need of no such things,
> For Thought has a pair of dauntless wings.

At night the speaker's thought is interstellar, but day brings him back to an earthly room. In the last stanza we note well the emphases: Love has earth, "Wall within wall to shut fear out"; Love is thralldom, bondage, which possesses all.

The poems thus far cited, except for "Bond and Free," a much earlier one, are in *A Witness Tree*. "The Silken Tent" is the first poem after "Beech" and the brief "Sycamore." This one-sentence sonnet is an unforgettable portrait. Love, grace, strength are in part made possible by, not in spite of, the ties and bonds, which are no bondage. One who knows well the poetry of Robert Frost knows that he himself, "though circumstanced with dark and doubt," is bound to earth with "ties of love and thought," and to more than earth. Both "Beech" and "Sycamore" are almost like subtitles to *A Witness Tree*. A tree may be not only a boundary marker but also a vantage point for looking out beyond terrestrial bounds for, as the short poem "Sycamore" tells us, Zaccheus "did climb the tree / Our Lord to see."

"Mending Wall" was published in *North of Boston*, 1914. Many first knew it among the readings in school books. Since the poem lends itself readily to thoughts about walls and fences, it is frequently alluded to, with varying implications. Years ago I read in the newspaper of a sermon preached in a New York cathedral. The bishop took as his text "Something there is that doesn't love a wall," and developed his theme that God doesn't love walls. This is a startling version of Frost's thought, and it is difficult to resist an image of the cathedral walls beginning to fall as he spoke. Because metaphor plays such a large part in poetry, it may be difficult at times to distinguish between our inferred meanings and those intended by the poet. There is no reason, however, why this clergy-man, or any reader should not take a line from anywhere, regardless of its import in the original context, and adapt it to his own purposes. We all do this sort of thing, justifiably. Single lines may be compelling and richly "negotiable" in our thought and feeling. And Frost is indeed skillful in writing memorable lines, such as these: "High purpose makes the hero rude" ("America Is Hard to See"); "The lesson for today / Is how to be unhappy yet polite" ("The Lesson for Today"); the spring "Too lofty and original to rage" ("Directive"); "Some mystery becomes the proud" ("Take Something Like a Star").

Not only bits—lines, stanzas, speeches from a play—but whole poems may play their part in our imaginations, for good, in ways which freely go beyond or are deflections from the poet's emphases and meanings. Some may be moved to respond to a poem with another, as Raleigh does in the nymph's reply to Marlowe's passionate shepherd who entreats her to "Come live with me and be my love." But the response may be so transmuted that we cannot be sure about the impulses which began it. And an experience, idea, mood may be so uni-versal that our creation or adaptations of poems may be nourished in many ways, in and out of books. In "Birches" the line "That would be good both going and coming back" expresses a theme as much a part of us as morning and evening moods. And we know variations of the theme in many poems, as in the great Greek and Roman epics, in the story of The Prodigal Son, in Words-worth's "Michael" or "To a Skylark," the bird singing far above the nest on the ground ("Type of the wise who soar but never roam"). Tennyson's Ulysses, with a quenchless thirst for roaming, sets forth to sail beyond the baths of all the western stars. All this, of course, is what may make source hunting dubious or unfruitful. But even as numberless variations on related themes may stimulate our imaginations and reflection, so also knowledge of them may help us target in on their treatment in a particular poem.

We do like to know what a poem means, what Frost's "Mending Wall" means, as distinct from meanings we may impose on it. We should recognize at the out-set, however, the difficulty, even the undesirability, of being definitively precise. A poem may be complete and yet not complete. It is complete in the sense that it has a beginning and end, it has as many lines and divisions as the poet wishes it to have, and it says all he wants to say. But it is not complete, for it may imply far more than it states. The reader must complete the poem, fulfill it in so far as possible on the beam which the poem, thought of as a light and focusing lens, projects. Thus we may say also that a poem is clear and yet not wholly clear. It may be clear in the sense that we are not puzzled by the plain sense of what is being said or by the images, the tone, the allusions, or the way the parts fit together. What may not be wholly clear is how we are to take the metaphors, of parts or of the whole, in what directions and how far we are to go with them. This inconclusiveness is the source of much dispute about the meanings of Frost's poems. Frost spoke often and well about the basic significance of metaphors in almost all our thought and about the importance of learning to think with and about them, of knowing where they break down and when to "push" them and when not, or recognizing the scope and subtleties of thought and feeling they arise from and may evoke.

Frost was asked many times, for example, about the "promises to keep" in "Stopping by Woods on a Snowy Evening." Once he said: "You have your promises and I have mine." Another time: "We could say that there are promises we make and promises made for us." To be specific about his own promises would not only abuse a reticence about "coming too much to the surface," but might also diminish and impoverish the reader's range of promises, from the least to the greatest. Impatient with some interpretations which he felt pressed the poem too hard, he said (as he said of Shakespeare): "It's straight stuff." What he wants to tell us is clear enough. As for the overtones, he must trust to our tact and temperance in attributing inferred or imagined meanings to him. A cautionary word. That a poem is clear, in the sense that there is no obfuscation, does not mean that it is "simple" and thus unworthy the serious attention of critics supposedly more knowing and sensitive than the "common reader." It may touch on matters profound and complex. Yet complexities need not be abstruse but rather may be the very stuff of experience and considerations common to all in this mortal life.

Anyone who knows Frost's poetry well, or knew him well, must be aware of his delight in clarifying thought, in play of mind. Some minds seem like filings arranged statically about a single magnetic pole; his is rather like electric charges arcing from pole to counter-pole. The word *play* suggests games, from tiddly-winks to a World Series, in which there is free performing, prowess, within agreed upon bounds, rules. Frost loved sports and liked to compare the poet to the athlete. Indeed, we find the figure of play occurring again and again in his poetry, even "play for mortal stakes." He praises E. A. Robinson: "His theme was unhappiness itself, but his skill was as happy as it was playful." All Frost's poems are not personal affirmations but the thought and moods of imagined speakers, not only in such dramatic narratives as "Home Burial," but in other poems as well, thus extending the scope of play of mind. He said of "The Road Not Taken" that it expressed an attitude more characteristic of Edward Thomas than of himself. He often prefaced his "saying" of "The Most of It" by remarking: "You know the kind of person who talks like that, 'He thought he kept the universe alone.'" And he spoke the line in a way suggesting more than a trace of mockery. Much of the play of Frost's poetry is in the tone: simple statement, ironies, humor, wit meant seriously, overstatement, understatement. As he acknowledged, "All the fun's in how you say a thing." Play of mind in the poet asks responding, fulfilling play of mind in us. He said he enjoyed friends with whom he could talk even contraries without fear of being misunderstood.

Granting the play of mind in Frost's poetry, from pleasing frivolity to high seriousness, granting the reticence, the uncommitted figurative, the inclusiveness of what we must fulfill, can we be reasonably sure that we are close to a poem? There is such a thing as fair consideration of lines in context, statement, tone, character, narration, dialogue. And we may be helped greatly by observing the poet's leanings in other poems where the ideas are similar or related. (We have already noted, for instance, several poems on the theme "not unbounded.") Sometimes, too, we can refer to Frost's own comments on the "point" of a particular poem. In reading and thinking about "Mending Wall," therefore, we may hope to come closer to what Sir Philip Sidney calls "conjectured likelihoods."

Walls, such as the walls of buildings or fence-like constructions, are manmade from a variety of materials. We speak also of natural objects as walls, such as mountain features or masses of rampaging waters. Living creatures and plants have their walls, partitions, passageways. And "walls" is a fruitful image for intangibles important in our perception of reality. But it seems that in the common figurative language of our times, the wall image primarily signifies that which is to be rejected. Over many years student responses to "Mending Wall" have proved very interesting to me, as have those of other commentators. An illustrative composite of those responses, primarily of figurative meanings of the wall, would include these: narrowing confinement, repression, withdrawal from reality, and especially unfriendliness—exclusiveness as opposed to inclusiveness. One understands the popularity of the 1940s song "Don't fence me in." It is contended that the narrator in "Mending Wall" does not approve the wall he is helping to repair, nor walls in general, that he is only humoring his dark-minded neighbor, with whose twice-stated folk saying he does not agree. Curiously, often those speaking thus are individualists, resentful of intrusions on their personal and private rights and privileges, alert to invoke constitutional protections—without any seeming awareness of possible contradictions. Although in proper contexts such figurative meanings for walls have validity, I think we may say that such readers do not go very far in exploring other possibilities, literal as well as figurative, especially in directions pointed to in this and other Frost poems.

In the poem what doesn't love this wall are destructive winter freezing and thawing and the hunters, eager to get at the game with little regard for other people's property. The narrator of "Mending Wall" has often repaired the wall after hunters. It is he who reminds his neighbor that it is spring mending-time. As they work, one on a side, the narrator, full of spring mischief, tries to tease the neighbor into defending this wall, which serves no such practical function as keeping cows from wandering. The neighbor only says, "Good fences make good neighbors." The narrator tries again: "Before I build a wall I'd ask to know / What I was walling in or walling out, / And to whom I was like to give offense. /

Something there is that doesn't love a wall,/That wants it down." And it is something other than fanciful elves. But he cannot get his neighbor to venture an opinion as to *why* fences make good neighbors or what it is that doesn't love them. In turn, the speaker offers no opinions himself or even hints at specific answers although there is the clear implication that something may be said against as well as for walls, that what wants them down may be good or bad. It amuses the narrator that his companion will not *go behind* (italics mine) his father's traditional folk saying but only repeats: "Good fences make good neighbors."

It is appropriate that the neighbors should together repair the wall, for it is a visible boundary of their two farms, a line not imaginary as in "Beech." Note again that the forces which necessitate the rebuilding are not wise and good, but destructive. Nothing in the poem said or done seems adequate grounds for doubting that both think this is a good wall, to be kept so. There is nothing in the poem to justify concluding that the narrator disagrees with his laconic friend, armed with stones and ancient wisdom—darkly, for in him there is no play of mind whatever.

In a radio talk taped in 1953 Frost, after reading "Mending Wall," commented on the abiding question of how much solitude and how much society we should have, and our need for prudence about both. He said of "Mending Wall," "The point of that poem is that you have to have walls even when there is no apparent need for them." And he said once: "The best line in the poem is the last, and I didn't write that." Lesley Frost, his eldest daughter, remarks about her childhood that "we were always welcome to hunt for flowers, gather chestnuts, or find a Christmas tree on the Gays' farm, which bordered ours, good walls and good axe helves having made us good neighbors" *Redbook*, Dec. 1963. (Napoleon Gay [or Guay] was the French-Canadian farmer who helped repair the farm's wall and who showed Frost "that the lines of a good helve / Were native to the grain before the knife / Expressed them.")

In the "Hill Wife" poems Frost writes of solitude become loneliness, desperate loneliness. In "Home Burial" and "A Servant to Servants" there is inner desolation. The "I" of the poem addresses the "Tree at My Window": "You have seen me when I was taken and swept / And all but lost." "Walls within walls" may protect us from outer but not from "inner weather." (In the same radio talk of 1953 he read and commented on "The Gift Outright," stressing the importance of our separateness from England, although we share so much in language, literature, common law, tradition.) In "A Time to Talk," although busy with his hoeing when a friend calls from the road, the speaker says, "I go up to the stone wall for a friendly visit." Yet in "A Mood Apart" there is intrusion, and the poet-narrator concludes, "For any eye is an evil eye / That looks in onto a mood apart." Both moods are in "A Serious Step Lightly Taken," the next to the last poem in *A Witness Tree*. The narrator says that the family lives "Aloof yet not aloof."

Replying once to my inquiry about a young poet he knew, Frost wrote: "He inclines to the school of attenuated content." And he said elsewhere that to write well is to have ideas. His thought ranges widely over those human concerns that touch us most nearly and deeply. No "poetry corner" of the mind for him. Frost writes in "The Constant Symbol": "Every single poem written regular is a symbol small or great of the way the will has to pitch into commitments deeper and deeper to a rounded conclusion and then be judged for whether any original intention it had has been strongly spent or weakly lost; be it in art, politics, school, church, business, love, or marriage—in a piece of work or in a career." It is inevitable that one who enjoys the play of wisdom and counterwisdom, who has clearly discernible leanings in matters political, social, religious, should arouse both sympathies and antipathies. Frost poses difficulties for those who recognize his stature as a poet, yet who sincerely reject, often with passion, many of his commitments. There is much critical magnanimity, yet sometimes approval is mixed, even harshly, with disapproval. One may sometimes be reminded of the lines in "The Literate Farmer and the Planet Venus." The literate farmer says:

> You know how cunningly mankind is planned:
> We have one loving and one hating hand.
> The loving's made to hold each other like,
> While with the hating other hand we strike.
>
> (*The Poetry,* p. 371)

Randall Jarrell contends that there are two Frosts, the great poet and the cracker-barrel philosopher. Lionel Trilling contrasts the Sophoclean, terrifying poet with the rustic affirmer of old virtues, simplicities, pieties. At one time the judgment seemed to be hardening into a creed that Frost was a good poet but a bad man. For those who knew him well as a friend this last was offensively untrue. One admits that all he wrote is not of equal excellence, that some is slight, that his jesting verse may trouble some, and that he had faults (unlike you and me); yet Robert Frost, the man and the poet, was one—not for ill but for good.

The idea of being bounded is an important element in Frost's thought generally, extending to science and the humanities, his country, the darkness of the world, and to religion. "There Are Roughly Zones" offers one more example of his concern about "this limitless trait in the hearts of men" that makes them want to grow the peach too far north, where it must perish. Frost pulls back from unrealities and extravagant hopes. In "Looking for a Sunset Bird in Winter," for me one of the perfectly etched short poems, the momentary impression that the poet has seen a summer bird alight on the tree only sharpens the crystal chill in a setting of gilded snow and an early piercing star. In "A Boundless Moment": the speaker and his companion, "too ready to believe the most," must admit that far in the maples it is not the Paradise-in-bloom they see. The speaker acknowledges this: "And then I said the truth (and we moved on). / A young beech clinging to its last year's leaves."

All his life Frost had a deep interest in science, not only in astronomy and archaeology but in botany, physics, and other sciences as well. Some of his favorite reading was in *Scientific American*, which in quality he considered the best magazine published in America. As shown by his 1931 Amherst talk "Education by Poetry," one thing that interested him especially is the necessarily metaphoric character of scientific thought in its descriptions of reality. He illustrates in his writing that although one cannot be scientific about poetry, one can be poetic about science. There is scientific thought in his poems, and scholars, properly, are studying that thought and tracing its origins. Science, for Frost, from the Greeks on, has been Western man's daring to risk spirit by plunging into matter (see for example, "Kitty Hawk"). But science, too, has its limits and boundaries; he had no illusions about science solving all man's problems, now or ever. The humanities, in his view, are concerned with those essential aspects of man's nature where "science can never come" (he emphasized that "never")—our loves, hates, fears, griefs, loyalties, infidelities, our passionate preferences, our failures and triumphs. He found in Shakespeare's Sonnet 116 a line expressive of a valid distinction between what science can and cannot do: Love is like the north star, an ever-fixed mark, "Whose worth's unknown although its height be taken." The measurable altitude will give us a line of position for navigation, but the worth of the star is immeasurable, helping both the evil and the good, friend and enemy. Indeed, Frost said once that "science has not come within a billion light-years of a first cause."

Frost's thinking about America is grounded in his deep love for his own land. When on his seventy-fifth brithday the United States Senate honored him, speaking of his poems that "have enhanced for many their understanding of the United States and their love of country," Frost wrote Senator Taft: "There is nothing I would rather be called than an American and a poet." His was "The Gift Outright." He even risks "flag-waving" successfully. For instance, in "Not of School Age," the very young boy shouts in the gale to ask one out walking if he would please go to school to see if the big red, white, and blue flag was out today and "He bet it was." He spoke clearly on "the nation belief," as in the prose of "A Romantic Chasm": "Isn't it true that the world is in parts and the separation of the parts is as important as the connection of the parts?" From "Education by Poetry": "Look! First I want to be a person. And I want you to be a person, and then we can be as interpersonal as you please . . . First of all, you have got to have nations and then they can be as international as they please with one another . . . And the national belief we enter into socially with each other, all together, party of the first part, party of the second part, we enter into that to bring the future of the country." And from the poem "For

John Kennedy": "And by the example of our Declaration / Make everybody want to be a nation."

What Frost admires and wants for his nation is what he admires and wants for individuals: initiative, performance, a will to achieve and win, "The Courage to Be New." We must work together but with a large measure of freedom to go it on our own. Between equality and liberty he leans a little to the latter, distrustful of our being so homogenized that the cream can't rise. He discounts any new paradise America in which there can be guaranteed freedom from fear, from struggle, from failure. Earth, even in America, will always be a hard place in which to save the soul, one's decency, one's integrity. And he accepts with pleasure, even zest, the struggles that go with initiative and prowess. He would not like "A ruler who pretended not to love / A turbulence he had the better of" ("For John F. Kennedy"). Years ago he spoke of our self-governing as characteristically "ramshackle." Like railroad cars we ram, but then we shackle and go on.

The volume *In the Clearing,* 1962, includes several poems expressing some anxiety about America ("Our Doom to Bloom," "America is Hard to See," and "Does No One at All Ever Feel This Way in the Least?"). The first has a subtitle quotation from Robinson Jeffers: "Shine, perishing republic." The poet remarks on the growing belief that the state's one function is to give: "The bud must bloom till blowsy blown." In the second his earlier belief that Columbus was like a god who had given us "A more than Moses' exodus" has become a doubt that perhaps he had simply put off the weary day "When we would have to put our mind / On how to crowd but still be kind." The third expresses regret that the vast sea that once separated us from the old, the sea "That should have made the New World newly great," is no more a protective moat (another wall down). But Frost's dominant mood about his nation is articulated in the poem "For John F. Kennedy, His Inauguration," in which he says we as a country are "Firm in our free beliefs without dismay, / In any game the nations want to play."

Frost unblinkingly acknowledges man's fearful limitations in a world beyond his comprehension. He has been highly praised for such dark poems as "Home Burial," "A Servant to Servants," "Design," "The Hill Wife," "Acquainted with the Night." In "The Lesson for Today" he recognizes that "The groundwork of all faith is human woe . . . / There's nothing but injustice to be had. / No choice is left a poet, you might add, / But how to take the curse, tragic or comic." An awareness of darkness and injustice, however, does not dictate an inevitable response, does not make bitterness, hopeless despair, cynical defeatism, or self-pitying plaintiveness compulsory: "Now let the night be dark for all of me" ("Acceptance"); "Let's let my heavenly lostness overwhelm me" ("Lost in Heaven"). He will not grant that our own age is essentailly different from any other: "All ages shine with equal darkness" ("The Lesson for Today"). And when caught up in the floods of destruction he saves himself by "One Step Backward Taken."

Frost is not tempted beyond restraint to see more darkness than there is. Looking out from the train at night in lonely Utah Frost imagines the "flickering, human pathetic light" as maintained by the people there "With a Godforsaken brute despair." But this poem is "On the Heart's Beginning to Cloud the Mind." He has second thoughts and gives us a happier interpretation. In "The Onset" the speaker, caught in winter desolation, is in a mood of defeat and despair, but he has better thoughts: "I know that winter death has never tried / The earth but it has failed." Trilling spoke justly of persons in Frost's poems: "When ever have people been so isolated, so lightning-blasted, so tried down and calcined by life, so reduced, each in his own way, to some last irreducible core of being." With amusement Frost told of a boy who came by after a lecture to bring him greetings from his great-grandmother. She was the prototype of the woman in "A Servant to Servants." "Tough, wasn't she?" he said.

Although both in imaginative perceptivity and personal tragedy he had reason enough, Frost refused to go into the dark and lament ("Come In"): "But no, I was out for stars; / I would not come in." "That means," Frost said, "that I was out for small hopes." In "The Ax-Helve" there is a fine image for the night and day of the mind and spirit. The Frenchman's wife:

> rocked a chair
> That had as many motions as the world:
> One back and forward, in and out of shadow.
> (*The Poetry,* p. 186)

Frost's response to the ultimate darkness in and beyond the world is religious. That one should feel accountable to that which is unknowable is a mystery. To many it is superstition. Frost boldly asserts that without superstition we are naught—not low but high superstition, the awareness that there is always something more to everything. *Masque of Reason* and *Masque of Mercy* are Witness Trees. In the latter Keeper says: "The uncertainty / In which we act is a severity, / A cruelty, amounting to injustice / That nothing but God's mercy can assuage." Paul replies: "We have to stay afraid deep in our souls / Our sacrifice . . . / Our very best . . . may not / Be found acceptable in Heaven's sight." The abiding need is courage "To overcome the fear within the soul / And go ahead to any accomplishment." There is design in the world, although it may be terrifying (as in "Design"). We have the best of all freedoms—to make and find form and meaning, not only in art but in the many endeavors of our lives as well. It is bounds that make attainments possible; bonds need not be bondage. What Frost says in the illuminating "Letter to *The Amherst Student*" should not be neglected if we are to come closer to the thought and impelling assumptions of this poet:

The background in hugeness and confusion shading away from where we stand into black and utter chaos; and against the background any small man-made figure of order and concentration. What pleasanter than that this should be so . . . We were born to it, born used to it and have practical reasons for wanting it there. To me any little form I assert upon it is velvet, as the saying is, and to be con-considered for how much more it is than nothing.

CLIFFORD LYONS

University of North Carolina

Notes

1. The Frost family were our neighbors in Gainesville, Florida the fall of 1937 and spring of 1938. For almost a year during the war I was stationed at a naval air base on the south border of Boston; we were often with Robert Frost at his home in Cambridge and he at ours in Squantum. For several days for fifteen consecutive years he came to the University of North Carolina in Chapel Hill, and was then a guest in our home. I have in my library unpublished tapes of Frost's lecture-readings given at the University and of talks and interviews recorded at the University radio station. During these twenty-five years we shared countless hours of walks and talks, often far into the night. I have heard him lecture or talk with smaller groups at least thirty times. When I report what he said, directly or in paraphrase, it is what I have heard him say. Primary sources for this discussion are Frost's published poems and prose, and all textural references to them are to *The Poetry of Robert Frost,* ed. Edward Connery Lathem (New York: Holt, Rinehart and Winston, 1969); and *Selected Prose of Robert Frost,* ed. Hyde Cox and Edward Connery Lathem (New York: Macmillan, 1968). Secondary source references for the two critics cited are Randall Jarrell, "The Other Frost" in *Poetry and the Age* (New York: Random House, 1955); and Lionel Trilling, "A Speech on Robert Frost, A Cultural Episode" in *Robert Frost: A Collection of Critical Essays,* ed. James M. Cox (Englewood Cliffs, N.J.: Prentice-Hall, 1962).

Problems of Biography

The essence of the many problems which can be discerned in regard to biography of Robert Frost (as indeed of many other people) is that Frost was fundamentally a writer of fiction. Naturally, these fictions were based on his own life. As he once told one of his most enthusiastic admirers, Professor Louis Mertins, (author of *Robert Frost: Life and Talks—Walking* [Oklahoma Press, 1965] and other Frost studies), the features of his life were the raw materials of his artistic creation. But he also issued on this reported occasion a successful imprecation against "digging into his life."

As is now generally known, Frost was a very paradoxical man. Not the least of his paradoxes was that concerning his biography. He both wanted and feared the study and recording of his life. A separate study could be made of that fact alone. A very full record of his dual attitude is found in the account of his relationship with Professor Robert S. Newdick of Ohio State University, who had a close friendship with Frost between 1934 and 1939, so close that he was fully involved with the writing of a Frost biography at the time of his sudden death in July, 1939.[1] Although the surviving correspondence shows that, in his own phrase, Frost had "blown hot and cold" about the biography and, I think, probably felt some secret relief on the death of Newdick (who published thirty-one articles on Frost between 1935 and 1939), he engaged a new biographer within three weeks after Newdick's early death.

The new biographer was the late Professor Lawrance R. Thompson, the third of whose three volumes on Frost was published posthumously in January, 1976. Thompson had met Frost at Wesleyan University in Connecticut when he was a student. Although he had, as a librarian, collected bibliographical material and arranged a display collection of Frostiana for Wesleyan in 1936, he knew and recognized in correspondence with Newdick his own qualifications and position of priority as a biographer of Frost.

When Newdick died, his wife naturally hoped that her husband's devoted work would be recognized and completed. Mrs. Newdick scheduled a meeting with Frost and with representatives of Henry Holt and Company early in August 1939, in an effort to arrange for that. There are, doubtless, missing factors involved, but it is apparent that Frost summoned Thompson, whose biographical work on Longfellow (a Frost enthusiasm) he admired, to his home in Ripton, Vermont. A letter of July 17 and a telegram of July 26 from Frost to Thompson resulted in Thompson's stay with Frost over the weekend of July 29–30, during which Frost proposed and Thompson accepted the role of authorized and only biographer, with the proviso that Thompson was not to publish the biography until after Frost's death. (It should be added that Thompson had also competed successfully with Newdick for Frost's uneasy blessing concerning an edition of Frost's prose.) In Thompson's account of Frost's choice, in the Appendix to *The Later Years,* Volume III of the biography, he says that Frost discussed with him the problem of a biographical successor to Newdick.[2] Thompson suggested Mark Van Doren, Bernard De Voto, and Louis Untermeyer. An ensuing monologue by Frost about the qualificatons of each of these lasted until after midnight. Finally, after Thompson pointed out that the poet would have to supply his own answer since Frost had not accepted any of those supplied by him, Frost proposed Thompson his "official biographer." Appreciating the intended honor and opportunity, Thompson noted he did not have the qualifications Frost had mentioned. Frost said he felt Thompson's work on Longfellow was sufficient basis for him to make the selection.

For a period of nearly twenty-four years thereafter, Thompson had an interesting and very trying time as Frost's supposed sole biographer. He found, however, as had Newdick and Mrs. Kathleen Morrison (his secretary-guardian-guide from 1938 to 1963, after the death of Mrs. Frost), that Frost was a very hard person to live with.[3] Probably Thompson's greatest difficulty was that he was a good researcher who did want to record Frost accurately. Being only human, he was so conscious of the previous biographical work of Newdick whose work he never examined or referred to in his own effort.

However, it might have made it easier for Thompson to stand the trial of trying to record Frost if he had known about the trials Newdick had had. Just before he died, for example, Newdick discovered that Frost had been born in 1874, instead of 1875, as Frost repeatedly had said and as he had allowed Newdick to believe. When Newdick wrote the opening chapter of his unfinished biographical manuscript, he recorded the date as 1875. In a later chapter he wrote 1874. The realization that he could not count of Frost to tell accurately his date of birth may well have been devastating. (Frost had given his brith date correctly when entering Dartmouth, for example.) A comparison of accounts given Newdick and Thompson might have made Thompson feel better about the inaccurate information he was being given.

Thompson tried to be a good sport about being misinformed by Frost after being asked to be his official biographer. He professed at times to enjoy the process of seeing Frost's creative mind at work, of witnessing Frost "improving" on a story. In essence, however, he could not be pleased about what amounted to an elaborate hazing of the factual-minded professor (for whose type and institution Frost apparently had little respect). It must have occurred to Thompson, even if subliminally, that he was being exploited, just as the schools where Frost taught and where he appeared were, in a sense, under his attack.

(On this point, the writer once asked Lesley Frost Ballantine, the poet's daughter, if she thought Frost had deliberately misled Thompson. "Oh, yes," she said. "Once he told me he had told Thompson a cock-and-bull story and that Thompson had swallowed the whole thing.")

Actually, Thompson kept records and had quite sufficient awareness to see that Frost, willfully or not, was not a reliable source. When Professor Daniel W. Smythe of Bradley University wrote Thompson about conflicting accounts he had heard from Frost, with whom Smythe had a valued friendship, Thompson replied that he had nine different versions of one incident from Frost. In a letter of July 15, 1964 to James de T. Abajian, librarian of the California Historical Society, discussing Frost's place of birth in San Francisco, Thompson remarked that over a period of thirty-seven years he had taken more than fifteen hundred typed pages of notes. He mentioned that he had fallen into a process of recording differing versions of events, not that he wanted to show Frost was falsifying, but rather to show the poet's imagination at work as his attitudes changed. He professed to find these changing accounts "fascinating." He explained that Frost could be expected to declare that the lastest account was accurate, to claim that Thompson's memory was at fault—a claim which, in effect, insulted or ignored Thompson's methodical note taking.

The student of Thompson's three-volume biography can see that Frost's lack of reliability became, for Thompson, an unsolvable problem. Although he mentions in his work that Frost's accounts were unreliable, he constantly depended on them. In certain cases, such as the matter of Frost's youthful trip to the Dismal Swamp in Florida in November 1894, he simply accepted the Frost account he preferred for his interpretation without any substantiating evidence. He could not cope with the fact that any matter which had to depend on Frost's evidence would remain in doubt. In regard to the Dismal Swamp trip, this writer has found five accounts based on Frost, all with just as much foundation as the one Thompson chose to use.

The result of being demeaned by Frost's lack of respect for his work shows in Thompson's biographical work on Frost through a constantly shifting pattern of inaccuracy, and it finally told on Thompson himself. Though he specifically wrote in the July 1964 letter to Abajian that he had no interest in showing that Frost lied, the fact that his own work and scholarly reputation were at stake continued to build his resentment. Fortunately, however, the choice of Thompson as Frosts' official biographer led to the crowning honor of Thompson's career—the Pulitzer Prize.

But the personal cost was great. Thompson evidently came more and more to resent Frost's treatment of him. By the time he began to work on the biography after Frost's death, he was probably thinking of Frost more as a liar rather than as a writer of poetic fictions. He had to be certain to tell Abajian he had no interest in proving the lies. With others, he was more overt. When he tried to interview Professor and Mrs. Clifford P. Lyons, Frost's devoted friends at the

University of North Carolina, he told them that Frost had lied to him. His attitude was so aggressive and negative that the Lyonses gave Thompson the most minimal cooperation. This rejection of Thompson was also true of Huntington Cairns, a Frost admirer in Washington and North Carolina.

Possibly a part of the problem was that in the nearly twenty-four years in which Thompson spent a great deal of time with Frost, acting almost as his servant at times, he was asked to perform duties which were beyond the call of biography and at times very onerous. Whatever the reason, as time went by Thompson became what Mrs. Morrison called "judgmental"; he lost his objectivity because of his own personal anguish over the situation.

One cannot fail to mention what was probably Frost's most damaging strategic error. He had offered Thompson the role of official biographer, which certainly can be taken to mean sole biographer. But this did not stop Frost from encouraging other biographers, most notably Louis Untermeyer, whom he specifically asked in the fifties to become his biographer. Thompson knew about this strange betrayal.

There is no particular explanation why Thompson's realization that his primary source actually was not reliable was not more significant to his methodology or interpretations. His preoccupation with Frost kept him from doing the broad-ranging research he could and should have done. Threatened as he was by Frost's invitation to Untermeyer, he may have been afraid to do penetrating research, afraid Frost might have felt threatened and broken off their relationship, thereby tarnishing Thompson's scholarly reputation. In any case, Thompson did not even use the observations of Lesley Frost, whose fifty-year witness of her father and his work began when she typed his manuscript for *A Boy's Will* in the English farmhouse where the family was living in 1912.[4]

Although much valuable data on Frost has been gathered and recorded, there is much, much more to be done. Subtleties and difficulties of work in Frost studies continue, indeed, beyond the lifetime of the poet, and we do not yet understand, may never understand, the elaborate relation between the complex man and the often superb poems from his pen.

WILLIAM A. SUTTON

Ball State University

Notes

1. Robert S. Newdick, *Newdick's Season of Frost: An Interrupted Biography of Robert Frost*, ed. William A. Sutton (Albany: SUNY Press, 1976). See Foreword by Lesley Frost [Ballantine].

2. Thompson and R. H. Winnick, *Robert Frost: The Later Years* (New York, Holt, Rinehart and Winston, 1976), pp. 351–66. This Appendix contains a revised version of a statement by Lawrance Thompson that gives his account of how he came to be Frost's official biographer. Other observations made in this essay are drawn from primary and secondary materials at my direct disposal, and the conclusions drawn are my own.

3. Morrison, *Robert Frost: A Pictorial Chronicle* (New York: Holt, Rinehart, and Winston , 1974). [Biographical material in this account is particularly interesting for a study of the poet's later years. Apparently Mrs. Morrison coped with difficulties she describes because of the poet's value she recognized and his unusual poetic gift.—vol. ed.]

4. Lesley Frost [Ballantine], *New Hampshire's Child: The Derry Journals of Lesley Frost,* notes and index Lawrance Thompson and Arnold Grade, facsim., (Albany: SUNY Press, 1969).

A Note On Bibliographical Problems

As in the reading of Wordsworth, it is time for criticism to find some way of showing that the surfaces are as important as the depths.[1]

RICHARD POIRIER

What Professor Poirier is saying in his excellent book on Frost is that criticism and bibliography have been impeded by the general misunderstanding of Frost's work. Poirier also writes, "Even now, Frost has not escaped the gravitational pull of general popularity which keeps him from orbiting in a constellation of 'great' poets."[2] This fact, coupled with Frost's own puzzling unreliability as a commentator on his prose and poetry, has made bibliographical exploration very difficult, and even at times impossible.

Adding to this basic problem, especially for the bibliographer of primary materials, is that Frost materials are scattered practically everywhere in this country and abroad. Here, the University of Michigan, Amherst College, Dartmouth College, New York University, and the University of Virginia are only some of the most well known primary source libraries. In fact, numerous small college libraries, because of the popularity of Frost poems, may be found to own valuable primary material, donated by scattered friends and relations of the poet. Agnes Scott College in Decatur, Georgia, has a fine collection of Frostiana, contributed by Frost himself. And there are, of course, all sorts of primary materials in the hands of private collectors, and not only held by those who collect literary artifacts, but also by persons who have corresponded, say, briefly with the poet—not always likely to be persons aware of the value of literary manuscripts.

Furthermore, for the primary materials bibliographer, the difficulties are compounded by the fact that Frost published his work in such a variety of ways—Christmas card poems, limited editions, interviews in newspapers, tape-recorded talks (many of which still remain unpublished),[3] and unique copies of poems written in undiscovered and unavailable letters. A glance at Clymer and Green's bibliography done at The Jones Library, Amherst in 1937, now being revised and updated, will attest to this unwieldy problem.[4]

For the bibliographer of secondary materials there are just as many difficulties to be confronted. Biographies begin to become more numerous among

Frost secondary materials, not only the few full-length literary biographical studies, but also the memoirs and reminiscences of all lengths and subject matter. And the biographers' problems apply as well for the bibliographer. Two factors must be kept in mind—the two kinds of error which insidiously and constantly creep into even the best work. The first is the error of facile interpretation which seems to arise from an admiration for the subject matter. There is the fairly well known but always startling example of an article by one distinguished scholar in a well-respected journal describing Frost's "Stopping by Woods on a Snowy Evening" as a poem really about Santa Claus, the little horse being a cleverly disguised reindeer. To compound absurdity of interpretation, another eminent scholar wrote a rebuttal to that interpretation. Over-simplification (or reductionism) is only one of many possible interpretative errors which find their way into annotated Frost bibliographies, as it is sometimes found in the biographical materials.

Another sort of error which both the bibliographer and the biographer must beware is the error of fact. Many scholars, along with Professor Poirier, have demurrers of Lawrance Thompson's accounts (as well as of his interpretations) of Frost's life and work. To illustrate how biographical data of some of Frost's outrageous behavior has been excised or minimized I would refer to Poirier's account of Frost's relationship with Stark Young at Amherst College. Although Young was instrumental in bringing Frost to Amherst, Frost frequently alluded to Young's effeminancy and possible homosexuality—bringing embarassment and, of course, anger, to Young. Years afterward, Young achieved his revenge by his contribution to the Robert Frost issue of the Amherst literary magazine, *Touchstone* (4 [Feb. 1939] p. 9). He wrote, "The thought that I had a share in the effort to bring Frost to Amherst College has always seemed to me part payment . . . . I can only hope that such a statement will carry with it the full meaning it has for me." Frost's gossip and ridicule of others may have been played down because of a view that he should, being a writer of cherished poems, be a sort of Santa Claus to everyone.

Obviously, with such a racy personality behind the literary subject matter at hand, the bibliographer must maintain a sense of the humorous along with a sense of the seriousness of his purpose. It is well known, of course, that Frost was the constant prankster and enjoyed "spoofing" even his closest friends. His official biographer, Lawrance Thompson, could never be certain whether Frost was providing him with accurate information or making up some yarn. Therefore the bibliographer must take his cue from the experience of the biograher and maintain a professional sense of distance. The mechanics of the task are sufficiently demanding, and the bibliographer can afford to profit by the greater hazards of the biographical scholar.

In addition to earlier established sources, two new journals may be helpful in reaching a clearer understanding of Frost's life and work. The *Robert Frost Newsletter,* 1976–, containing news notes of events, meetings, publications and holdings along with MLA abstracts and other pertinent materials related to Frost scholarship, is helpful to Frost scholars. Dealing, on the other hand, with all aspects of bibliography, is a new journal, *Literary Research Newsletter,* 1977–, edited by Vincent L. Tollers (SUNY, Brockport), which is generally helpful in matters which today trouble the sincere researcher or bibliographer.

It really is not possible for me to guess, from having tried to cope with Frost bibliography myself, what direction present and future research needs to take. From the overview, I would say that a new sophistication must be present in material added to the secondary file. But some new areas of interest have been suggested by others in the recent primary and secondary materials. In biographical studies perhaps the question of the poet's intense sexuality and its subliminal appearance in the poems needs inquiry. Then there is Frost's relationship with professionals and with his family. The life and literary or other ambitions of Elinor White Frost, the poet's wife, has not been documented to any degree. What was her role in the development of Frost's career? It does not seem to be explained fully as yet. And, of course, biography is not the only area of interest in Frost studies. When will the poems be dated as to their original drafts and revisions? Will dating be a feasible subject of inquiry for Frost's poetry? Much textual scholarship would seem to be needed in the sorting out of memoirs, tapes, documents. What is to be decided regarding Frost's punctuation and spelling and his deliberate misuse of grammar? Generally speaking, future work in Frost studies will require more awareness of sources (of what as been done and what has not) and helpful documentation.

Undoubtedly there is an upswing of interest in the poetry of Robert Frost which was initially felt by so many to be very well understood. As Frost's reputation turns from that of America's most popular poet to that of a serious poet to be dealt with seriously, the number of theses and dissertations, articles and books of independent research increase. Frost and his poetry are now beginning to be read and accepted as genuine art, by a true artist, not a Santa Claus. It is about time.

PETER VAN EGMOND

University of Maryland

Notes

1. Richard Poirier, *Robert Frost: The Work of Knowing* (New York: Oxford Univ. Press, 1977), p. 7.

2. Poirier, pp. 226, 227.

3. Please see note to Clifford Lyons's essay in this volume regarding his collection of unpublished tapes.

4. Peter Van Egmond, *The Critical Reception of Robert Frost* (Boston: G. K. Hall, 1974), pp. ix–xiv.

IV BACKGROUND

Creative Borrowing:
Auditory Memory and Latin Heritage

I. Auditory Memory

Before issuing the English edition of Robert Frost's *Selected Poems,* the publisher, William Heinemann, objected to the poet's unacknowledged borrowings from a celebrated ballad and from a Shakespearian sonnet. The ballad lines occur in "Love and a Question": "The bridegroom looked at the weary road / Yet saw but her within. / And wished her heart in a case of gold / And pinned with a silver pin." As Heinemann notes, the ballad source is familiar; most readers recognize the lines from the ballad, "Waly, Waly": "But had I wist before I kissed / That love had been so ill to win / I'd locked my heart in a case o' goud / And pinned it wi' a siller pin." Frost owned William Allingham's *Selection of the Choicest British Ballads,* which contains this poem. It is also in *Percy's Reliques,* one of the books his mother read to him.

The Shakespearian image from sonnet 116, Frost's favorite, is in "Into My Own," the first poem in *A Boy's Will:* "One of my wishes is that those dark trees, / So old and firm they scarcely show the breeze, / Were not, as 'twere, the merest mask of gloom, / But stretched away unto the edge of doom." Lawrance Thompson suggests that Frost might have defended himself as he later defended a group of undergraudate poets at Dartmouth: "A [poet] has to begin as a cloud of all the other poets he ever read."[1]

As a mature poet, Frost continued to be haunted by, to echo, and to use creatively an amazing variety of lines from other poets. For the development of his remarkable auditory memory he was indebted to his mother, who not only read to him but recited from memory her own favorite poems as well. One of these was Bryant's "To a Waterfowl." Later, working by himself as a teenager, Frost discovered that though he had never tried to memorize it, he could recite the entire poem. He also knew by heart almost all of Poe's poems and many by Keats and Arnold.[2]

Frost retained this auditory memory throughout his life and tried to develop it in his children. After reading to them, he had them take turns reading aloud and memorizing poems. Among the writers familiar to the Frost children were Blake, Milton, Luther, Watts, Christina Rossetti, Poe, Longfellow, and Eugene

Field. Beginning with Mother Goose rhymes, they learned other verses as they grew older.[3]

Several anecdotes give evidence of Frost's own ready memory. In 1932, when T. S. Eliot was reading one of his poems at a banquet in his honor, Frost mischievously offered to compose a poem while Eliot was reading. Pretending to be in the throes of creation, he wrote out from memory "My Olympic Record Stride," which he had composed during the previous summer.[4] On another occasion he "suddenly broke out with the ballad, 'O my father was the keeper of the Eddystone Light.' . . . He sang well, with a clear voice and a fine sense of sound and tone."[5] Once when he failed to recognize his Amherst friend, Edward M. Lewis, in a dimly lit railway station, Lewis put his hand on Frost's arm and quoted the first lines of Browning's "Memorabilia": "Ah, did you once see Shelley plain, / And did he stop and speak to you?" Frost immediately responded with lines from Browning's "Time's Revenges": "I've a Friend from over the sea; / I like him, but he loves me. / It all grew out of the books I write . . ."[6]

In his lectures too Frost drew effortlessly upon his stored memory. Louis Untermeyer writes: "He never 'recited' his poems; he 'said' them—sometimes, especially if they were new or short, he 'said' them twice. 'Would you like to hear me say that one again?' he would inquire." In his commencement address at Oberlin College in 1938 he introduced two stanzas from Christopher Smart's "A Song to David" by saying, "I'll tell you one of the poems which came out of the eighteenth century."[7]

The same ease of reference is notable in Frost's letters, particularly those written to Louis Untermeyer, with whom he corresponded from 1915 until his death in 1963. The poet quotes from the Bible, spirituals, proverbs, nursery rhymes, slogans, popular songs, and ballads; he draws on Shakespeare, Raleigh, Milton, Collins, King, Dryden, Coleridge, Emerson, Lewis Carroll, Tennyson, Browning, Dobson, Kipling, Arnold, Stevenson, Landor, Lionel Johnson, Southey, Keats, Gilbert and Sullivan. Untermeyer concludes that "Frost's letters supplement his life and work in the same way that Keats's letters round out his poetry."[8] The quotations are usually handled informally, often combined or playfully revised. As he says, "Why shouldn't we [rewrite] dead poets?"[9] The following passages from Frost's letters illustrate the range of his borrowings and his easy manipulation of what he has taken.

> "I feel as if my poetry and pretty much all the rest of me under a heap of jarring atoms lay." To Wilbur Cross Feb. 18, 1918. (Dryden, "A Song for Saint Cecilia's Day")[10]
> "There's twa fat hens upo' the coop / Been fed this month or mair. Well death to them, thraw their necks about, feed for the welcome guessed! [sic]" To Louis Untermeyer, Nov. 4, 1918 (M. J. Mickle, "The Sailor's Wife")[11]
> "[The name Stork] almost more unwelcome to the married ear than cucoo even." To Untermeyer, Dec. 8, 1919. Shakespeare, "When Daisies Pied and Violets Blue")[12]

"Jean Ingelow says Lascelles Abercrombie is old, so old he can't write a letter." To Untermeyer, Jan. 5, 1920 ("Seven Times One")[13]

"Spring, I say, returneth and the maple sap is heard dripping in the buckets. Allow me to sell you a couple." To Untermeyer, March 21, 1920 (*Song of Songs* 2:12; Lewis Carroll, "You Are Old, Father William")[14]

". . . if in these bad days I propped your mind so also you might be expected to prop mine." To G. R. Elliott, March 20, 1920 (Arnold, "To a Friend": "Who prop, thou ask'st, in these bad days, my mind?")[15]

"The children are all already back and at the farming. There shall they see no enemy but foul weather." To Lincoln McVeagh, May, 1922. (Shakespeare, "Under the Greenwood Tree": "Here shall he see no enemy but winter and rough weather.")[16]

"You were their man and you done them brown." To Untermeyer, May 2, 1922 ("Frankie and Johnny": "He was her man and he done her wrong.")[17]

"I have got to confess to someone. It gives me strange powers of speech." To Untermeyer, April 10, 1925. (Coleridge, *Rime of the Ancient Mariner*: "I have strange power of speech.")[18]

"You would only have to call on him to comfort you with slogans and he would touch your various stops." To Untermeyer, May 3, 1927. (*Song of Songs* 2:5; Milton, "Lycidas": "He touched the tender stops of various quills.")[19]

"Ink, mink, pepper, stink, I, am, out!" To Untermeyer, June 6, 1930. (Counting-out rhyme)[20]

"Pacifism . . . is a dream of wiping out the last infirmity of noble minds." To Untermeyer, Feb. 18, 1935. Milton, "Lycidas": "That last infirmity of noble mind.")[21]

"But I was not born an immortal bird to be served up on peacock's tongues among many . . . If I am, trust me to be found singing when the pie is opened." To Untermeyer, June 24, 1935. (Keats, "Ode to a Nightingale": "Thou wast not born for death, immortal Bird!"; "Sing a Song of Sixpence": "When the pie was opened, the birds began to sing.")[22]

"Time is long and theories are fleeting." To Ferner Nuhn, 1936(?) (Longfellow, "A Psalm of Life": "Art is long and Time is fleeting.")[23]

"My days among the dear are passed." To Untermeyer, May 9, 1936. (Southey, Title and first line)[24]

"Oh sweet, oh sweet content, as Dekker says." To Untermeyer, Jan. 2, 1937. (From *Pleasant Comedy of Patient Grissill*, "Art thou poor, yet has thou golden slumbers? Oh, sweet content!")[25]

"And I the last go forth companionless." To Hervey Allen, April 12, 1938. (Tennyson, "Morte D'Arthur")[26]

"Home is the farmer, home from the Untermeyer farm." To Untermeyer, July 14, 1938. (R. L. Stevenson, "Requiem": "Home is the sailor, home from sea . . .")[27]

"Stay for me there, I will not fail / To meet thee in the hollow vale."
To Bernard De Voto April 12, 1938. (Henry King, "The Exequy")[28]
"You 'flattered to tears this aged man and poor.' " To Untermeyer,
July 5, 1949. (Keats, "Eve of St. Agnes")[29]
"All is well and wisely put. / If we cannot carry mountains on our
back / Neither can we crack a nut." To Untermeyer, April 14, 1962.
(Emerson, "Fable": "Talents differ; all is well and wisely put; / If I
cannot carry forests on my back / Neither can you crack a nut.")[30]

Considered in their entirety, Frost's letters show many aspects of this complex, tormented, and gifted man. Although the present study focuses only on his
easy, informal use of poems long familiar to him, even this scrutiny reveals a
remarkable assimilation and utilization of a vast store of quotations. In general,
the quotations in Frost's letters are amusing, showing, as Untermeyer points out,
"the extraordinarily playful spirit of a great poet."[31] In letters written at the
time of his wife's death, March, 1938, some of the quotations are somber, but
these are exceptions. The examples given above contain only two attributions
to their authors, Ingelow and Dekker; there are no contemporary poets. The
passages are drawn from the Bible, Shakespeare, Milton, two other seventeeth-
century writers, Romantics, Victorians, and nineteenty-century Americans.

In Frost's poems echoes of remembered poems are also discernible—less
numerous than in the letters, but equally diverse. If these echoes have com-
manded little critical comment, it may be because they are so expertly integrated into his verse. Arnold E. Grade has remarked that "it is worth noting . . .
that Frost's assimilation was so complete as to afford but a handful of frank or
discernible borrowings in his poetry."[32] This statement may be questioned.
from his first volume *A Boy's Will*, whose very title is a discernible borrowing
from Longfellow, to his last volume, *In the Clearing*, Frost incorporates lines
from other poets. With the publication of "New Hampshire," title poem of the
1923 volume, this practice becomes observable. Into the easy, conversational
flow of this, his longest poem to that date, he introduces passages from Shakespeare, Emerson, Marlowe, Arnold, and Bryant. In most instances he gives the
author's name. The first quotation, from the "Ode Inscribed to Mr. W. H.
Channing," comes approximately halfway through the poem: "Emerson said,
'The God who made New Hampshire / Taunted the lofty land with little men.' "
He next refers to Amy Lowell without naming her, designating her "another
Massachusetts poet": "But when I asked to know what ailed New Hampshire /
She said she couldn't stand the people in it, / The little men. (It's Massachusetts
speaking) / And when I asked to know what ailed the people, / She said, 'Go
read your own books and find out.' "

A few lines further on Frost quotes from *Dr. Faustus*: "Kit Marlowe taught
me how to say my prayers: / 'Why this is Hell, nor am I out of it.' " Returning
to the passage previously quoted from Emerson, he writes: "The glorious bards
of Massachusetts . . . taunt the lofty land with little men."

Frost puts his own stamp on whatever he borrows. (For example: "Choose which you will be—a prude or puke / Mewling and puking in the public arms.") While aware of the familiarity of the words, the reader of "New Hampshire" is not likely to be distracted by the echo of the melancholy Jacques in the Forest of Arden.

Although in his letters Frost several times refers to Arnold's "Cadmus and Harmonia" as "my favorite poem," he treats the poet mockingly and even unfairly by quoting him out of context in "New Hampshire." The passage in question begins with a description of a man who goes into the woods with an ax, "But his heart failing him, he dropped the ax / And ran for shelter quoting Matthew Arnold: / 'Nature is cruel, man is sick of blood.' " This is from Arnold's sonnet "In Harmony with Nature," where the title is sarcastic. The unfair manipulation of Arnold's lines occurs when Frost writes that the poet "owned himself 'a foiled circuitous wanderer' who 'took dejectedly / His seat upon the intellectual throne.' " Arnold "owned" no such thing. The "foiled circuitous wanderer" is the river Oxus in *Sohrab and Rustum;* the one who "took dejectedly his seat" is Goethe as described in "The Scholar-Gypsy." Lawrance Thompson has called attention to these misapplied quotations.[33] "New Hampshire" also includes a line from Bryant's "Forest Hymn": "Even to say the groves were God's first temples" and completes it wryly: "Comes too near to Ahaz' sin for safety."

"I will Sing You One-O" in the same volume is the first line of a traditional English folk song. In "Build Soil," the political pastoral in *A Further Range,* 1936, Frost adapts a well-known spiritual: "Steal away / The song says. Steal away and stay away. / Don't join too many gangs. Join few if any." A passage in "A Moth Seen in Winter" contains the familiar words from the dedication to Shakespeare's sonnets: "The old incurable untimeliness / Only begetter of all ills that are." In "From Plane to Plane," a dialogue between an old farm worker and a college student, the final passage includes a line from Milton's *Comus* and Frost's favorite quotation from *Hamlet*: "Shall I go on or have I said enough / To convey my respect for your position? / 'I guess so,' Pike said, innocent of Milton." The poem ends: " 'So I have heard and do in part believe it,' / Dick said to old Pike, innocent of Shakespeare."

Frost's last collection, *In the Clearing,* 1962, contains strikingly diverse quotations. In addition to the Virgilian echoes in "For John F. Kennedy, His Inauguration," which are discussed in the second part of this study, there are two lines from nursery rhymes and a pun from Christopher Smart. "A-Wishing Well" begins "A poet would a wishing go," an adaptation from the children's Mother Goose rhyme about the wooing frog. The children's charm, "Star Light, Star Bright," supplies another line: "I wish I may, I wish I might . . ." In the long poem "How Hard It Is Keep from Being King," Frost makes a startling pun in the middle of a line from Smart's "A Song to David": "Tell them Iamb, Jehovah said, and meant it, / Free verse leaves out the meter . . ."

Frost's virtuiosity in weaving quoted lines into the fabric of his poems is most abundantly demonstrated in *A Masque of Reason* and *A Masque of Mercy*. In the former, Job, speaking to his wife, Thyatira, quotes from the seventeenth-century lyric, "Go, Lovely Rose": "Suffer yourself to be admired, my love, / As Waller says." The original lines are "Suffer herself to be desired / And not blush so to be admired." In the same masque, Jehovah says: "You would have supposed / One who in the beginning *was* the Word / Would be in a position to command it." (Reference is to John 1:1) Later, speaking to God about Thyatira, that prototype of the liberated woman, Job says: "Kipling invokes You as Lord God of Hosts, / She'd like to know how You would take a prayer / That started off Lord God of Hostesses." The reference is of course to Kipling's "Recessional." In a subsequent speech God refers to originality as "the sin / That felled the angels, Wolsey would have said." The reference is to *Henry VIII* (act 4, sc. 1, 440–41): " . . . fling away ambition / By that sin fell the angels."

Later, speaking of "the way all things come round," Job paraphrases Emerson's "Uriel," calling it "the greatest Western poem yet." The pertinent lines are "Line in nature is not found; Unit and universe are round; / In vain produced, all rays return . . ." The next quotation occurs when Thyatira speaks in pretended admiration of Satan: "Oh, he speaks! He *can* speak! / That strain again! Give me excess of it!" (*Twelfth Night* [act 1, sc. 1, 2,4]). Continuing her adjuration to Satan, she quotes lines from Herrick, with a characteristic alteration: "Please don't go. Stay, stay / But to the evensong, and having played / Together we will go with you along." Two lines are here omitted from the poem, "To Daffodils," and "played" is substituted for "prayed" in the original.

In the longer *A Masque of Mercy* Frost uses even more quotations, beginning as early as the second line: "Late, late, too late, you cannot enter now." This closely resembles the line in Tennyson's "Guinevere" from the *Idylls of the King*: "Too late, too late, ye cannot enter now." The line is repeated toward the end of the masque. The next quotation is from Thompson's *Hound of Heaven;* it is smoothly integrated into the dialogue. Paul: "I fled Him, down the nights and down the days, / I fled Him down the arches of the years." Keeper: "This is a bookstore, not a sanctuary." Keeper's wife, Jesse Bel, whose name exemplifies Frost's verbal manipulations, makes a startling juxtaposition in a subsequent speech: "Them is my sentiments, and, Mr. Flood, / Since you propose it, I believe I will." The first half line is Fred Bullock's speech in Thackeray's *Vanity Fair* (Chapter 21). The remainder, immediately recognizable from E. A. Robinson's "Mr. Flood's Party," is a rare example of a quotation from one of Frost's contemporaries. Jesse Bel's next remark follows her husband's sardonic reproof to Jonah: "You've lost your faith in God? How wicked of you." Jesse Bel: "You naughty kitten, you shall have no pie." Possibly the last words of the nursery rhyme quotation are meant to suggest "pie in the sky." Given the context, this seems not unlikely.

When the books fall from the shelves, Jonah's exclamation amalgamates two scriptural passages: "you see the Lord God is a jealous God. / He wrote one book. Let there be no more written. / How are their volumes fallen!" (Deut. 5:9; Sam. 1:19: "How are the valiant fallen!"). A witty combination of names and images occurs in a speech by Jonah and in Keeper's comment on it: Jonah: "My tongue's my own, as true Thomas used to say." Keeper: So you've been Bohning up on Thomism too." Jonah's speech is from the ballad of Thomas the Rhymer, as found in Scott's *Minstrelsy of the Scottish Border:* "My tongue is mine ain, True Thomas said." Keeper's rejoinder equates the ballad Thomas with Thomas Aquinas, some of whose works had been issued by the publisher, Henry Bohn. Two of Frost's letters cast some light on the complimentary "true" applied to Thomas Aquinas: "It's the frosting on the cake for me to discover Thomas Acquinas' [sic] explanation of the Holy Ghost." And, "Thomas was a good boy from first to last. I believe he weighed too much, but the Church will have it his weight was glandular."[34]

Into a later speech by Paul to Jonah a Miltonic quotation is smoothly inserted: ". . . after doing Justice justice / Milton's pentamenters go on to say, / But Mercy first and last shall brightest shine. / Not only last, but first, you will observe" (*Paradise Lost,* III, 134). Two Shakespearian echoes follow shortly: "I choose the star-crossed as a star-crossed lover" (*Romeo and Juliet,* Prologue), and ". . . it wasn't down a well / but in a butt of malmsey I was drowned." The latter reference is to the death of Clarence in *Richard III* (act 1, sc. 4).

In his essay "Robert Frost's Masques and the Classical American Tradition," Peter J. Stanlis comments on the poet's parody in *A Masque of Mercy* of Yeats, unnamed but designated as "Bel's favorite poet / Who in his favorite pose as poet thinker . . . / Once charged the Nazarene with having brought / A darkness out of Asia that had crossed / Old Attic grace and Spartan discipline / With violence."[35] Finally, an effectively assimilated passage from Bunyan forms Jonah's response to Paul's question: "But you, what is your answer, Jonas Dove?" Jonah: "You ask if I see yonder shining gate, / And I reply I almost think I do." Frost has here telescoped two speechs from *Pilgrim's Progress*: "Then said Evangelist, pointing with his finger over a very wide field, Do you see yonder wicket gate: The man said no. Then said the other, Do you see yonder shining light? He said, I think I do."

The foregoing survey has illustrated Frost's use of quotations in several areas: his conversations and lectures, his letters, and his poems. An auditory memory developed from childhood became a ready resource for both formal and informal use. Though for the most part familiar, his quotations are not hackneyed, often occurring in unexpected contexts. His variations, adaptations, and combinations of quoted passages are frequently highly original and well integrated into his own writings. That he maintains the unity of his longer poems while incorporating passages of diverse character is a mark of high craftsmanship. One might answer William Heinemann and any others troubled by Frost's borrowings by quoting Dryden's comment on Ben Jonson's use of the ancient writers: "You track him everywhere in their snow . . . . He invades authors like a monarch, and what would be theft in other poets is only victory in him."[36]

II. Latin Heritage

When Robert Frost's *Collected Poems* appeared in 1939, William Sloane, the editor, sent him a telegram ending with an adaptation of the famous line from Horace: *Exegi monumentum aere perennius* [I have erected a monument more lasting than bronze] (*Odes* 3, 30). By changing *exegi* to *exegisti* [you have], Sloane paid Frost a compliment that touched him deeply. Frost wrote to Untermeyer: "The Latin gave me a stir that I never expected to have again in this world from publication."[1]

As Helen H. Bacon observes, his talks, letters, and poems give evidence that "Frost read and pondered classical literature intensely and subtly all his life."[2] A survey of his experiences as student and teacher of the classics, his casual use of Latin in his correspondence, but above all, the adroit and masterly integration of the classics into his poetry will give a deepened understanding of the intellectual background of Frost's writing.

The influence of his parents no doubt contributed to an early and enduring interest in the classics for Frost. As a child, he had listened to his mother's stories of Greek and Roman heroes. His father, a graduate of Harvard, had distinguished himself in classical studies. Although Frost was only eleven when his father died, his example may have had some influence on the son's decision to concentrate on the classics in high school and college. A classmate in the local academy remembered Frost as "the eager, rosy-cheeked boy who stuttered a bit in his enthusiasm over his ready translations of Cicero, Virgil, and Homer."[3] Two poems written during these years were "A Dream of Julius Caesar" and "Caesar's Lost Transport Ships." Frost also wrote an editorial for the school paper, praising the students who elected the classical program.

At Dartmouth he did superior work in Greek and Latin but left before the end of the first semester in order to help his mother, who was having trouble with unruly pupils in the Methuen district school. Here Frost had his first experience in teaching Latin as well as other subjects. Meanwhile, he continued his own studies, and it was while reading Tacitus that he expressed the desire to teach Latin and Greek in college. With this goal in mind, he entered Harvard as a special student. Before his withdrawal from the university in March of his second year, he had taken courses in Livy and Terence; lyric, elegiac, iambic poetry; and the eclogues of Virgil. Robert Newdick reports that "simply for his own gratification he committed to memory passage after passage . . ."[4]

Reading and memorizing the Latin poets led to Frost's recognition of the "speaking voice" in poetry—a concept that was to form a major portion of his theory and practice. He wrote: "First heard the voice from a printed page in Virgilian Eclogue and in *Hamlet*." Commenting on his poems "The Black Cottage," "The Housekeeper," and "The Death of the Hired Man," he wrote: "Virgil's Eclogues may have had something to do with them."[5] More than thirty-five years after he had left Harvard University, in replying to an invitation to give a reading there, Frost wrote, "It is good of you not to let Harvard forget the old regular poet to whom she taught Latin and Greek."[6]

An opportunity to teach Latin came when Frost took his family to England. Dissatisfied with the local schools and unable to afford better ones, he and his wife decided to teach their children themselves. Frost wrote to a friend: "Lesley . . . reads a decent paragraph of Caesar off without looking up more than a couple of words."[7] Many years later, in a letter to his son-in-law, Willard Fraser, he said that teaching was "one of the four things I most wanted to go into in life." (The other three were archaeology, astronomy, and farming.)[8] For years he toyed with the idea of teaching, but except for his brief experience in his mother's school and in England as Lesley's tutor, Frost never had a regular appointment as a teacher of Latin. When an opportunity did occur, as for example, in 1894 when he was offered a position at Elizabeth City Academy in North Carolina, he did not accept it. Forty-five years later, he was suggesting to the chairman of the Classics Department at Harvard that he would be in interested in teaching "the Roman classics" there. Although he received a cordial reply, it included the proposal that he might like to have Professor John Huston Finley as a "watcher" (Frost's word) in his class. This was enough for Frost. He wrote to John Hillyer: "It won't do for me to profess Latinity. I've been warned off already. Don't I know those bozos from of old? They are too humanistic to be human."[9]

A year later, when he wrote to President Conant, accepting the appointment of Ralph Waldo Emerson Fellow in Poetry at Harvard, he said, "At the first serious suggestion of my pretending to Latinity or any other kind of scholarship, I am struck as school-shy as in the nineties when I fled uneducated to the Philistines.[10] All in all, it seems that like the college boy in "The Death of the Hired Man," Frost "studied Latin like the violin / Because he liked it."

How well he liked the language is clear from the easy, playful, and sometimes punning use of Latin in his letters and speeches. Such common expressions as nihil obstat, requiescat, in medias res, obiter dicta, mea culpa, felix culpa, since they are usually Anglicized, are perhaps not of sufficient importance to note, but possibly (to use Frost's own words) "well worth preliminary mention." He sometimes tacks English endings onto well known Latin phrases—for example, Cato's *"Delenda est Carthago"* [Carthage must be destroyed]. In a letter to Louis Untermeyer he writes, "It is amusing to see Russia yawn and stretch at word that Geneva is delended." After reporting that his fingernails had been cut in Connectuciut, his hair trimmed in Maine, and a tooth extracted in Vermont, he lifts a phrase from Horace; "Nothing but the Resurrection will ever reassemble the disjected members" [*disjecta membra*] (*Odes* 4, 9).[12] He sometimes Latinizes his own name, signing himself "Robertus Geler." In a letter to F. S. Flint, he puns on his friend's name: "I ought to know by the length of your silence that you don't want to write to me any more—cor silicis" [heart of flint]. The expression which is familiar in the Latin poets, is here probably suggested by a line in Tibullus.[13]

The well-known *Cave canem* [beware the dog] supplies the pattern for "Cave poetam when he gets a little power in his hands."[14] Frost writes to Mark Sullivan, "How'd I look asettin up as an arbiter poetarum [judge of poets]?[15] To another friend who had promised a book he writes, "I thought something was said about your looking in on us this summer donum ferens [bearing gifts]."[16] In a letter to Untermeyer he alters a line from Virgil's first eclogue, "Deus nobis haec otia fecit [the god has given us this leisure], "changing it to "A goddess haec otia frangit [a goddess breaks up this leisure] to bring forth a book again."[17] The "goddess" is evidently his devoted secretary, Kathleen Morrison. He tells in Latin a joke about a man who, startled from sleep when the clock struck four, cried out, "Nae horologium delirat [The crazy clock struck one four times]."[18] One of several echoes of Virgil is in a letter to his former pupil, John Bartlett, written while the Frosts were in England: "Sic ad astra itur in London town [Thus one goes to the stars]" (*Aeneid* 9.638).[19]

The poet's somewhat defensive attitude toward formal scholarship has been shown by his reaction against the prospect of having Professor Finley associated with him in teaching Latin. Another instance of his defensiveness is found in a letter: "Erudita inscita est, which I choose to translate from Scaliger, as Erudition is a form of ignorance." In the same letter he quotes, "Sapientiae pars est quaedam aequo animo nescire velle [There is a kind of wisdom in calmly choosing not to know]."[20]

On more serious occasions as well Frost drew upon his store of Latin language and literature. He called E. J. Bernheimer, a wealthy collector, by the name of the patron of Horace and Virgil, addressing him as "my one and only Maecenas." When he gave Bernheimer a copy of the limited edition of *A Masque of Reason*, he wrote on the flyleaf: "Anno poetae edite LXX."

At Oxford, on the occasion of receiving an honorary degree, he said: "Poetry is the thoughts of the heart. I'm sure that's what Catullus meant by mens animae" (65.4). He uses the phrase again in "Kitty Hawk" (1. 390).[21]

His friend Rabbi Reichert once asked Frost to preach at his temple. On this occasion Frost attributed to Ennius, the early Roman historian and dramatist, the assertion that courage is only the second greatest of the virtues. Many bad men, according to Ennius, are brave. Wisdom is better than bravery. Frost was was paraphrasing a passage from the play, *Hectoris Lytra* [The Ransom of Hector]: "Melius est virtute ius, nam saepe virtutem mali nanciscuntur." This is Priam's speech, which has been rendered: "A better thing than bravery is justice / For bravery the wicked oft attain."[22]

The most noteworthy evidence of Frost's familiarity with Latin is in his poems. The Title in his *Collected Poems* include "Carpe Diem," "Pertinax," "Auspex," "Haec Fabula Docet," "Lucretius Versus the Lake Poets," "Canis Major," and "Triple Bronze"—the last a translation of the famous Horatian *aes triplex* (1, 28). An unpublished poem, "On the Question of an Old Man's Feeling," refers to the "combination hate and love" affirmed by "Catullus whose address was Rome" [*Odi et amo*] (85. 1). Helen H. Bacon points out that another unpublished poem, a Latin limerick, is based on a rare word in Catullus.[23] The use of Catullan hendecasyllabics in "For Once, Then, Something" has been noted by several commentators. Frost himself proudly referred to it as his "hen dekkers."

When Frost was reading "West-Running Brook" at Rutgers University, his biographer, Lawrance Thompson, who was in the audience, noted that when the poet came to the line "Not just a swerving, but a throwing back," he "paused after 'swerving' and said parenthetically to the audience, 'as in Lucretius.'" His reference was apparently to *De Rerum Natura* (2. 216-93).[24] In "Iris by Night" the mysterious reference to the "confusing lights, . . . Before the fragments of a former sun / Could concentrate anew and rise as one" Newdick traces to a blend of *De Rerum Natura* (5. 663-65) "with another passage from classical literature, a passage yet to be found."[25] Frost once admitted, "You know how I am about chapter and verse—somewhat irresponsible some would say."[26]

Many of the quotations and allusions in the poems are from Virgil. In the draft of a projected preface for an enlarged edition of *North of Boston,* Frost writes: *"North of Boston* (I want to say) was not written as a book nor towards a book. It was written as scattered poems in a form suggested by the eclogues of Virgil."[27] In "Build Soil" the names Tityrus and Meliboeus are from the first eclogue. Lines 19-23 in "For John F. Kennedy, His Inauguration" are drawn directly from the fourth eclogue and Book One of the *Georgics.* The passage reads:

> Now came on a new order of the ages
> That in the Latin of our founding sages . . .
> God nodded His approval of as good.

The "new order of the ages" represents the *novus ordo seclorum,* the "founding sages'" adaptation of Virgil's Latin. It appears on the great seal of the United States. In a parenthetical couplet Frost points this out: "Is it not written on the dollar bill / We carry in our purse and pocket still?" Similarly, "God nodded His approval of as good" translates the *annuit coeptis* on the great seal.

In a verse letter that Frost wrote to Carl Burrell, Francis Utley sees an adaptation of Virgil's description of the Cyclops in *Aeneid* 3. 658. His ingenius argument reaches a conclusion different from Thompson's, which is that the passage is based on Milton.[28]

Those who believe that Frost's poetry is georgic rather than pastoral may find suppport for their conviction in "Something for Hope." The last line of the poem includes a quotation from Tibullus (3. 6): "Hope may not nourish a cow or a horse / But *spes alit agricolam*, 'tis said." The original Latin has the plural *agricolas*; by changing it to the singular, Frost avoids an unnecessary sibilant and makes his statement more immediate.[29]

Several writers have seen a resemblance between the tone of Horace's satires and that of Frost's long so-called sociopolitical poems—"New Hampshire," "Build Soil," "Hard Not to Be King," and "The Lesson for Today." The last-named poem, addressed to Alcuin, eighth-century preceptor at the court of Charlemagne, is of particular interest. Frost imagines that he can hear Alcuin calling to "every sheepish paladin and peer": "Come learn the Latin *eheu* for alas / You may not need it and perhaps you may." Thereupon these unlettered warriors sit down and try to write "Like Horace in the true Horatian vein." At the same time, since they are Christians they must always remember: "*Memento mori* and obey the Lord."

Whatever Horatian undercurrent may be discerned in "The Lesson for Today," some of us may find more pleasure in the haunting and elusive quotations from later, anonymous poets. These are the writers, post classical and pre-Renaissance, "who could calmly take the fate / Of being born at once too early and late." They sang of "Dione in the woods / And *ver aspergit terram floribus.*" The reference to Dione in the woods is from the famous fourth-century *Pervigiliam Veneris* (*regnet in silvis Dione*, 1. 47). The next line in Frost's poem, less easily recognizable, is from the eleventh-century lyric *Levis exsurgit Zephirus*, one of the so-called Cambridge songs. Helen Waddell says of it: "It is like nothing else in mediaeval Latin," and Frederic Raby calls it "the first 'dramatic lyric' of the Middle Ages."[30] Frost takes the first word of the second stanza and joins to it the third line of the same stanza. The delicacy and adroitness of his handling may be judged by a glance at the stanza in the original:

> Ver purpuratum exiit,
> ornatos suos induit:
> aspergit terram floribus,
> ligna silvarum frondibus.

[The rosy spring goes forth, clad in her own adorning, over the earth she sprinkles flowers, and over the woodlands, leaves.]

As Raby says, "Here is all the promise of the years to come, but nothing can equal the freshness of this lyrical spring."[31] The fragile lines are like gracenotes counterpointing the steadier music of lines written in "the true Horatian vein." Helen Bacon says that the "Hyla Brook is to Frost's New England farm what the *fons Bandusiae* was to Horace's Sabine Farm—an ordinary water-course in a humble, alien setting far from Greece, transformed by its owner's powers of song into another spring of the Muses."[32]

It seems that the lifelong attraction that Latin held for Frost had many stages. As noted earlier, the ground had been prepared by his parents. When he studied the classics in high school, he was ready to enjoy them. His classes at Dartmouth and at Harvard deepened and widened his knowledge. For all these advantages Frost was indepted to others—his parents and his teachers.

But Frost was never a passive redcipient of knowledge. Even in high school he made creative use of what he was learning. The two poems on Caesar and the editorial in praise of the classical program show independent active involvement in his favorite study. Similarly, at the university when he encountered in the eclogues of Virgil and in *Hamlet* the "speaking voice," he was able to realize its potential for the evolution of his own style. He had been prepared for this realization by the development of a strongly auditory memory, fostered by listening to his mother's reading and by his own habit of memorizing poems.

His interest extended to the technical aspects of Latin poetry. Newdick reports that he and Frost discussed the development of the meter of accent from the meter of quantity.[33] A passage in "The Lesson for Today" is pertinent. It was, Frost says, the postclassical poets who "slowly led old Latin verse to rhyme / And to forget the ancient lengths of time / And so began the modern world for us." Classical theory as well as practice may have been influential, according to the comment of David Allen Sanders, who remarks that Frost's dictum "No tears in the writer, no tears in the reader" suggests Horace's advice to poets in the *Ars Poetica* (102–03).[34]

Concurrent with this serious interest is the vein of playfulness that marks Frost's humorous references to Latin, particularly in his letters, as has been pointed out. He wrote to Untermeyer, relating a dream in which he was reading "a new elaborate law in very fine print. It was designed to keep any poet from reading in public for a larger fee than any other poet . . . . There was a good deal of Latin in it."[35]

In Frost's writings his use of the Latin classics is never obtrusive but always assimilated to the totality of his art. Nevertheless, it is unmistakable. Those who designated the poet "the Old Roman" had more to warrant their attribution than his rugged profile and the calculatedly gnomic style of some of his utterances.

SISTER JEREMY FINNEGAN

Rosary College

I. Notes

1. Lawrance Thompson, *Robert Frost: The Years of Triumph, 1915–1938* (New York: Holt, Rinehart and Winston, 1970), pp. 649–50, 355.

2. Thompson, *Robert Frost: The Early Years, 1874–1915* (New York: Holt, Rinehart and Winston, 1966), pp. 69–71, 500.

3. Thompson, *Early Years*, pp. 304–07.

4. Thompson, *Years of Triumph,* pp. 402–03.

5. Louis Mertins, *Robert Frost: Life and Walks-Talking* (Norman: Univ. of Okla- Press, 1965), p. 275.

6. Thompson, *Years of Triumph,* p. 468.

7. *Letters of Robert Frost to Louis Untermeyer,* ed. Louis Untermeyer (New York: Holt, Rinehart and Winston, 1963), p. 5; Thompson, *Years of Triumph,* p. 484.

8. Louis Untermeyer, "Robert Frost" in *Makers of the Modern World* (New York: Simon and Schuster, 1955), p. 472.

9. *Letters to Untermeyer,* p. 205.

10. Thompson, *Years of Triumph,* p. 549.

11. *Letters to Untermeyer,* p. 78.

12. *Letters to Untermeyer,* p. 93.

13. *Letters to Untermeyer,* p. 94.

14. *Selected Letters of Robert Frost,* ed. Lawrance Thompson (New York: Holt, Rinehart and Winston, 1964), p. 244.

15. *Selected Letters,* p. 243.

16. *Selected Letters,* p. 277.

17. *Letters to Untermeyer,* p. 147.

18. *Letters to Untermeyer,* p. 172.

19. *Letters to Untermeyer,* p. 187.

20. *Letters to Untermeyer,* p. 200.

21. *Letters to Untermeyer,* p. 257.

22. *Letters to Untermeyer,* pp. 258–59.

23. Thompson, *Years of Triumph,* p. 458.

24. *Letters to Untermeyer,* p. 277.

25. *Letters to Untermeyer,* p. 286.

26. *Selected Letters,* p. 470.

27. *Letters to Untermeyer,* p. 350.

28. *Selected Letters,* p. 471.

29. *Letters to Untermeyer,* p. 309.

30. *Letters to Untermeyer,* p. 384.

31. *Letters to Untermeyer,* Foreword.

32. "A Chronicle of Robert Frost's Early Reading, 1874–1899," *Bulletin of the New York Public Library,* 72 (1968), 611.

33. Thompson, *Years of Triumph,* pp. 595–96.

34. *Selected Letters,* pp. 530–31.

35. Stanlis, in *Frost: Centennial Essays,* ed. Jac Tharpe (Jackson: Univ. Press of Mississippi, 1974), p. 445.

36. "Essay of Dramatic Poesy," in *Essays of John Dryden,* ed. W. P. Ker (New York: Russell and Russell, 1961), I, 43, 82.

II. Notes

1. Lawrance Thompson and R. H. Winnick, *Robert Frost: The Later Years, 1938–1963* (New York: Holt, Rinehart and Winston, 1976), p. 38.

2. Bacon, " 'In- and Outdoor Schooling:' Robert Frost and the Classics," in *Robert Frost, Lectures on the Centennial of his Birth* (Washington: Library of Congress, 1975), pp. 3–25.

3. Robert S. Newdick, *Newdick's Season of Frost: An Interrupted Biography of Robert Frost,* ed. William A. Sutton (Albany: SUNY Press, 1976), p. 307.

4. Newdick, p. 61.

5. Newdick, pp. 60–61.

6. Thompson, *Years of Triumph,* p. 670.

7. *Selected Letters,* p. 124.

8. *Selected Letters,* p. 385.

9. *Later Years,* p. 6.

10. *Later Years,* p. 49.

11. *Letters to Untermeyer,* p. 318.

12. *Letters to Untermeyer,* p. 110.

13. *Selected Letters,* p. 152. Helen H. Bacon also notes this source; see her "In- and Outdoor Schooling," p. 6.

14. *Letters to Untermeyer,* p. 36.

15. *Years of Triumph,* p. 607, n. 21.

16. *Selected Letters,* p. 449. The allusion is to the *Aeneid* (2. 49): *Timeo danaos et dona ferentes.*

17. *Letters to Untermeyer,* p. 330.

18. *Letters to Untermeyer,* p. 335.

19. *Selected Letters,* p. 90.

20. *Letters to Untermeyer,* p. 343.

21. *Later Years,* p. 238.

22. *Remains of Old Latin,* ed. E. H. Warmington, rev. rpt. (Cambridge: Harvard Univ. Press, 1956), I, 291.

23. "In- and Outdoor Schooling," p. 6.

24. *Years of Triumph,* p. 624, n. 9.

25. Newdick, "Robert Frost and the Classics," *Classical Journal,* 35 (1940), 412. n. 37.

26. *Later Years,* p. 407, n. 35.

27. *North of Boston* (New York: Dodd, 1977), Foreword, p. v.

28. "Robert Frost's Virgilian Monster," *English Language Notes,* 10 (March 1973), 221–23. Cf. *Early Years,* pp. 551–52.

29. Helen H. Bacon makes the same identification and suggests the same reason for Frost's changing the noun to the singular. The clarifying description of Frost's poetry as georgic is also hers. See "In- and Outdoor Schooling," p. 11.

30. Waddell, *Mediaeval Latin Lyrics* (Harmondswood, England: Penguin Books, 1952), p. 169; Raby, *A History of Secular Latin Poetry in the Middle Ages* (Oxford: Clarendon Press, 1934), I, 305.

31. Raby, I, 305.

32. "In- and Outdoor Schooling," p. 17.

33. Newdick, p. 270.

34. "Revelation as Child's Play in Frost's 'Directive,' " in *Frost: Centennial Essays* II, ed. Jac Tharpe (Jackson: Univ. Press of Mississippi, 1976), p. 277, n. 6.

35. *Letters to Untermeyer,* p. 259.

36. "Frost's Virgilian Monster," p. 222.

A Road Taken:
The Romantically Different *Ruelle*

To J. Ryan Brownfield, author of "La Ruelle
    De Mon Choix"
Up! up! my Friend, and quit your books . . .
Let Nature be your Teacher.
                Wordsworth, "The Tables Turned"

Scatter poems on the floor;
Turn the poet out of door.
                Frost, "The Thawing Wind"

Clearly one of Frost's little ironies is the title of perhaps his most characteristic and controversial lyric, "The Road Not Taken." His main concern in the poem is evidently with the road he or the persona *did take*, and in this paper I shall identify it as the aesthetic route. The textual testimony indicates that the road is Wordsworth's. In particular, it is related to the path of the Lucy lyric that has become known to us rather by its first line that its title, "She Dwelt Among the Untrodden Ways." Wordsworth himself had a simpler lesser-known title for it: "Song." When the more common title is conflated with that by which Frost knew it, "The Lost Love," then we have a combination of two ideas subjoined in Frost's own title: an untaken path and an accompanying feeling of aloneness. "The Lost Love" is the title bestowed on the Lucy lyric by Palgrave in *The Golden Treasury,* Frost's favorite *vade mecum,* and hence I shall refer to the poem's title as such in this paper. When we raise the question of how Frost's sense of isolation in "The Road Not Taken" came into being, the answer is, again, Romantic. It is also, however, as we may find, ultimately more reminiscent of Keats in this respect than of Wordsworth, for although Frost has been related more to Wordsworth than to any other Romantic, he has deeper affinities with Keats, and the end of Keats's "Ode on a Grecian Urn" had a mythopoeic value for him that he was able to transform abstractly by way of a very concrete design in the two roads of his poem.

But is Frost truly a Romantic? In recent years various responsible scholars have from time to time called that designation into question, in effect qualifying his connection with Wordsworth. Indeed, Frost himself is on record for doubting whether the Romantic path was the one he should follow; he considered it perilously allied to escapism, which he found pusillanimous. Two well-known verses that serve as caveats against Romantic over-indulgence are "Lucretius Versus the Lake Poets" and "Escapist (?)—Never." Still, he could not fully abandon the legacy of Romanticism; in many a verse he adopts a Romantic famework almost in spite of himself. True, he insisted he was writing about man in nature, not merely about nature itself; he claimed to deplore a brand of Platonism which he found unscientific. Yet the Romantics have also put man back into nature; the image in Wordsworth's Lucy lyrics indicating that her hiddenness stems from nature refers to mankind. In any case, it is fortunate that the grounds we have for labeling one of Frost's best-known poems as Romantic have a solid objective or verbal basis.

Along with the critics who have qualified Frost's link to Romanticism are some who have recently observed that he was especially dependent on it. Any overall consideration of his sources cannot fail to cite his debt to the English, as well as American, Romantics.[1] Although Frost frequently made ambivalent remarks with regard to influences upon him or source study in general, a few key statements stand out, notably that a true poet "has to begin as a cloud of all the other poets he ever read."[2] Indeed, an excellent recent scholarly summing up of scholarship on Frost maintains that the name most often associated with him has been Wordsworth's.[3] Should we hesitate at this juncture and not travel on to his famous two roads because we recall only too well Wordsworth's admonition about the dangers of probing into a poet's raw material ("We murder to dissect")? Let us recollect Dryden's defense of Jonson's use of ancient writers: "What would be theft in other poets is only victory in him."[4] With his scientific concerns, Frost also would hardly have been apodictically opposed to dissection —whatever the specimen before us in the lab.

So let us examine with impunity his use of Wordsworth. Although, on one hand, he had claimed that Wordsworth's mind was "not . . . of the very first class,"[5] on the other, he eulogized him, especially during a Wordsworth Centenary address at Cornell during which he made the seeming casual confession:

People ask me what I read. Why, I read Wordsworth . . .[6]

This admission, which went on to include other poets whose influence he conceded, was inspired at least as much, say, by the "nature" of the centennial occasion as it was by a Wordsworthian sense of "Nature." Yet, naturally enough, a poet like Frost who claimed to speak poems rather than recite them because he wanted his speech as much like that of ordinary people as possible, would find much kinship in the leading English Romantic who shifted from stilted eighteenth-century diction to a selection of the words used by everyday man. Nevertheless, Frost was cagey in admitting any link with a poet whom he had dubbed a somewhat-less-than-first-class writer. "No," he once said apropos of his possible debt to Wordsworth, "you couldn't pin me there."[7] A strong statement, but then he straightaway allowed that he would "read all sorts of things," certainly including the arch-Romantic. We know also that his mother read Wordsworth to him when he was a child, that he often spoke of his delight in the Palgrave anthology and *The Oxford Book of English Verse* with their selections of Wordsworth and Keats which he so much admired.

Less known but nonetheless characteristic of Frost is that he indulged even in textual criticism of Wordsworth: he submitted an emendation for a line of the Lake Poet's, contending that "Bound each to each by natural piety" was in fact a misnomer and had better read "Bound each to each by nature piety."[8] Piety, to him, was not per se "natural." Bypassing the patristic commonplace that the natural builds on the supernatural, he evidently thought of piety as basically preternatural; or, if he did not think specifically of "nature piety" as peity toward nature rather than God, what he meant was simple or unsophisticated piety. With the hindsight of John Stuart Mill's essay "Nature," which allows for the complexity of meanings inherent in this abstraction, we can duly appreciate Frost's gloss—even if we do not count him here as a full-fledged textual emendator. But that is hardly irreverent, because he did not mean to be thought of as a scholar concerned with determining a substantive text based on authorial meaning. What is of more basic interest, ultimately, is that just as he realized that nature and piety are technically two very different universals, so he likewise found it difficult to combine two other Romantic abstractions: beauty and truth. The distinction between them is central to his thought, not only in "The Road Not Taken," as we shall see, but in "Two Tramps in Mud Time" as well, regardless of whether or not he was specifically indebted to Keats's ode in each case. In so saying, I have no wish to contravene Louis Untermeyer's detection of a more comprehensive association of beauty and truth in Frost: "For him poetry was not only beauty but, in the Keatsian equivalent, truth."[9] I claim only that Frost himself would have been chary of it.

My purpose in this paper is not to start off on an ambitious road trip by showing Frost's major indebtedness to, say, parts of Wordsworth's epical vision in *The Prelude*; I leave that undertaking to such Frost scholars as Reuben Brower and Richard Poirier. My attempt is more modest. I propose that in "The Road Not Taken" we find that Romantic individualism is expressed in its very windings. Knowing some of the poet's background helps. Dissatisfied with academic life, Frost had chosen the bonafide American path of the rugged individualist, even as did his persona in the poem, but he also felt a hankering for the roadway he had failed to take. So the poet returned to academia to teach classes at Amherst, ones which inevitably turned out to be anything but "academic."[10] In his very rebelliousness, he was thus akin to the early Wordsworth. If we should ponder his more conservative interests, he would be like the older Wordsworth, though a better poet. He even predicts this comparison when, in "Precaution," he slyly counters that he did not want to be radical when young for fear of becoming reactionary when old. Such a dichotomy already points to a kind of intellectual crossroads, as also depicted in "The Road Not Taken," as we shall see. The concept of a "moral or mental cross-roads" intrigued him, and he wrote, as Elizabeth Shepley Sergeant tells us, that "some of the world's great geniuses (Goethe is one of them) have recorded similar meetings with their own images at a moral or mental cross-roads in life."[11] When we recall this summation—redolent as it is with the seeds of Goethean Romanticism in Germany—do we not find it helpful that two of his English predecessors also engaged in such troublesome roadwork, John Stuart Mill and William Hale White's Mark Rutherford, both of whom overcame their dilemmas expressly through their rediscovery of the heartfelt nature poetry of Wordsworth? What could then be more "natural" than to seek for similar Wordsworthian recollections in Frost's own poetic crossroads in "The Road Not Taken"—especially when we recollect that it was initially called "Two Roads"?

Frost's first published lyric, "My Butterfly," is in the Wordsworthian mode, comparable to the Lake Poet's "To a Butterfly."[12] Both W. W. Robson and Reuben Brower have found traces of "Michael" in Frost.[13] But the most convincing interrelationship I have been able to detect in terms of verbal evidence is that between "The Road Not Taken" and "The Lost Love." This kinship, although extraordinary enough in its precise parallels and reversals, is most interesting thematically, but in that respect not as important philosophically, as what I should call the Keatsian subsurface, which represents the gravel base beneath the concrete. For Frost finally preferred the intensity of Keats to the plain style of Wordsworth. But let us start with the surface appearances and with Wordsworth—after the Edward Thomas matter is taken care of.

In any competent overview of source materials, previous "road crews" should be given their due. Sergeant and Thompson treat the genetic material in detail.[14] Among well-known views that have been proposed, the most common is that Frost remembered his poet friend Edward Thomas. As Reginald L. Cook tells us, " 'What I had in mind that night,' Frost explains, 'was not myself but a friend of mine (Edward Thomas) who had gone to war. No matter what road he took, he would always have missed not having taken the other. I was thinking of him.' "[15] To some scholars, such a statement would amount to a donnée. Why, they might ask, should we search about for other possible sources when the poet himself has assured us of what made him write what he did?

In answer, let us broach certain qualifications. First, I had my doubts that Frost told the whole story when he made this remark, so I put the matter to Cook, who knew the poet well, by asking if "The Road Not Taken" did not deal with something "more than Edward Thomas," and he readily agreed.[16] Second, Frost's statement could apply to certain other questions raised by the poem, specifically if it was about his problem of whether to stay in England (where he started writing it) or come to America (where he finished it). A further view has been that an experience on a "Plymouth wood road" led him to write what he did. Still another is Allen Tate's recent submission that Frost's road was his choice not to follow the learned style of Pound; thus since Pound was in the vanguard with his Chinese calligraphy and imagism, Frost's pastoral road was scarcely Pound's route.[17] On the other hand, the speaker's choice of the road less traveled by would point toward Pound's esoteric style, in a sense, not away from it.

In the light of Frost's specific statement, let us now discount these other views as not specifically bearing upon the occasion of the poem—that prompted by Thomas. Yet the occasion and the meaning are two very disparate matters. When we get to the significance of the road poem, we have to travel further than merely acknowledge that Frost, say, "parodied and quietly mocked" Thomas.[18] (The point was that Frost felt that whatever path Thomas would choose, he would always wish he had taken the other.) To say that the poem is "a joke at the romantic self-consciousness of making such a choice"[19] is better but not good enough, because it tends to disparage the very Romantic ingredients intrinsic to it. (Interestingly, however, Hartley Coleridge himself parodied "The Lost Love.")[20] Thompson helpfully posits eleven items relating to "the writing and reception of the poem," and two of them are relevant in that indirectly they also point to the Wordsworth poem.[21]

Thompson's item "g" claims attention first. He quotes from Frost as follows:

> That poem: there's a hint intended there. But you ought to know that yourself. One of the things I suffer from, you know, is being taken as intending a double meaning when I don't. Sometimes I do, and sometimes I don't. And I can't mark 'em—there's no way of marking them. I have to leave it to nice people to know the difference.[22]

Now the hint that I cull from that comment is in the last two words: "the difference." The last line of "The Lost Love" contains the key phrase "The difference," and the concluding line of "The Road Not Taken" echoes it—*au pied de la lettre*: "And that has / made all the difference." Whether or not Frost intended the last words in his comment as a hint would be curious but no great help because deep-seated indebtednessif often below the surface and not a matter of specific intent (though it should not contradict the latter). The Wordsworthian echo in Frost paradoxically represents a "difference" that conveys a similarity, one that is more than merely verbal. Aside from slyly informing the literary historian that what "made the difference" in Frost was Wordsworth's "the difference" transposed—in itself a rather simplistic gloss—the line is soulful. Wordsworth's speaker specifically sighs, and Frost present that exhalation in his own way. Whereas Wordswroth writes, "O!" Frost utters, "And I— / I . . . ." The sigh becomes a dash, almost a stutter, a pause easily stimulated by the earlier dash in "The Lost Love." In a similar manner, there are exclamation points in both lyrics, one seemingly transferred from the other; thus whereas Wordswroth's point follows the "O," Frost's also does but at the end of the line instead. Whether these shifts are substantive effects rather than accidentals is hard to determine but at least they offer evidence for claiming influence. It might also be noticed that Frost's "ohs" are not always or merely sighs.

Next let us look at Frost's other comment (item "h") as cited by Thompson, who writes:

> On one occasion [Frost] told of receiving a letter from a grammar-school girl who asked a good question of him [on "The Road Not Taken"]: "Why the sigh?" That letter and that question, he said, had prompted an answer. End of the hint.[23]

Not much help? It is of some if we recall the Wordsworthian sigh. For Frost made much of sighs. During his unpublished lectures at the New School for Social Research, he said:

> Sometimes [some people] get a tone of grandeur . . . it starts with "oh," usually "oh world" "oh life" "oh time." You get to a prolonged "oh-ing" until you are dead . . . the same in speech . . . "oh thou that rollest about . . ." "oh king live forever" . . . one tone . . . probably a better one, I don't know whether it is or not. But there is a place where you show a difference.[24]

(Again that "difference.") Now "oh world, oh life, oh time" comes directly from Shelley.[25] But the phrase "rollest about" surely conjures up one of Wordsworth's other Lucy lyrics, "A Slumber Did My Spirit Seal," with its pantheistic ending, "Roll'd round in earth's diurnal course / With rocks, and stones, and trees." The poem appeared with "The Lost Love" in Palgrave. And once again Frost relates his exhalation to a "difference," recalling "The Lost Love."

In his lectures at the New School, Frost had more to say about "oh-ing," as he called it. His account of whether "ohs" should be pronounced long or short suggests, at least on one level, the height of emotional Romanticism recollected, as Wordsworth had it, in tranquility. "One of my favorite places to have it out," he said, "was on the word 'oh.' " He contended that "those 'ohs' are subject matter of poetry . . . subject matter, not technique," and he claimed that he would like to exhibit his resources by the variety of "ohs" he could invent. With such emphasis upon this long vowel sound, is it any wonder that he took a hint from Wordsworth's "O!" in "The Lost Love" when he composed "The Road Not Taken"? Not only is the exhalation itself transformed, but also the long vowel sound at the end of a line becomes, for him, such a sound at the beginning of one. The "ways" of Wordsworth's lyric are echoed in Frost's "how way leads on to way," and "Fair as" at the start of line six becomes "as fair" at the conclusion of Frost's own line six.

With Frost's reference to "subject matter," we are back to meaning per se rather than merely occasion, so let us regard the intrinsic significance of Frost's Romantic *ruelle* (or metaphoric poetic alley). Lawrence Perrine is certainly on the right track when he analyzes the exhalation as not simply for "the road not taken," but instead a "sigh of regret that *both* choices were not possible" (italics Perrine's).[26] Such a positive interpretation removes the lyric from the realm of someone's "being different" (with modern negative connotations for twentieth-century Americans) and brings it into the arena of being "something different" (with more positive associations). These designations, after all, appealed to the conventions of the common man for whom Frost wrote. The speaker, in other words, is not sighing with regret because he finds himself "different" but observing that it would have also been a comfortable experience if he had been both layman and poet.

Ben W. Griffith notes that the two roads are described as "fair," an adjective which he takes to mean favorable (as in "a fair choice") because they diverged but did not separate at right angles.[27] One was therefore hardly bad and the other good. Consequently, it is probably being good—but too narrow—to claim, as Sister Catherine Theresa does in her otherwise expert analysis of Frost's religious imagery, that the source is the scriptural passage "It is a narrow gate and a hard road that leads to life, and only a few find it" (Matt. 7:13-14).[28] Yet the roads, although "about the same," are still different; that is the point of the poem. Ambivalence in the adjective "fair" implies that one road was fair in the ethical sense (thus "a fair choice") whereas the other was propitious in an aesthetic one. The effect is closely comparable to the meaning of "My right might be love but theirs was need," the key line in "Two Tamps in Mud Time." The road not taken becomes the way of prosaic truth; the pathway selected, the *ruelle* of beauty, "decadent" though it sometimes may seem to be. When the speaker sighs that he was incapable of accepting both roads, he is ruefully aware that, to him, truth and beauty are irreconcilable. Again compare a line in "Two Tramps in Mud Time": "where the two exist in twain."

At this point, it is convenient to turn directly to Keats, since the Truth-Beauty calculus ushers in the ending of "Ode on a Grecian Urn." On one level, Frost's speaker finds himself a Romantic, seemingly escapist poet who would like to travel two routes but cannot because the creative artist is, *sui generis,* set apart from the multitude; on another, the persona expresses his inner doubts about the / mythopoeic Truth-Beauty identification at the end of Keat's poem, albeit indirectly. Since Frost is on record as having questioned the inherent meaning of the famous Keatsian equation, contending, for example, that truth is sometimes ugly—although he conceded that Keats got away with his Platonic formula poetically—[29] there is thus more to "the difference" in "The Road Not Taken" than initially would alert the eye. The sigh is not merely one of regret, but concomitantly one of gratitude. Herein lies the implicit paradox of the poem. The speaker inwardly is pleased that he is not run-of-the-mill. He is not harking back to the idea, now corrected by Perrine in his interpretation cited above, that there was no essential difference between the two roads.

It is time for a short, but required digression of Frost and his understanding of Keats's ode, because I wish to propose that he is the one who should be given credit for finally solving the famous problem at the end. His gloss on it elsewhere has a seemingly offhand quality but in point of fact it makes a good bit of sense. In a letter to Sidney Cox, he began, "You aren't influenced by that Beauty is Truth claptrap"; yet he hastened to add, "In poetry and under emotion every word is 'moved' a little or much—moved from its old place, heightened, made, made new."[30] Although his initial criticsm very likely indicated his inability to resolve the life-versus-art dilemma as hinted at in the Keatsian equation, his qualification is of substantial value. Any scholarly consideration of the text of the lines has to take into account how the words "move"—that is, the "full set" of quotation marks, viz.:

> . . . to whom thou say'st,
> " 'Beauty is truth, truth beauty.' That is all
> Ye know on earth, and all ye need to know."[31]

Although all these quotation marks are not formally found in the text, a modern emended edition could well put them in (or at least call attention to a grammatical need for them), because they reveal the critical consensus that the transcripts are, at least in part, superior to the printed versions. The purpose of the inverted commas around only the first five words found in the printed versions, however, far from indicating the specific words of a speaker or a quotation from someone like Shaftesbury (the most recent conjecture),[32] was most certainly to show (and correctly so) that these words invoke a special meaning. Indeed, one accepted usage of quotation marks has always been to point to the special sense. Did not Frost himself intuit this sense when he said that "every word is 'moved' a little or much," even as his use of the participle is put within inverted commas to indicate *his* special sense? After noting that Keats's equation represents "a fine beautiful-sounding phrase as far as it goes,"[33] he remarked that ugliness is also truth; yet he was scarcely rejecting the Transcendentalist label of truth per se, if what he meant—and he surely did—was that beauty is simply not the whole of truth. Although Frost hardly admitted to being a Transcendentalist, at the same time his liking for Emerson showed that he was not apodictically opposed to such a philosophical position; time and again I find he is exhibiting Transcendentalist qualities in spite of himself.

Metaphysically, the issue that arises is the following: Transcendentals may be accepted for what they are without their having to be equated; Aquinas, to cite a standard authority to whom Frost had explicit recourse, posited that there are three Transcendentals as aspects of God's Nature (that is, transcending His Being and found in His Creation): the *Unum* (Oneness), *Verum* (Truth), and *Bonum* (Goodness)—not, however, *Pulchrum* (Beauty), which, though related, is not the same. Admittedly, Jacques Maritain interprets Aquinas somewhat differently, although associating beauty with goodness rather than truth,[34] but he is not in the mainstream, which has followed the age-old dictum that "beauty is in the eye of the beholder." Interestingly, Keats would have reversed the relationship imputed above to Frost (namely that ugliness is also truth or beauty is but a part of truth) by claiming that "truth is not all of beauty" in that a life of sensations, as he put it in his letters, or the aesthetic life, was superior to him than thought. What Frost's Puritanism reacted to was the patent affront to commonsense hazardously resonant in the Keatsian lines. It would be of interest if Frost was indebted in this respect to Ruskin's well-known essay "The Greatness of Style," with its own famous critique of the Keatsian passage, but in any event other major writers of our time have criticized the equation as well.[35]

Although Frost intuitively grasped the special use of quotation marks—implying that Keats was not referring to beauty and truth as absolutes per se—did he also see that Keats evidently meant the speaker of the final two lines not to be the poet but the urn? Doubtfully so, because most readers have not, although that reading now has the endorsement of the Harvard Keatsians. As the leading expert on the crux informs us, "It seems better for the urn to tell us what we know and need to know than for the poet to do so."[36] Keats's idea was that the Truth-Beauty equation was merely an earthly solution to a mystery to be finally resolved in the afterlife. So the urn addresses the lovers on its surface, themselves things of beauty, and not primarily the speaker or reader at all. (If it is objected that commonsense is at stake with such a reading, we can respond that it makes as much sense for the urn to speak to the lovers as to speak in the first place.) How then would it "tease us out of thought"—like Keats's "life of sensations"? How else but by inviting a teasing bit of paronomasia on the words *on earth*? The wordplay implies that the lovers are depicted on an earthen vessel, one made of terra-cotta; their meaning is thereby based not on a worldly existence alone, or on an otherworldly one, but on an artistic one.[37]

If Frost did not catch on to Keats's meaning *in toto*—"How do I know," he once wrote, "whether a man has come close to Keats in reading Keats? It is hard for me to know"[38]—his limited formal understanding was prompted by his own difficulty in coming to terms with Platonism, a point frequently reiterated in the Thompson biography. In "Boeotian," he says, "I love to toy with the Platonic notion"; he thereby opposes what he designates "systematic" wisdom, presumably that, say, of Aristotle rather than Plato; yet at the same time he is more a disciple of Aristotle than Plato in his insistence on a formal or structured dimension to art, as in his poem "Pertinax." What might be called his unsystematic ordering of form, or his creative ability to make order out of chaos, pertinently, and pertinaciously, stands also behind the artistry of Keats.

But let us get back to "The Road Not Taken." Why did Frost shift poetic gears by changing the title from "Two Roads"? Since the reason is Wordsworthian, Keats must temporarily take a back seat. Did not the title derive from "The Lost Love"? As hinted at in the titles, both poems delineate a similar sense of deficiency. Frost's feeling of loss is a far cry, however, from what Yvor Winters unfortunately dubbed "spiritual drifting" in the seeming paradox of the two roads—that is, that one appears less worn, yet both are actually more or less alike.[39] The true deficiency described is also different from what a more recent critic terms the poet's rationalization in coming to a decision.[40] For these Frostian crossroads do not represent a vague turning off. Winters is quite wrong. The important point made is that their being described as "about" the same craftily indicates (as Perrine argues in his analysis cited earlier) that they are not really the same. To put it another way, roads that are "about" the same are *only* "about" the same, and therefore not equivalent. The word *about* should be stressed, not the word *really*.

Thus the intricate intersection of these roads is more evident than most critics have surmised: Frost interconnects with Wordsworth and, indirectly yet more basically, with Keats. Aside from the strong verbal parallels with Wordsworth that I have already shown ("The difference"—"the difference"; "O!"—"Oh . . . !" and "I–I," "ways"—"Way . . . way"; "Fair as"—"as fair"), Lucy's "untrodden ways" are re-presented as Frost's "leaves no step had trodden black"—both phrases signifying the immediacy and freshness of experience. Whereas Wordsworth tells of a landscape that is "mossy," Frost produces one which is, analogously, "grassy." From an elementary verbal perspective, however, the "-trodden" echo is the most remarkable.

But does Frost express regret at the symbolic death of *his* Lucy? Yes, inasmuch as Lucy is hardly a mere allusion to Dorothy Wordsworth, Marie-Anne Vallon, or Mary Hutchinson—recent "psychobiographical" criticism notwithstanding.[41] Derivable from the Latin *Lucia* (itself derivable from "light" in Latin), Lucy has a function that is largely, if not entirely, symbolic. Now Frost too expresses regret at a symbolic passing away and imagines reciting the event in old age ("ages and ages hence"). Just as Lucy reflects Wordsworth's feeling of heavenly light or creative afflatus in terms of the diminution of his childhood vision as he gets older, Frost too finds his vision darkened. His lyric tells of a similar loss—not of untrodden ways by themselves but of the youthful dream encompassing both roads of life. Interestingly, Keats, like Frost, found the final words of "The Lost Love" exceptionally meaningful; he spoke them as "the best . . . that Wordsworth ever wrote."[42] This correlation enhances the overall Wordsworth-Keats-Frost relationship.

In sum, the road leading into the undergrowth in "The Road Not Taken," the one which the speaker does not take, is that of the common man and his way of life, that of humdrum "truth" and thereby closer to "reality" in an ordinary sense. The other road may not seem to be beautiful at the outset, but it is the lonely road of the artist and it can lead to beauty. Frost does not of course make it that crystal clear, but we are at least on the road to the road. Frost's is certainly the road of the individualist, which the New Englander was, leading to isolation and longing, especially in old age. The reader can then draw out the more universal meaning.

Ultimately Frost's poem is more significant than Wordsworth's because, behind the façade of the commonplace, our Puritan is able to imply that the basic philosophical dichotomy between ethics and aesthetics is by no means foreign to the nature of the artistic mind, that he is destined to come out on top even if, in the process, he has to forsake some of ordinary humdrum reality, or the "pedestrian" path. The aesthetic route, the speaker well realizes, is not identifiable with the whole truth of realiy—except possibly on the anagogic level—but it is surely part of the reality of truth. The lyric informs us that when the road of "pedestrian" truth is passed by, the optional road of beauty may yet remain and that route is not essentially a detour at all. On the other hand, some modern critics who have compared the two poets aver that the Englishman is superior to the New Englander.[43] Louis Simpson has an apt reply for one of these castigators: "The reviewer compares Frost with Wordsworth, as though they were in some sort of competition."[44] Such competitive evaluation is indeed irrelevant. Frost did not personally accept the Lake Poet's special brand of pantheism. Yet in utilizing some of the aesthetic qualities of the English Romantics, Frost arrived at a new synthesis, which became a product all his own. In the process "The Road Not Taken" has ironically become, at least for numerous readers and scholars, a well-traveled thoroughfare.

ROBERT F. FLEISSNER

Central State University, Ohio

The Wordsworthian Parallels

Wordsworth	Frost
Titles: "The Lost Love" (the title of "She Dwelt . . ." in Palgrave)	"The Road Not Taken"
Lines: "among the untrodden ways" (1.1)	"In leaves no step had trodden black" (1.12) "way leads on to way" (1.14)
"mossy" (1.5)	"grassy" (1.8)
"Fair as" (1.6)	"as fair" (1.6)
", and, O!" (1.11)	", and I— / I . . ." (11.18-19) "Oh" (1.13)
"The difference" (1.12)	"the difference." (1.20)
Punctuation: The use of the single dash to indicate a sharp pause at the beginning of a line. (1.7)	The use of the single dash to indicate a sharp pause at the end of a line (1.18)
The exclamation point (11.6, 11, 12)	The exclamation point (1.13)
Poetic Devices: Use of conjunction at the start of a line "And" (1.4) "But" (1.11)	Use of the conjucntion at the start of a line "And" (11.2, 3, 4, 7, 11, 20) "Yet" (1.14)

Notes

1. The most comprehensive recent paper I have seen dealing with such literary indebtedness is by Sister Jeremy Finnegan, O.P., "Creative Borrowing: Auditory Memory in Robert Frost," presented at the annual convention of The Midwest Modern Language Association in 1976. (See her essay on this same topic in this volume.) See also Charles Carmichael, "Robert Frost as a Romantic," in *Frost: Centennial Essays* ed. Jac Tharpe (Jackson: Univ. Press of Mississippi, 1974), pp. 147-65. I have published separate studies on Frost's debt to individual Romantics; e.g., "Frost's Response to Keats's Risibility," *The Ball State University Forum* (Frost issue), 11 (1970), 40-43; on Coleridge: "Frost on Frost . . . at Midnight," *Studies in the Humanities*, 5 (1976), 32-38; on Tennyson as a Victorian Romantic "Like 'Pythagoras' Comparison of the Universe with Number': a

Frost-Tennyson Correlation," in *Frost: Centennial Essays,* pp. 207-20; " 'Frost . . . at . . . Play': a Frost-Dickinson Affinity Affirmed," *Research Studies,* 46 (1978), 28-39. Quotations from Frost are from *Complete Poems of Robert Frost* (New York: Holt, Rinehart and Winston, 1949) because Frost used that volume himself, but I have also consulted *The Poetry of Robert Frost,* ed. Edward Connery Lathem(New York: Holt, Rinehart and Winston, 1969). Lathem's more recent edition has an optional comma in the text of "The Road Not Taken." [Lathem's description of his textual scholarship on the Frost poems appears in Vol. I of the two-volume edition, *The Poetry of Robert Frost* (Barre, Mass: Imprint Society, 1971), pp. vii-xxvii.] Quotations from Wordsworth are taken not from the De Sélincourt edition, but from that to which Frost had access, Palgrave, *The Golden Treasury* (New York: Random House, 1944).

2. Lawrance Thompson, *Robert Frost: The Years of Triumph, 1915-1938* (New York: Holt, Rinehart and Winston, 1970), pp. 355, 650.

3. Reginald L. Cook, "Robert Frost," in *Fifteen Modern American Authors: A Survey of Research and Criticism,* ed. Jackson R. Bryer (Durham: Duke Univ. Press, 1969), p. 270.

4. "Of Dramatick Poesie," in *Essays of John Dryden,* ed. W. P. Kerr (New York: Russell and Russell, 1961), I, 43, 82. (As cited by Sister Jeremy Finnegan.)

5. Radcliffe Squires, *The Major Themes of Robert Frost* (Ann Arbor: Univ. of Michigan Press, 1963), p. 8.

6. This talk was published for the first time as "A Tribute to Wordsworth," *The Cornell Library Journal,* No. 11 (1970), 76-99. (Reference here is to p. 91).

7. Interview with Richard Poirier, *The Paris Review,* as cited in *Interviews with Robert Frost,* ed. Edward Connery Lathem (New York: Holt, Rinehart and Winston, 1960), p. 88.

8. Elizabeth Shepley Sergeant, *Robert Frost: The Trial by Existence* (New York: Holt, Rinehart and Winston, 1960), p. 88.

9. *Robert Frost: A Backward Look* (Washington: Library of Congress Ref. Dept., 1964), p. 23.

10. Thompson, *Years of Triumph,* p. 100.

11. Sergeant, p. 87.

12. In a recent study, however, George Monteiro traces "My Butterfly" to both Frost's stay at Dartmouth College in 1892 (as Thompson also did) and his reading of Dickinson: "Over the memory of the autobiographical moment which moved Frost to attempt this elegy hovered Dickinson's 'butterfly' poems." "Emily Dickinson and Robert Frost," *Prairie Schooner,* 51 (1977/78), 369-86. (This quotation from p. 374).

13. Robson, "The Achievement of Robert Frost," *The Southern Review,* NS 2 (1966), 735-61; Brower, *The Poetry of Robert Frost: Contellations of Intention* (New York: Oxford Univ. Press, 1968), pp. 174-79. Brower has a great deal to say on the Frost-Wordsworth-Keats relationship.

14. Sergeant, pp. 87-89; Thompson, *Years of Triumph,* pp. 88-89, 544-48.

15. "Frost on Frost: The Making of Poems," *American Literature,* 28 (1956-57), 65.

16. Quoted by permission from Reginald L. Cook.

17. Allen Tate, " 'Inner Weather': Robert Frost as a Metaphysical Poet," in *Robert Frost: Lectures on the Centennial of His Birth* (Washington: Library of Congress, 1975), p. 65. Tate also relates Frost to Wordsworth (p. 66).

18. Thompson, *Years of Triumph*, pp. 88–89.

19. See Millicent Travis Lane, "Agnosticism as Technique: Robert Frost's Poetic Style," Diss. Cornell 1967, p. 128. The gravamen of this thesis should, however, be compared with the essay on Frost's religion by Dorothy Judd Hall, "An Old Testament Christian," in *Frost: Centennial Essays* III (Jackson: Univ. Press of Mississippi, 1978), pp. 316–49.

20. The poem is cited by G. E. (in "Wm. Wordsworth," *Notes and Queries*, 4th ser., 3 [1869], 580) in answer to a query. It is also cited by Herbert Hartman ("Wordsworth's 'Lucy' Poems: *Notes and Marginalia,*" *PMLA*, 49 [1934], 134–42) but only in part, which is misquoted, with an incorrect reference as to its source. The parody is interesting to compare with Frost's use of the same poem (but for more than parodic reasons); it is very amusing.

21. Thompson, *Years of Triumph*, pp. 545–48.

22. Thompson, *Years of Triumph*, p. 547.

23. Thompson, *Years of Triumph*, p. 547.

24. Lecture of 5 Feb. 1931, recorded by Genevieve Taggard in The Dartmouth College Library and cited with permission but with my pointing.

. 25. Frost quotes the line again, labeling it "Shelleyan," in his Cornell speech, p. 98. He discusses Wordsworth in close proximity.

26. Robert Frost, 'The Road Not Taken,' " *The Explicator Cyclopedia*, ed. C. C. Walcutt and J. E. Whitesell, (Chicago: Quadrangle Books, 1966), I, 140. This explication counters David Wyatt's "Choosing in Frost," in *Frost: Centennial Essays* II, ed. Jac Tharpe (Jackson: Univ. of Mississippi Press, 1976).

27. Griffith, "Robert Frost, 'The Road Not Taken," in *Frost: Centennial Essays*, pp. 139–140.

28. Sr. Catherine Theresa, "New Testament Interpretations of Robert Frost's Poems," *The Ball State University Forum* (Frost issue), 50–54. Other religions have had similar maxims, notably Hinduism, which has a saying that the road to salvation is as straight as a razor's edge (thus influencing Maugham's *The Razor's Edge*). I do not see how Frost's poem is explicitly Christian, especially since he called himself an Old Testament Christian; in other words, that it is based at all on the New Testament has not been proved. But I like the idea.

29. *Selected Letters of Robert Frost*, ed. Lawrence Thompson (New York: Holt, Rinehart and Winston, 1964), pp. 140–42.

30. *Selected Letters*, pp. 140–42.

31. See Jack Stillinger's seminal article, "Keats's Grecian Urn and the Evidence of Transcripts," *PMLA*, 73 (1958), 447–48; and also the appendix "Who Says What to Whom at the End of Ode on a Grecian Urn?" in his book *The Hoodwinking of Madeline and Other Essays on Keats's Poems* (Urbana: Univ. of Illinois Press, 1971), pp. 167–73. I would add, however, one more category to his four: *(5) Urn to figures on the urn.*

32. Harry M. Solomon, "Shaftesbury's *Characteristics* and the Conclusion of 'Ode on a Grecian Urn,' " *Keats-Shelley Journal*, 24 (1975), 89–102.

33. See Daniel Smythe, *Robert Frost Speaks* (New York: Twayne, 1964), p. 62.

34. "So, although the beautiful is in close dependence upon what is metaphysically true, in the sense that every splendour of intelligibility in things presupposes some degree of conformity with that Intelligence which is the cause of things, the beautiful nevertheless is not a kind of truth, but a kind of good." *Art and Scholasticism with Other Essays*, tr. J. F. Scanlan (London: Sheed and Ward, 1949), p. 21.

35. E.g., T. S. Eliot, I. A. Richards, and William Carlos Williams. For a convenient reference work, see Harvey T. Lyon, ed., *Keats' Well-Read Urn: An Introduction to Literary Method* (New York: Holt, Rinehart and Winston, 1958), passim.

36. Stillinger, *Hoodwinking*, p. 173.

37. There has been disagreement in the scholarly ranks regarding the material out of which the Grecian Urn was composed. A typical reaction is the following one from a professor at St. Peter's College, Oxford during the summer of 1978: "Keats did not have in mind some great big marble thing." Such a reading ties in with my view that the last lines of the Ode suggest an earthen vessel ("That is all ye know on earth"). Yet the poem does refer to "marble," possibly because the poet had in the back of his mind the Elgin Marbles, about which he also wrote. Thus Keats biographer Amy Lowell asserted that "the inspiration . . . came from the Elgin Marbles" and that "no urn had anything to do with it," a view then accepted by Walter Jackson Bate. Miss Lowell's comment is of interest with regard to Frost because of his interest in her (he once memorably referred to a special dinner to which she had invited him as her "Keats eats"). Perhaps the best article on the subject of the Urn's composition is James Dickie's ("The Grecian Urn: An Archaeological Approach," *The Bulletin of the John Ryland Library*, 52 [1969], 1-19). Although Dickie apodictically contends that the urn is marble, as also in Keat's "Ode to Indolence," he remarks in regard to the latter reference that "Professor Corbett of University College, London, makes the interesting suggestion that Keats was here 'unconsciously thinking of a clay vessel, which you can turn easily by hand, unlike marble' " (p. 5). The same could apply to the Grecian Urn Ode, especially since Dickie believes that "the poet turns the urn round between stanzas 3 and 4" (p. 8). Moreover, "green altar" suggests a painted vessel.

38. *Selected Prose of Robert Frost,* ed. Hyde Cox and Edward Connery Lathem (New York: Holt, Rinehart and Winston, 1966), p. 43. Yet Frost later revised this essay and crossed these lines out. The article as initially revised appeared in *Amherst Graduates' Quarterly,* 4 (Feb. 1931), 5-15, and the crossed-out lines appear in the copy published in facsimile as a keepsake of a Robert Frost gathering held at Dartmouth, Baker Memorial Library, on July 3, 1966, and preserved now at Cornell. He cut the lines after the speech was published in the *Quarterly* as "An Uncompleted Revision of 'Education by Poetry,' " thus in effect revising his revision. To my knowledge, the final deletion is found only in the Cornell copy. Frost was this way denying any belief in what has now been paraded as "The Intentional Fallacy." He wanted instead to stress the need for seeking poetic intent, his own included, and he felt a close attachment to Keats's own meaning.

39. Winters, "Robert Frost; or, The Spiritual Drifter as Poet," *The Sewanee Review,* 56 (1948), 564-96. In spite of its negative verdict, Winters' article has become the most often cited critical article on Frost—thus underscoring *en passant* the popularity of "The Road Not Taken."

40. William B. Bache, "Rationalization in Two Frost Poems," *The Ball State University Forum* (Frost issue), 33-35.

41. Richard E. Matlak, "Wordsworth's Lucy Poems in Psychobiographical Context," *PMLA*, 93 (1978), 46-65. Matlak argues that Wordsworth was unconsciously basing Lucy on his sister Dorothy because he wanted to be free of her (and thus had Lucy die) to join Coleridge—a view with which I disagree.

42. See C. D. Narasimhaiah, "The Reputation of Robert Frost: A Point of View," *The Literary Criterion,* 9 (Winter 1969), 1-10. (This reference is to p. 5.) Narasimhaiah compares "The Road Not Taken" and "The Lost Love" critically, not historically.

43. Narasimhaiah, 1-10; see also the review of Thompson in The *Times Literary Supplement,* 16 April 1971, pp. 434-35; George W. Nitchie, *Human Values in the Poetry of Robert Frost* (Durham: Duke Univ. Press, 1960), pp. 27-28.

44. *TLS,* 30 April 1971, pp. 504-05.

A Way Out: Pastoral Psychodrama

When he died in 1963, Robert Frost had received more official and academic honors than any other poet who had lived and written in the United States. He had won four Pulitzer Prizes, received forty-four honorary degrees, been invited to read his poetry at a Presidential Inaugural, and been sent to Russia as a cultural ambassador. But despite these triumphs in the academic and literary world, Frost owed much of his poetic reputation to his identification with farming. His mannerisms and the years he had spent farming in New Hampshire seemed to guarantee that his poems were a uniquely authentic vision of a pastoral existence in which man is "closer to reality" and "independent of the complicated social structure" of urban society, because he "earns his living from the soil."[1] As Professor George Whicher, who saw him give his first reading in Amherst in 1916, later recalled, "Frost was dead set not to appear either academic or literary. He was all farmer. When it came my turn to speak with him, we spent an animated ten minutes discussing the healthful properties of horse-manure."[2]

Acutally, as Frost was sometimes quick to admit, he was never a very successful farmer. He was a part- or full-time teacher for five of the ten years he lived in Derry, and after he established himself as a poet in 1915 he held a great many appointments as an English professor or poet-in-residence. However, he was often unhappy with academic life, and when his difficulties became critical on several occasions he resigned and retreated back to his farm in Vermont (or New Hampshire).

When he first began to try to earn his living as a poet in 1913, his dream was to start his literary career in London and then retire to a New England farm where he could write and "live cheap." By November of the next year, his desire for recognition and financial security led him to amend this dream significantly. "I should awfully like a quiet job in a small college," he decided, where he could receive some honor for what he had achieved as a poet. In 1916 when he had returned to America and New Hampshire, he told a reporter that he was a good teacher and a poor farmer, but he disliked teaching because it did not allow him time to write and because he hated "academic ways." A decade later—after he had taught at Amherst and Michigan—he complained half jokingly that colleges kept intruding on his "pastoral serenity" by offering him teaching jobs. "I want to farm," he said, ". . . Amherst, Dartmouth, Bowdoin and Connecticut Wesleyan are going to give me a living next year for a couple of weeks in each of them. The rest of the time I shall be clear away from the academic, feeding pigeons, hens, dogs, or anything . . . for the pleasure or profit of it." However, in 1930 when he was worried that his *Collected Poems* would not be well received and that his poetic career had been eclipsed by Robinson's, he complained to Louis Untermeyer: "I don't want to raise sheep; I don't want to keep cows; I don't want to be called a farmer . . . What am I then? Not a farmer—never was— never said I was."[3]

These letters as well as many incidents in Frost's life suggest that he needed both the simple, "pastoral serenity" of farming and the more complex milieux which he inhabited as a professor or poet-in-residence. He needed both the relative isolation and the simplicity of rural life *and* the honors and financial security which academic appointments gave him. However, it was not easy for him to reconcile the very different values represented by these two ways of life.

The tensions which were created by Frost's efforts to live in both of these worlds are expressed obliquely but forcefully in his one-act play, *A Way Out.* This work was first published in the February, 1917 issue of *The Seven Arts.*[4] This was only a month after he started his first major academic appointment as a professor of English at Amherst. Frost was offered this position during the summer of 1916, when he was living at his farm in Franconia, New Hampshire, shortly after he had returned triumphantly to Harvard, as Phi Beta Kappa poet in June of 1916. He was still not certain whether he would accept the Amherst appointment as late as December, 1916, and so he must have written the play when he was still struggling to decide whether or not to become a professor. Also, during the summer and fall of 1916, Frost was preparing the manuscript for *Mountain Interval,* which was published in December of that year. At least eleven of the thirty-two poems in that book were written or begun between 1900 and 1911 during the lonely years at Derry when Frost was an unrecognized and virtually unpublished farmer and teacher. Thus as he was writing *A Way Out* and making up his mind about Amherst, he was rereading and finishing poems like "An Old Man's Winter Night" and "The Hill Wife" which must have reminded him of how hard and lonely his years as a New England farmer had been.[5]

The action of *A Way Out* is simple but rather mysterious. It begins when a hunted murderer identified only as the "stranger" invades the home of a New England hermit named Asa Gorrill. The criminal is a tough, fairly sophisticated man who questions Gorrill about the way he lives. He then reveals that he plans to hide with him by "mixing" their identities. They will, the murderer plans, take turns appearing in the barnyard and visiting town to sell eggs so that no one will know that there are two of them. In effect, they will be two persons with one identity—Gorrill's. To achieve this "mixing," the stranger performs a ritual. He puts on the hermit's spare clothing, imitates his voice and posture, and asks him, "Are you happy? Have you anything to live for?" He then forces Gorrill to dance with him to complete the merging of their identities. He says:

> I'm going to mix us up like your potato and stringbeans [Gorrill's supper], and then see if even you can tell us apart. The way I propose to do is to take both your hands like this and then whirl around and round till we're both so dizzy we'll fall down.

When the two men fall, each claims the other is the criminal. They struggle, one falls unconscious, and the other drags him outside into the woods. The posse suddenly arrives, and Asa—or the stranger dressed as him—rushes back into the farmhouse to say that the fugitive has escaped. The pursuers leave to search for him, and the hermit goes to bed.

The play's ending is quite ambiguous. Frost's stage directions and dialogue make it difficult to be sure which man won the fight or returned to the house. The scene is dimly lit, and when the two fall Frost identifies them only as the "First to Speak" and the "Second." The pursuers do not find Asa's corpse in the woods, and the man who returns is called "Asa"—which suggests that Gorrill won the fight and the stranger escaped. But according to the stage directions, when the posse leaves the hermit throws his socks and the strangers shoes into the fire—which is something the murderer would do since earlier in the play Frost emphasizes that Gorrill wore only slippers. Moreover, when a returning member of the posse calls goodnight to the hermit, he gets "into bed so as to answer with his face in the pillow"—an action which the murderer might perform to disguise his voice.[6]

In his preface to the 1929 edition of the play, Frost remarks that "here for once I have written a play without (as I should like to believe) having gone very far from where I have spent my life." Taken literally, this statement would suggest that the play's events might have been based on incidents which happened near Derry. The stranger mentions that he worked in a shoe factory before he committed the murder, and there were some industries—including shoe factories —in Derry Depot.[7] But on a deeper level the play may be interpreted as expressing some of Frost's feelings about how he had spent his life—particularly his life as a farmer in New Hampshire. His characterization of Gorrill and the stranger's taunts reveal what must have been some of his own doubts about the merits of a purely pastoral existence.

The opening dialogue between Gorrill and the stranger is virtually a parody of the traditional pastoral convention that the swain is happy because he chooses to be poor and to have few needs. When the stranger enters he remarks that Asa locks up early and asks, "What you afraid of?" " 'Fraid of nothing, because I ain't got nothing—nothing't anybody wants,' " Gorrill replies. In Renaissance pastorals like Book VI of *The Faerie Queen,* for example, the swain is a man who chooses to live in poverty in the country so that he will be happy and serene. Thus Meliboee tells Sir Calidore that he is content with his pastoral life because "having small [needs], yet do I not complain / Of want, not wish for more it to augment."[8] In contrast, Gorrill is poor and seems proud of it because he lacks the imagination to choose any different, richer way of life. Later in the play the stranger asks:

> You haven't got any real prejudices in favor of this way of living then? I mean you didn't take it up as a man goes into the Methodist Church in preference to the Baptist or the Orthodox?
> ASA. Dunno's I did.

In some respects, Gorrill lives the kind of life that the Frosts lived in Derry between 1900 and 1911—but without the compensations which made their life there bearable and sometimes even enjoyable. Like Frost when he was at Derry, Gorrill is a particularly poor kind of farmer—a chicken farmer or "hen man"— who lacks the capital, good land, or farming skills needed to raise something more profitable. Frost must have been remembering those lean years when he has Asa explain that he cannot even buy flour to bake bread if his hens are not laying. "Oh, eggs are at the bottom of it," the stranger exclaims in dismay, "Nothing unless eggs. God, it's worse than I thought." When he started teaching at Pinkerton Academy in 1906, Frost was so enraged when a student wrote "Hen Man" on the blackboard of his classroom that he had the boy expelled. But afterwards he insisted that the years of poverty in Derry had been an ordeal which had tempered his character and somehow contributed to his creativity. In fact, on some occasions he made his economic plight seem even worse than it really was by not mentioning—or by discounting—the five-hundred-dollar annuity which he received each year from his grandfather's estate.[9]

Moreover, Asa is a hermit who lives in isolation without any friends. In his descriptions of the Derry years to his biographers, Frost emphasized that his family was so isolated that no neighbors visited them socially for eight years and that he was out later than eight o'clock at night only twice. However, Frost claimed that this "lack of company" meant that he had

> plenty of solitude. And solitude was what I needed and valued . . . . It couldn't have been more perfect if we had planned it . . . I botanized a lot. One of my favorite plays was making paths in the woods and bushes. We were showing the country things to the children as they came along.[10]

But Gorrill has neither a family nor any interest in nature. "Ever been heard to say you like the innocent woods and fields and flowers like a poem in print?" the stranger demands. "Dunno's I have," Asa replies; and the stranger disgustedly concludes, "I supposed people that lived alone had to have something to say for themselves . . . You haven't got ideas enough to make a hermit's life interesting.

Gorrill's existence represents the New England pastoral way of life reduced to its lowest, barest essentials. Such an existence, as the stranger's taunts indicate, is not the way an adult, male human being should live. He might murder him, the stranger warns Asa, because "it wouldn't amount to another crime to kill a half man like you . . . Does anyone know for certain you're not a woman in man's clothing anyway?" He repeatedly calls the hermit "old boy," implying that he has gotten old without becoming mature; and at the end of the play he speaks to him as if he were a child: "I'm putting you to bed tonight. I'm going to let you stay up later than usual on account of company."

A number of Frost's symbols in the play also suggest the limited, uncompleted nature of Gorrill's existence and personality. His name Asa (or "Asie") Gorrill can be read as a pun on the phrase "as a gorilla"—which suggests that though he may be a primate, he is not fully human. His house contains a locked, unused room which has no relevance to the plot but is an archtypal symbol for unknown, unlived, or secret parts of the personality. ("That door's closed with nails," Asa tells the stranger. "You can't get in there. This is all the room I live in.") Finally, the house is surrounded by dark woods which are the symbol Frost uses for unknown, alternative ways of life in "The Road Not Taken" and "Stopping by Woods on a Snowy Evening."

Frost makes the same association between the theme of loneliness and the image of New England woods in his poem "The Hill Wife," which he began at Derry and finished in 1916 in Franconia.[11] In that poem he expresses this theme as a pathetic tragedy by describing how a young New England farm wife becomes so nervous and depressed by her loneliness that she disappears into the forest and dies there. *A Way Out* is a kind of dark comic, or melodramatic, version of the same theme. Asa is a kind of dark comic, or melodramatic, version of the same theme. Asa is too unimaginative to be troubled—as the wife is—by bird songs, a "lonely house," and a "dark pine that kept / Forever trying the window-latch."[12] Instead the stranger invades his house and forces him to recognize the emptiness of existence. "Are you happy?" the stranger asks twice as he is about to spin Asa in his dance. "Have you anything to live for? Lord, didn't you ever ask yourself a question like that—with so much time on your hands?"

The plot of *A Way Out* also can be considered a variation on the theme of the uninvited guest, an archetypal motif whose best known modern examples are probably Camus's "The Guest" and Conrad's "The Secret Sharer." In this plot motif, a person living a relatively settled but unimaginative and limited way of life is visited by a criminal or outcast under mysterious circumstances. In the course of the story, a strange kinship is established between the reluctant host and the outcast—giving the host some insight into previously unknown or undeveloped aspects of himself, things which he has "cast out" of his consciousness.

The antithetical yet complementary characters of the two men and the actions at the end of the play, particularly the dance and wrestling match, suggest not so much "The Secret Sharer" but other stories of doubles and opposites—such as Gilgamesh and Enkidu or Jacob and Esau—in which two partial individuals struggle with one another in their efforts to achieve a state of psychic completion. Asa is innocent and ignorant. The stranger is guilty and worldy-wise. Asa is a poor and unreflective hermit, and the stranger is a clever, self-reliant wanderer and outcast. Asa is a man who is passively indifferent to humanity because of the way he has cut himself off from the community. The stranger has expressed his indifference to the value of life and his hostility to the community in an aggressive way by committing murder. Consequently the play's title has a double meaning. Sharing Asa's life is a "way out" for the stranger since it will enable him to survive. But his plan to unite his life with Asa's is also a "way out" for the hermit since it will end his isolation and ignorance.

A Way Out is Frost's harshest portrayal of how limited and limiting New England rural life could be. The passive existence of an Asa Gorrill is not enough. It must be supplemented by the more aggressive and urbane qualities which are present in the stranger's character. However, these qualities—particularly the aggressiveness—were by no means alien to Frost's personality. His letters as well as many incidents in Thompson's biography reveal that he had a capacity for resentment and a fearsome temper which he controlled with considerably difficulty. So it is very possible he feared the possibility that someday he might lose control of himself completely and actually kill someone while in a rage.[13] For this reason it is significant that the stranger is a murderer who accepts Gorrill's way of life almost as a kind of self-punishment—to escape from justice. If Gorrill represents an aspect of Frost's life which he was dissatisfied with and wished to change, then the stranger represents a part of his personality which he feared and distrusted.

When it is considered in this context, the play's ambiguous conclusion is very significant. In his preface to the 1929 edition of the play, Frost emphasizes that writing had to be "dramatic . . . heard or sung or spoken by a person in a scene— in character, in a setting. By whom, where and when is the question." But it is this fundamental question of *who* is speaking that Frost leaves uncertain at the end of *A Way Out*. If it is the stranger, then he has survived by consciously putting himself in the hermit's persona—by mimicking his stooped walk and piping voice, by living on his farm and tending his chickens. "It will take me to do this thing right when I come into office," the stranger says, speaking of Gorrill's way of life as if it were a political position like a governorship which he could take over and occupy. Analogously, Frost may have implicitly rejected his earlier, simple pastoral existence by becoming a professor of English, but for the rest of his life he continued to cultivate the persona of the New England farmer-poet. In private he may have sought literary awards and recognition and wanted to be considered a better writer than sophisticates like Joyce and Eliot.[14] But in public he often presented himself in the role which he expressed so well in "New Hampshire"—as the witty country poet ("a plain New Hampshire farmer" with a generous publisher) who is proud of his regionalism and regards the aspirations of his New York and Boston contemporaries with tolerant amusement.

A Way Out reveals more about Frost's life and personality than many of his poems do. As I have pointed out, it was written during a particularly crucial watershed in his development when he was choosing between farming and academic life as a way to support his poetic career. Thus it is also a retrospective work in some respects. In his characterization of Asa Gorrill, he was recalling some of the bleaker aspects of his own pastoral way of life as a New Hampshire farmer and implicitly rejecting that kind of existence. Moreover, it is significant that the stranger's taunts are not only criticisms of Gorrill; they are also a sarcastic assault on writers who idealize farm life because it is so "innocent" and "close to nature." In fact, though Frost may not have been conscious of it, the stranger's contemptuous remarks about "the innocent woods and fields and flowers like a poem in print" could be applied to some of his own early, idyllic pastoral poems like "The Pasture," "Going For Water," and "The Tuft of Flowers."

Interpreted in the context of Frost's later poetry, the play may be related to the increasingly explicit intellectual content of his work. The stranger berates Asa for not "thinking," and in many of the poems in *New Hampshire* and *West-Running Brook* Frost is much more deliberately intellectual than he had been in *North of Boston* and *Mountain Interval*. He had always been an intelligent, well-read man with an ability to philosophize about life; but in many of his poems written after 1917 he seems to place a quiet but deliberate emphasis on his thoughtfulness, on the fact that he is thinking about his rural subjects as well as describing them lyrically.[15]

A Way Out can also be interpeted as an oblique rationale for Frost's acceptance of the appointments which he received at Amherst, Michigan, and other universities starting in 1917. However, the play may also suggest one reason why he had so many difficulties, disappointments, and misunderstandings in some of these academic appointments. He may have rejected the simple, passive pastoralism of Asa's hermitage, but he made the stranger a murderer who invades and then symbolically "kills" a part of Frost's own life and personality. As the stranger tells Asa at the end of the play, "If you won't go to life, why life will come to you." And, as the action of the play reveals, this is a painful rather than an easy process.

Finally, the play suggests strongly that it may have been difficult for Frost to integrate the different aspects of his personality and his career. Publicly, he often gave the impression that it was relatively easy for him to do this, that it only took a bit of Yankee common sense to be a farmer, a great poet, and a good college teacher all at once. In a 1923 interview in the *New York Times* he criticized authors whose lives were different from their works. These writers, he explained, tried to "straddle between two realities, like a man trying to ride two horses at once." "I have no straddle," Frost said:

> Perhaps it is because I am so ordinary . . . I have given thought to this business of straddling, and there's always seemed to me to be

something wrong with it, something tricky . . . It isn't the natural
way, the normal way, the powerful way to ride. It's a trick.

Indeed he saw himself as ordinary: "That's what's the trouble with me. I like
my school [Amherst] and I like my farm and I like people. Just ordinary, you
see."[16] But *A Way Out* and many incidents in Frost's career suggest that at best
he was able to create a tense, difficult synthesis between farming and academic
life, that is between the pastoral and the urbane sides of his personality. Asa
and the stranger may become symbolically "mixed" at the end of the play, with
the audience unable to tell which is dead and which is alive, but they never
become friends.

JAMES K. GUIMOND

Rider College, New Jersey

Notes

1. John Lynen, *The Pastoral Art of Robert Frost* (New Haven: Yale Univ. Press,
1960), pp. 10–11.

2. Whicher, *Mornings at 8:50* (Northampton, Mass.: The Hampshire Bookshop,
1950), p. 35.

3. "To Ernest L. Silver," 8 December 1913, Letter 68, *Selected Letters of Robert
Frost*, ed. Lawrance Thompson (New York: Holt, Rinehart and Winston, 1964), p. 103;
"To Sidney Cox," October 1914, Letter 90, *Selected Letters*, p. 138; the 1916 interview
is quoted in Lawrance Thompson, *Robert Frost: The Years of Triumph* (New York: Holt,
Rinehart and Winston, 1970), p. 67; "To John T. Bartlett," 26 May 1926, Letter 259,
Selected Letters, pp. 329–30; To Louis Untermeyer, 6 June 1930, *The Letters of Robert
Frost to Louis Untermeyer*, ed. Louis Untermeyer (New York: Holt, Rinehart and Winston,
1963), p. 200.

4. *The Seven Arts*, 1 (1917), 347–62. *A Way Out* was also published in *More One-
Act Plays by Modern Authors*, ed. Helen Cohen (New York: Harcourt, Brace, 1927), pp.
359–69; and in a limited edition with a preface by Frost (New York: Harbor Press, 1929).

5. Thompson, *Years of Triumph*, pp. 80–86, 540–42. Frost expressed his uneasiness
about accepting the Amherst appointment in a letter: "This [information] about the college
must be a secret. I haven't decided yet." "To Alfred Harcourt," December 1916, Letter
153, *Selected Letters*, p. 208.

6. Thompson says that the stranger kills Asa and hides the body off-stage. See *Years
of Triumph*, p. 109.

7. When Frost lived in the vicinity, Derry Depot had about five-thousand inhabitants
and a fair amount of industry. See Gorham Munson, *Robert Frost* (New York: George H.
Doran, 1927), p. 37. According to Thompson, Frost's "An Old Man's Winter Night" may
have been based on the character of a hermit named Charles Lambert who lived near Derry
and was well-known locally. See *Years of Triumph*, p. 540. Thus it is possible that Asa
Gorrill—or the play's references to a hermit who has been written up in the newspaper—may
also have been based on Lambert.

8. *FQ* VI. ix. 20. 3–4.

9. Lawrance Thompson, Robert Frost: *The Early Years* (New York: Holt, Rinehart and Winston, 1966), pp. 330–331, 412; Thompson, *The Years of Triumph,* p. 322; Munson, p. 39.

10. Robert Newdick, *Newdick's Season of Frost: An Interrupted Biography of Robert Frost,* ed. William A. Sutton (Albany: SUNY Press, 1976), p. 74. The quotation from Frost is from a letter to Gorham Munson, 16 June 1927, quoted in Thompson, Years of Triumph, pp. 322–23. Thompson is skeptical about whether the Frosts were really so isolated in Derry. See his notes to the letter to Munson in *The Years of Triumph,* p. 635.

11. Thompson, *Years of Triumph,* p. 541.

12. "The Hill Wife," in *Complete Poems of Robert Frost* (New York: Holt, Rinehart and Winston, 1949), p. 161.

13. See Thompson, *Years of Triumph,* p. 109.

14. Thompson, *Years of Triumph,* p. 200.

15. E.g., "New Hampshire," "A Star in a Stone-Boat," "I Will Sing You One-O," "The Aim Was Song," "Good-By and Keep Cold," "The Need of Being Versed in Country Things," "West-Running Brook," and "Tree at my Window"

16. Rose C. Feld, "Robert Frost Relieves His Mind," *New York Times Book Review,* 21 Oct. 1923, pp. 2, 23. Portions of this interview are quoted in Munson, pp. 84–86.

Lyric Impulse:
Birds and Other Voices

I. What the Birds Say

The symbolism in Frost's poems is synecdochic. Particular birds, for instance, represent a larger meaning or law of nature. That is, they characterize that perceived actuality through what they say and what they act out. At the same time they actually behave like birds so as not to violate the law of verisimilitude: a bird *is* a bird. When they talk we have fable, and occasionally a comic effect, but most of Frost's birds are fabulously serious, even tragic, actors. What they say moves us closer to psychological or other scientific views of nature.[1] Frost's birds are those common to North America: the blackbird, bluebird, sparrow, robin, thrush, phoebe, crow, and the existential oven bird.

The traditional nightingale sits in the background in a white thorn tree singing in full-throated ease. She is the same tragic bird Philomela (Greek for love of song) from which all lyric poetry is descended, and her legend is truly terrible. Her sister Procne was married to a king who grew tired of her, tore out her tongue, and then forced Philomela to marry him and bear him a son (Itylus). When Procne wove a web-like tapestry that told her sister everything, Philomela killed her own son and served him up to the king. These horrors angered the gods who nevertheless decided to be merciful and turned the king into a hawk who forever chased but could not catch Procne, now changed to a swallow, and Philomela, now the nightingale. Out of this terrifying tale came the tradition that song is triumphant over horror and suffering. As Matthew Arnold wrote:

> Listen, Eugenia—
> How thick the bursts come crowding through the leaves!
> Again—thou hearest?
> Eternal passion!
> Eternal pain![2]

It seems to me that the entire canon of Frost's poetry, except for the light verse of course, belongs in this tradition of the lyric voice whether the poems are brief sonnets and ballads or extended blank-verse narratives. In any case, Frost's birds seem to have a special relationship to the nightingale myth of song's deep meaning.[3]

Frost's synecdochic sense of the metaphorical symbol allows a good variety of expression. Going the old gods one better, he has restored Philomela's ability to talk, and in rendering the actual sounds birds make has struck dissonant chords. His birds talk, twitter, murmer, whimper, screech, chop, shout, cluck, hush, argue, bring messages from other birds, sing "out of sleep and dream," show the way through the forest to an abandoned wood-pile, run, swoop, almost cough their tailfeathers off, and shake snow dust onto the poet's head. They never do or say the same thing twice. They speak love lyrics and engage in philosophical discussions. A bird is the occasion for a lyric about the evolutionary survival of the lyric voice, and other poems on birds examine the sources of the lyric and its strength in our time, the special knowledge the poet gets from listening to birds, a certain attitude of ruthlessness in the behavior of poets, the fragmentary nature of beauty, the tenacity of song quality and its seasonal rebirth, a sense of blind instinct in the poet, and a preference for the tone of truth in the poetic voice. Birds even tell of times when one may tire of hearing birdsong. Birds are featured as guides to revelation or as prophets of either geological or psychological "weather." In an early poem the speaker, Pan, tosses away his pipes to listen to the voices of blue jays and hawks.

The two people who are most obviously associated with birds in Frost's poems are his friend Edward Thomas, an English poet who died in the First World War, and Frost's wife Elinor. Of Edward Thomas Frost wrote, just after his friend's death in April 1917:

> Edward Thomas was the only brother I ever had. I fail to see how we can have been so much to each other, he an Englishman and I an American and our first meeting put off till we were both in middle life. I hadn't a plan for the future that didn't include him.[4]

Thomas's death occasioned both the dove wings image that opens "To E. T." as well as the elegiac "Looking for a Sunset Bird in Winter" which is placed very near the E. T. poem in the 1923 volume.

The significance of Frost's wife to the poems is best told in a letter (which he later considered suppressing) that he wrote to Louis Untermeyer in 1937 shortly before her death:

> She has been the unspoken half of everything I ever wrote, and both halves of many a thing from My November Guest down to the last stanza of Two Tramps in Mud Time—as you may have divined.[5]

It was just after the death of Elinor White Frost in 1938 (and the death of their son Carol in 1940) that two elegies associated with her appeared in *A Witness Tree,* 1942. These are "Come In," which is concerned with the voice of a thrush who does not invite the poet into its woods, and "Never Again Would Birds' Song Be the Same," which in its description of the "voice of Eve" metaphorically indicates that Frost's wife had been responsible for the tone of his lyrics, as his letter to Untermeyer had earlier acknowledged.[6]

After *A Witness Tree* (1942) there are no more direct references to birds. Birds do not speak again, nor are they used to reveal anything by their actions. (Here and there they are suggested in images such as the "pecker-fretted" apple trees of "directive" and the "migratory" leaves of November.") The Eden which had not come to grief in which the "daylong voice of Eve" had added to the birds' voices an "oversound . . . / Her tone of meaning but without the words," had been the farm at Derry, New Hampshire. It had been that existentially pastoral time when Frost was composing the nucleus of his poetry and gathering poems together. *A Boy's Will* (1913) tells us most about that time and that Eden filled with birds and flowers. In "My November Guest" Sorrow strikes the tragic tone, saying she's "glad the birds have gone away." Other birds of the first volume are woodpeckers in the orchard, and a whippoorwill who "comes to shout" in "Ghost House." And in "A Late Walk" there is the "whir of sober birds," while a motion image of "the last swallow's sweep" appears in "Waiting." The hawks' whimper and the blue jay's screech were "music enough" in "Pan With Us."

Further in the same volume "A Prayer in Spring" sings the transitory nature of life and love, wedding flower and bird in this unforgettable metaphor of a hummingbird:

> That suddenly above the bees is heard,
> The meteor that thrusts in with needle bill
> And off a blossom in mid-air stands still.[7]

And "In a Vale" declares that by listening to nature the poet knows well "Why the flower has odor, the bird has song." Flowers and birds also mingle in the metaphor and simile of Frost's most passionate love lyric, "A Line-Storm Song." In this poem, the poet presents his love the hardy common goldenrod rather than the fragile rose. The birds are in the woods even today, he tells her, although they do not sing as often because of the world's despair.

Moving chronologically through the volumes of poems, we notice that in *Mountain Interval* (1916) birds indicate Frost's conscious awareness of himself as a poet, of the hazards his role as poet may include, and of the whole estate of poetry. "The Exposed Nest" tells of society's carelessness toward poets and their children, "Range-Finding" observes a groundbird still revisiting her young although the meadow has been used as a battlefield, and "The Oven Bird" explains the wisom "in singing not to sing." Oven bird is a name for various birds in England and the Americas who build their nests in the shape of an oven, with the roof and basement continuous. This loud bird may not have much of a lilt and trill to his voice, but he has resonance. He "makes the solid tree trunks sound again." Most of the images he presents indicate that summer is ending when "comes that other fall we name the fall." As William R. Osborne writes in an explication of the poem, "The bird can raise his not so puny voice to frame questions about the nature of things, even to quarrel with a world that is not nearer to the heart's desire."[8] A whole chorus of Frost critics and scholars is pleased to recognize the tragic tone of Frost's lover's quarrel with the world in the voice of the oven bird. On that point at least we are generally in accord.

In *New Hampshire* (1923) "The Valley's Singing Day" and "Our Singing Strength" are celebrations of the lyric voice. The first pays tribute directly to the poet's wife for being "the songbird that awakened all the rest," so that the birds symbolize the poems as inspired by her. The poems are "the pent-up music of overnight." The second poem names a number of ordinary birds migrating north in spring who are brought down by a snowstorm into the road where the poet is walking. They gather in a striking metaphor of brook or channel water: "The road became a channel of running flocks / Of glossy birds like ripples over rocks." But the most difficult poem about birds for the early critics to interpret was "The Need of Being Versed in Country Things." Frost objected to the view that his poetry was primarily designed to point up a need for social reforms. As he wrote to Louis Untermeyer in 1938, "The best of your criticism of me all these years is that you have never treated me as welfare-minded or of social significance. *North of Boston* is merely a book of people, not of poor people . . . all the rich who ever came to my door were the condescending welfare-minded . . ."[9] Therefore the phoebes who are versed in country things are not planning agrarian reform. But it is not a sad time for them because they are nesting in the barn of the abandoned farm. Men may weep to see a home abandoned where there had been so much life, but the birds' springtime duty is nesting and they rejoice in it. Their murmuring may sound like weeping to man unless he is versed in the understanding that the task at hand takes all one's energy in country life. This poem is the last in the volume *New Hampshire*. Frost's penultimate poem voiced and acted out by birds on the theme of a stoical acceptance of death was to follow in the next book, *West-Running Brook* (1928).

Lawrance Thompson interprets "Acceptance" as Frost's attempt to reconcile the feelings of rage, resentment, and desire for revenge with those of Christian submission and obedience taught him by his mother. Whether or not that analysis is correct, the poem seems to be the poet's attempt to see death within the framework of the laws of nature, in something of the attitude of Emerson's "Brahma," perhaps. Elsewhere I have described this poem as a metrical accomplishment, with the movements of the two birds and the movement of the approaching night combining with the prosody in a very satisfying way.[10] And this accomplishment occurs along with that modification of the lyric voice that was the poet's intention when he commented: "I am only interesting to myself for having ventured to make poetry out of tones that if you can judge from the practice of other poets are not usually regarded as poetical ... They are always there—living in the cave of the mouth."[11] The male bird of the pair in "Acceptance" is given that voice tone that after the female bird has gone to sleep says:

> "Now let the night be dark for all of me.
> Let the night be too dark for me to see
> Into the future. Let what will be, be."

This somber idiomatic bird is advising acceptance of the laws of nature, the same thing the phoebes say in an entirely different situation and season of the year.

An ironic bird appears in *A Further Range* (1936) in the poem "On a Bird Singing in Its Sleep." The poet notes that evolution has somehow spared the lyric voice, although this seeming miracle may be due partly to the wisdom of songbirds. The bird who sings half asleep in the moonlight must be relatively safe because it sings an ordinary "inborn" tune (nothing new), because it sings from a low unimposing bush, and because it sings briefly—not long enough to awaken "hostile ears." The bird's tune could not possibly have continued to evolve through the era of man, the poem continues, if such singing had made it more vulnerable to "prey." Perhaps within the laws of nature, after all, poetry is not going to become extinct, even through man's doing. The metaphor this bird provides allows the poet to analyze the attitude that he takes toward his audience—a certain animal cunning taught him by the birds and other wild creatures.

But of Frost's gallery of tough-witted birds there is none so worldly-wise as the bluebird of "Two Tramps in Mud Time." Frost's wife inspired the poem. Bluebirds, it might be remembered, were at the time of the poem's publication beginning to be an endangered species. And this bird indicates, I think, the way Frost thought about birds and other natural organisms in relation to his poems. They were harbingers of poetic insight and at the same time messengers of natural law. In this way they could be helpful harbingers. The bluebird sings quietly, "His song so pitched as not to excite / A single flower as yet to bloom." The poem has, again, no social importance. The two tramps and their "logic" with which the poet agrees are merely the occasion for the poem's explanation that all activities of a poet's life have direct bearing upon his writing, as the poem's early subtitle, "A Full-Time Interest," indicated. But the poem does have psychological importance as a declaration of identity. Frost sees himself fully dedicated to the role of poet in both vocation and avocation and recognizes the necessity for bringing both into harmonious vision. His friend the bluebird suggests that hazards may exist also *within* the poet: he should beware that "lurking frost" may reappear and "show on the water its crystal teeth." Although the birds of the poems are not without a sense of humor, what they say—the words to go with the "tone of meaning" that modified birdsong in Frost's Eden—is deeply serious, and not without the sound of mourning either. That is, their song, as long as it lasted, had depth and range.[12]

Frost Poems Referring to Birds

A Boy's Will, 1913
Ghost House 5, 6*
My November Guest 6, 7
A Late Walk 8, 9
A Prayer in Spring 12
Waiting 14, 15
In A Vale 15, 16
Pan With Us 23, 24
Now Close the Windows 25
A Line-Storm Song 26, 27
October 27, 28

North of Boston, 1914
The Wood-Pile 101, 102

Mountain Interval, 1916
The Exposed Nest 109, 110
The Oven Bird 119, 120
Range-Finding 126
The Last Word of a Bluebird
135, 136

New Hampshire, 1923
Fragmentary Blue 220
Dust of Snow 221

To E. T. 222
Looking for a Sunset Bird in Winter
232, 233
The Valley's Singing Day 235, 236
Our Singing Strength 239, 240
The Need of Being Versed In Country
Things 241, 242

West-Running Brook, 1928
Acceptance 249
A Minor Bird 250, 251
A Winter Eden 254

A Further Range, 1936
Two Tramps in Mud-Time 275–277
A Blue Ribbon at Amesbury 279–281
On a Bird Singing in Its Sleep 302

A Witness Tree, 1942
Come In 334
Never Again Would Birds' Song
Be the Same, 338

Dates of Related Biographical Events

May, 1885: death of William Prescott
Frost, Sr., the poet's father

July, 1900: death of first child, Elliot

November, 1900: death of Işabelle
Moodie Frost, the poet's mother

June, 1907: death of sixth child,
Elinor Betina

April, 1917: death of Edward Thomas,
the poet's closest friend

September, 1929: death of poet's sister
Jeannie, after long hospitalization for
mental illness

May, 1934: death of daughter Marjorie
from childbed fever

March 21, 1938: death of Elinor White
Frost, the poet's wife

October, 1940: death of the poet's son
Carol by suicide

January 29, 1963: death of Frost

*All page references are to Lathem edition of *The Poetry*

II. Imagination's Fire

And a voice that has sounded in my room
Across the sill from the outer gloom.[1]

According to Lawrance Thompson, Yeats was Frost's favorite among contemporary living poets during the years he taught at the Pinkerton Academy.[2] Frost directed his students in at least two Yeats plays. When the poet went to London with his family, Pound arranged a meeting for him with Yeats who then invited Frost to his Monday evening gatherings. Frost attended twice, but the two poets did not become close friends. Probably Frost had been interested to meet with Yeats for several reasons in addition to admiration for his writing. Yeats was said to have seen spirits and experienced auditory hallucinations. Frost himself had "heard voices" as had his sister when they were very young children, and his own first poem was composed as if given to him by a "voice." As Thompson has noted of the writing of "La Noche Triste," it seemed "to him that he could hear the lines spoken, almost by the same voice which had puzzled him years ago in San Francisco."[3] The possibility of sharing thoughts in this rare area of experience was probably also important to Frost at this time because he was firmly formulating, stating, and restating his poetic theories including the sound of sense. His heightened sense of the sound of the human voice was at least one motivation for his sound of sense theory which begins to illustrate itself especially well with the use of many voices in the second volume *North of Boston.* (1914).

Frost letters are the best source for showing his struggle, indeed his excitement and enthusiasm, in the formulation of his own poetic theory around the time of his visit to England and his return home.[4] In his letters Frost refers a number of times to "Yates," spelling the name phonetically just as he had learned to write phonetically and as he taught his children as well.[5] In a letter to Sidney Cox from Beaconsfield, England, he praised some of Yeats's lines and poems, stating: "One is sure of them. They make the sense of beauty ache." Yet he qualified:

> He is not always good .... The thing you mention is against him. I shouldn't care at all if it hadn't touched and tainted his poetry. Let him be as affected as he pleases if he will only write well. But you can't be affected and write entirely well.[6]

Much later in a 1934 letter to his daughter Lesley, Frost observed that the new Imagist poets did not have much to say about "ear images," as he termed the auditory imagination, one of his own strong points.[7] Sister Jeremy Finnegan documents at length the operation of Frost's auditory memory, that is, his remembrance of heard literary and other material, and his rearrangement and use of it for his own artistic literary purposes, not only in the poems themselves but also in his talks and letters.[8]

Frost had something else in common with Yeats, which has direct bearing upon the matter of "hearing voices," and that is that they had both been strongly influenced by Swedenborg. Yeats writes about the importance of Swedenborg to his own poetry in his book of reminiscences, *If I Were Four and Twenty*.[9] It is the religious nature of the Swedenborgian influence that Thompson emphasizes in his biographical interpretation of Frost's San Francisco boyhood, and I think it is true that Swedenborg fascinated the young poet particularly for the hagiological account of his life.[10] Swedenborg, an eminent scientist, turned primarily to theological writings following a series of visual and auditory hallucinations he believed to be religiously mystical in nature. In the development of his elaborate doctrine, everything in the visible world became symbolic of a spiritual reality—a *correspondence*—a concept which must have had impetus for Yeats's and Frost's (and many other poets') sense of symbol and which in Frost's poetry became modified into metaphorical symbol. Frost was careful to qualify his own attitude toward Swedenborg when he stated in 1923:

> I was brought up a Swedenborgian. I am not a Swedenborgian
> now. But there's a good deal left in me. I am a mystic. I believe in
> symbols. I believe in change and in changing symbols.[11]

As far as I have read, this is the only time Frost ever spoke of himself as a mystic, and the reader may expect the possibility of ambiguity or irony in the self-designation: some of Frost's "kind of fooling." He may also have been remembering his love of the early Greek literatures or the lost origins of Greek lyric poetry in the "mystical experience which the 'poet' or speaker" underwent in the early Greek mystery ceremonies.[12] Kathleen Morrison, Frost's devoted secretary in the later years, has said of Frost's mother, Isabelle Moodie Frost: "She was a mystic, and also, like her son, a very intellectual person."[13] Frost's mother was converted to the Swedenborgian Church of the New Jerusalem from her Scottish Presbyterian girlhood church, and she died in the Swedenborgian faith. Frost was both baptized and married in the Swedenborgian Church, as the Robert Newdick biographical materials attest.[14] And yet his marriage may have been performed by a Swedenborgian minister more to pay respect to his mother's beliefs than to his own at the time.[15] It is difficult to ascertain just when Frost became "not a Swedenborgian" or what aspects of Swedenborgianism remained in him, at least up until the time of his 1923 statement—except for the hint he gives about mysticism and change and "changing symbols."

There are distinctions as well as similarities between Yeats's voices and Frost's voices. In Richard Ellman's standard critical biography of Yeats, the voices of the poet are associated with the theatrical masks through which they speak— and are said to be representative of aspects of Yeats's personality, disparate aspects which, after long and bitter struggle, Yeats was able to integrate and affirm into a coherent personality.[16] On the other hand, in Frost's poems there is insistence on an already established unchanging self: "They will not find me changed from him they knew." And yet the poet Frost is constantly restating, according to Howell Chickering, Jr., that already established self as if in a process of ego-strengthening.[17] The analysis of Yeats cited uses the Jungian framework, and the analysis of Frost uses the ego-psychoanalytical theory based on Freud's work. But these two analyses point up the difficulties in psychoanalytic biography, for where is the basic difference really, in the poet under discussion and his work, or in the psychoanalytic framework chosen to elucidate the subjects? Nevertheless, one becomes more acquainted with the man and his poetry regardless of the specific method: the critic wants to find the most appropriate method for the particular poet and poetry under discussion.

Apparently the two poets did not communicate easily with each other in every respect. Frost wanted to know at his first meeting with Yeats which poems Yeats had written out easily as if given (by a voice?), and when Frost suggested "The Song of the Wandering Angus" as one such poem, he was wrong. Yeats said it had been written "in agony during his terrible years."[18] As to the difficulty Frost had with Yeats following their meeting, it is helpful to look again at Ellman's fortuitous examination of Yeats's own concept of *masks* in his plays and theatrical productions. Here is the affected pose, the playacting, the wearing of a large cape (Frost himself had worn his coat as a cape when teaching at Pinkerton and afterwards, according to both Thompson and Newdick), and other theatrical trappings which may be associated with Yeats's establishment of the professional theatre in Ireland.

Distinguishing himself thereafter from any hint of affectation, Frost made a virtue of the ordinary, casual manner, but any student of Frost will see the mask of self-evasive protection in this although it is the opposite of the flamboyant pose. Drumlin woodchucks, moreover and more importantly, oven birds, are in less peril than unicorns and nightingales. Frost's manner was by now on the upswing of acceptance by world audiences and explains one reason for his unusual success in his perilous vocation. The psychodynamics of Irish and American cultures may also be involved here. Yeats's interesting masks must have appealed sufficiently to the Irish public which had a good sense of the theatrical and of historical anachronism. Frost's mask of ordinary poet-teacher-farmer, in turn, certainly appealed to American readers. One sees more clearly how Frost's own path was to bend in the undergrowth after his meeting with Yeats and his subsequent determination to delete anything artificial or archaic from his poetry or his manner of life, for the poet Frost was on the threshold of fame.[19]

In at least five poems Frost alludes to the experience of "hearing voices": "The Telephone," "Voice Ways," "The Generations of Men," "The Lovely Shall Be Choosers," and "In a Vale," which contains a direct allusion to voices and is, perhaps, the most revealing. Of the mysterious voices of one poem, later to be recognized as referring to the life of Frost's own mother, F. Cudworth Flint writes:

But he once said to me, by way of comment on the uncharacter-
istically mysterious poem, "The Lovely Shall Be Choosers,"—"I
have sometimes had the experience of hearing the voices of unseen
beings mocking at me."[20]

And, indeed, the poem Flint cites *was* mysterious until the Thompson and Newdick biographical materials which suggest that the poem is about Frost's
mother, possibly about voices that she herself had heard, became available.
Flint's report glosses the terrible voices of the poem. Certainly Frost did not
publicly make much of the matter of "hearing voices." Yeats, of course, wrote
bout his hallucinatory experiences and their relation to his poetry in *A Vision*.
His voices were not always friendly. As for Frost, although there are many
tones in his work, a consensus is beginning to form that Lionel Trilling's word
terrible best describes the best in the poems. I would add that just as the myth
of the nightingale combines lyricism and terror, so when the "sense of beauty
aches" in Fost's poetry, there is indeed an undercurrent of terror. As J. Dennis
Huston notes:

Frost does not altogether dismiss the possibility that some alien
daemonic power, some "heartless and enormous Outer Black" may
be inexorably working its malevolent purpose out in man's universe
—intimations of violent and imminent destruction run through
poems like "Design," "The Bonfire," and "A Loose Mountain"—
but he is much more interested in the part that man himself ultimately plays in structuring experience.[21]

In some of the poems references to witches suggest that alien power. Frost's
witch of Coös tells a fine ghost story: The pauper witch of Grafton muses about
her younger years when her witchery in sexual matters was appreciated by her
husband although her knowledge apparently more than isolated her from town
society.[22] In "New Hampshire" Frost mentions a modern witch and the other
reference to witches appears in *A Masque of Reason*. Job's wife, in defense of
her sisters, the witches, berates the character God:

I want to ask You if it stands to reason
That women prophets should be burned as witches,
Whereas men prophets are received with honor.[23]

But God is only a little surprised by her query and asks her, "You're not a
witch?" So there are degrees of the tone of terror in Frost's characterization of
witches. Closely related to Frost's witches is the hag in "Provide, Provide" who,
like the Grafton witch, has somehow not played her cards right and come to
penury. But the most frightening witch figure of all, though not called a witch,
appears in "The Bonfire" and refers to the story of Joan of Arc, burned at the
stake as a witch or heretic because she would not declare that the voices she
heard were of the Devil and repent. According to Thompson, Joan of Arc was

one of the stories of heroic figures, along with the story of Swedenborg of course, that Frost's mother told to her children when they lived in San Francisco. The story must have stayed with Frost vividly, and, as it is a well-known myth, could be successfully woven in with the main business of "The Bonfire" to increase the sense of terror. In the poem the poet-speaker has gone uphill with his children to light a bonfire. The children wonder why their father would be afraid of the bonfire, and he begins to explain that it might get out of control:

> "Why wouldn't it scare me to have a fire
> Begin in smudge with ropy smoke, and know
> That still, if I repent, I may recall it."[24]

"Ropy" and "repent" recall Joan, as well as phrases like "A little spurt / of burning fatness" and "sweeping round it with a flaming sword." But the poet balances the description of all the terror the bonfire can evoke with: "Done so much and I know not how much more / I mean it shall not do if I can bind it." The speaker thus at once identifies himself with the ropes of the executioner and assures the children that he does not intend to let the fire become wild and cause harm. The imagination's fire must be bound. As Huston notes, Frost's interest is ultimately with man's structuring of his life. In "The Bonfire" we see how Frost uses the terrifying spectre of witch burning to balance the sense of the necessity of the self-structuring of life, and, of course, of the formal elements in art as well.

One of the most important books read to Frost in childhood was, as noted earlier, George MacDonald's *At the Back of the North Wind*.[25] From Chapter Six, "Out in the Storm," come references found in at least five Frost poems. North Wind says, "My dear boy, I never talk: I always mean what I say." ("Ends" from *In the Clearing*, 1962: "But some mean what they say.") The chapter concludes with " . . . but it seemed to Diamond that North Wind and he were motionless, all but the hair. It was not so. They were sweeping with the speed of the wind itself towards the sea." These lines surely bring to mind both "The Master Speed" (*A Further Range*, 1936) and "The Secret Sits" (*A Witness Tree*, 1942). Then there is, in reference to numerous poems, but to "West-Running Brook" in particular, this extraordinary compression of thematic material in Frost's poems:

> Did you ever watch a great wave shoot into a winding passage amongst rocks? If you ever did, you would see that the water rushed every way at once, some of it even turning back and opposing the rest; greater confusion you might see nowhere except in a crowd of frightened people.

The discussion in this chapter from *At the Back of the North Wind* of the double nature of North Wind is basic, it seems to me, to an understanding of Frost's poems, to his view of human nature and the nature of the universe.

The chapter begins with Diamond's (the boy's) question as he rides at the wind's back: "Then you do mean to sink the ship with the other hand?" But more to the point of Frost's heightened sense of sound, are passages and incidents throughout the book, such as this one from the same chapter:

> Her voice was like the bass of a deep organ, without the groan in it; like the most delicate of violin tones without the wail in it; like the most glorious of trumpet ejaculations without the defiance in it; like the sound of falling water without the clatter and clash in it: it was like all of them and neither of them—all of them without their faults, each of them without its peculiarity: after all, it was more like his mother's voice than anything else in the world.
>
> "Diamond, dear," she said, "be a man. What is fearful to you is not the least fearful to me."

The voices of Frost's poems might be said to be the voice of his mother, the voice of North Wind, mysterious mocking voices, bird voices, the sounds of trees, the brook voices—any one or even all of these are true yet not inclusive of all the poet's soundings. Indeed, the aesthetic gift, like the innocent, amoral, Edenic North Wind character in the children's book, is at once beautiful and terrible, having both creative and destructive potential. And sometimes the voice or voices in the poems speak accompanied (as if by music) by other sounds—for instance, in "Mowing" by the whispering of the scythe: "The fact is the sweetest dream that labor knows. / My long scythe whispered and left the hay to make."[26] Probably the poet did consciously heighten his ability to "hear voices" by practice, by listening. The listening part of the process was something Frost was apparently familiar with as early as "In A Vale," first published in A Boy's Will, which describes the "vale" of childhood. Just as the voice of North Wind came into Diamond's room at night, so in "In A Vale" a voice from the "outer gloom" sounded in the speaker's room and he cultivated the ability to hear it: "No, not vainly there did I dwell, / Nor vainly listen all the night long."[27]

The love story in "The Generations of Men" is the fullest description of the creative make-believe of the voices in Frost's poetry. The young man who is smitten by love at first sight courts the girl by telling her about the voices. She says, "The voices give you what you wish to hear," but he replies, "Strangely, it's anything they wish to give." His effort to impress the girl is poignant and it is clear that they have fallen in love. He tries to hear the voices against "the noise that the brook raises," and this knack of his, he says, is "Something I must have learned riding in trains / When I was young. I used to use the roar / To set the voices speaking out of it."[28] Frost alludes to the hearing of voices a bit too often for us to think he made up the claim that he heard them merely to identify himself with Joan of Arc or Swedenborg. Even with the poems' internal evidence, we can probably be assured that this aspect of the creative process of poem-making occurred to the poem-maker as a gift outright.

KATHRYN GIBBS HARRIS

Michigan State University

I. Notes

1. Kathryn Gibbs Harris, "Robert Frost's Early Education in Science," *South Carolina Review*, 7, No. 1 (1974), 13–33.

2. Charles Mills Gayley, *The Classic Myths in English Literature and Art,* 2nd ed. (New York: Blaisdell, 1963), pp. 249–250.

3. Arthur M. Young, "Of the Nightingale's Song," *The Classical Journal,* 46, No. 4 (1951), 181–82.

4. *Selected Letters of Robert Frost,* Lawrance Thompson (New York: Holt, Rinehart and Winston, 1964), p. 217.

5. *Selected Letters,* p. 450.

6. See chart on p. 148 for poem reference.

7. *The Poetry of Robert Frost,* ed. Edward Connery Lathem (New York: Holt, Rinehart and Winston, 1965), p. 12. All references to the poems are to this edition.

8. William R. Osborne, "Frost's 'The Oven Bird,'" *Explicator,* 26, No. 6 (Feb. 1968), Item 47.

9. *Selected Letters,* p. 467.

10. Kathryn Gibbs Harris, "Robert Frost and Science: The Shaping Metaphor of Motion in the Poems," Diss. Michigan State 1976, pp. 325–326.

11. *Selected Letters,* p. 191.

12. After reading this essay, Lesley Frost added, "My father often read us Maeterlinck's *The Blue Bird.* Often."

II. Notes

1. *The Poetry,* p. 16.

2. Lawrance Thompson, *Robert Frost: The Early Years* (New York: Holt, Rinehart and Winston, 1966), pp. 412–414.

3. Thompson, *Early Years,* p. 93.

4. Kathryn Gibbs Harris, "Frost's Early Education," pp. 28–30.

5. *Selected Letters,* pp. 92–95.

6. *Selected Letters,* pp. 93, 94.

7. *Family Letters of Robert and Elinor Frost,* ed. Arnold Grade (Albany: SUNY Press, 1972), p. 162.

8. See Sr. Jeremy Finnegan's essay in this volume.

9. William Butler Yeats, *If I Were Four and Twenty* (Dublin: Cuala Press, 1940).

10. Thompson, *Early Years,* Chapters 5–7.

11. Rose C. Feld, "Robert Frost Relieves His Mind," *New York Times Book Review*, 21 October 1923, p. 2.

12. Alex Preminger, et al., *Princeton Encyclopedia of Poetry and Poetics* (Princeton: Princeton Univ. Press, 1965), p. 462.

13. Personal interview with Kathleen Johnston Morrison, August 1975, at the Homer Noble Farm, Ripton, Vermont.

14. *Newdick's Season of Frost: An Interrupted Biography of Robert Frost*, William A. Sutton (Albany: SUNY Press, 1976), pp. 53, 390.

15. Newdick, p. 53.

16. Richard Ellman, *Yeats: The Man and the Masks* (New York: Macmillan, 1948), pp. 171-76, 186, 187, 226, 227.

17. Howell Chickering, Jr., "Robert Frost: Romantic Humorist," *Literature and Psychology*, 16, No. 3/4 (1966), 139-50.

18. Quoted in Thompson, *Early Years*, p. 414.

19. The word *mask* does not appear in Frost's poems. The two theatrical masques are actually antimasques (see Preminger, p. 475), hence the common language used in them and the oddly disparate props and subject matter which troubled the reviewers (see Linda Wagner's discussion of their bafflement in the introduction to *Robert Frost, The Critical Reception* [Burt Franklin, 1977], p. xviii.) The question may be whether as antimasques they were *sufficient* travesties on the human condition.

20. F. Cudworth Flint, "A Few Touches of Frost," *The Southern Review*, 2, No. 4 (Autumn 1966), 830-38.

21. J. Dennis Huston, " 'The Wonder of Unexpected Supply': Robert Frost and a Poetry Beyond Confusion," *Centennial Review*, 13, No. 3 (1960), 317-29.

22. See Mordecai Marcus, "The Whole Pattern of Robert Frost's 'Two Witches': Contrasting Psychosexual Modes," *Literature and Psychology*, 24, No. 2 (1976), 69-78.

23. *The Poetry*, p. 476.

24. *The Poetry*, p. 130.

25. Harris, "Frost's Early Education." This article applies the background from George Macdonald's children's novel primarily to "The Trial by Existence."

26. *The Poetry*, p. 17.

27. *The Poetry*, p. 16.

28. *The Poetry*, pp. 77, 78.

Comic Exegete

It is indisputable that the Bible has replaced the Greek and Roman classics as the principal mythological source in our literature. Robert Frost shares with such contemporaries as Yeats, Robinson, Eliot, and Stevens the practice of making frequent allusions to the Bible, but with the important difference that he often treats these references in a comic manner. Such treatment is relatively rare since the Bible maintains a religious as well as literary significance to our culture. An interesting result of Frost's juxtaposition of humorous poetry and Biblical reference, beyond an incongruity valuable for aesthetic effect, is the reinterpretation of certain difficult scriptural passages. These exegetical exercises are numerous enough to be considered one of Frost's characteristic and significant poetic devices.

It should not be inferred, however, that Frost's Biblical references are always humorous. For instance, "Before God's last *Put out the Light* was spoken," the resounding last line of "Once By the Pacific," might be, as one critic has claimed, a quotation from *Othello,* but it clearly is also a reversal of the first act of creation recorded in Genesis.[1] "A Servant to Servants" gets its title from Noah's curse to Ham: "Cursed be Canaan; a servant to servants shall he be unto his brethren" (Gen. 9:25). The reference is particularly apt, for the speaker of the monologue is literally a servant to the servants her husband hires, and she is also fearful that she is a victim of the family curse of insanity. These are only two of many examples of the direct use of the Bible in Frost's darker poetry. Such use is effective, but it is not so striking as his lighter treatment.

The most pervasive appearance of the Bible in Frost's poetry is that most archetypal of patterns, the loss of paradise. George Nitchie, having devoted an entire chapter to this subject in his study of Frost, says that his exploitation of the Eden myth is a major theme both qualitatively and quantitatively.[2] He says that the ambiguous quality of the poetry can be seen through the use of the myth. It is used both seriously and comically. "So Eden sank to grief" from "Nothing Gold Can Stay" is positively Miltonic in its earnestness. On the other hand, "Never Again Will Birds' Song Be the Same" is sufficiently ambiguous to incite an argument in a recent *Atlantic Monthly* as to whether or not the protrait of Eve there is ironic or sentimental.³ Whatever the intention of the poem "Away," the coloquial word choice is clearly comic in the lines

> Don't think I leave
> For the outer dark
> Like Adam and Eve
> Put out of the Park.⁴

And the analogy in "The Ax-Helve" is similarly humorous:

> . . . the ax there on its horse's hoof,
> Erect, but not without its waves, as when
> The snake stood up for Evil in the Garden.
> (p. 188)

And in "Quandary" one finds the lines "We learned from the forbidden fruit / For brains there is no substitute" (p. 467).

As Nitchie maintains, the Eden myth has been used so often in literature and is so deeply inherent in the collective unconscious that it is no longer necessary to read Genesis to use it in poetry. That Frost makes the common mistake of assuming the forbidden fruit was an apple, as he does in "Unharvested," confirms this idea. There is no question, however, that Frost knew the Bible very well indeed, as is demonstrated by his use of non-Edenic materials. Frequently the attitude he takes is one of a somewhat ingenuously superior knowledge. He either misquotes or attempts to explain something but gets it deliberately wrong. These poems that make rather arcane Biblical references can be divided into two categories: those that make only casual reference for the purpose of a meta-phorical "grace note," and those in which the Biblical metaphor is central to the meaning of the poem. In both instances the Bible is used comically.

The most outrageous Biblical pun is found in "How Hard it is to Keep from Being King When It's in You and in the Situation." The speaker is objecting to free verse and is discoursing on the importance of writing poetry that is metri-cally sound. Then comes the line "Tell them Iamb, Jehovah said, and meant it" (p. 460), a reference from Exodus to the conversation between God and Moses during the episode of the Burning Bush (Ex. 3:14). The same subject is used in "Sitting By A Bush in Broad Sunlight," again with a pun: "God once declared He was true / And then took the veil and withdrew" (p. 266), as though God were on his way to a nunnery. Frost deliberately misquotes the line from the Sermon on the Mount, "Do men gather grapes of thorns or figs of thistles?" (Matt. 7:16) in "Wild Grapes":

> What tree may not the fig be gathered from?
> The grape may not be gathered from the birch?
> It's all you know the grape, or know the birch.
> (p. 196)

He has the quotation substantively right but the source wrong in these lines: "To quote the oracle of Delphi / Love thou thy neighbor as thyself, aye," but in the next line he gets it wrong again: "And hate him as thyself thou hatest" ("Quandary," p. 467). Presumably the speaker is dabbling in Biblical scholarship in these lines from "Kitty Hawk":

> Someone says the Lord
> Says our reaching toward
> Is its own reward.
> One would like to know
> Where God says it, though.
> (p. 438)

In other words, people erroneously attribute to the Bible Plato's dictum "Virtue is its own reward." In the same poem is Frost's humorous account of the idea of incarnation as well as a gloss on the earlier and more serious "Trial By Existence." In "Kitty Hawk" he says:

> . . . God's own descent
> Into flesh was meant
> As a demonstration
> That the supreme merit
> Lay in risking spirit
> In substantiation.[5]
> (p. 435)

These snippets from poems indicate the range and the kind of humor of Frost's Biblical allusions.

The poems that use the Bible in a more significant way are rarely simply comic. One exception is "The Objection to Being Stepped On" in which Frost takes literally and for purely comic effect the famous metaphor from Isaiah in which peace is prophesied: "They shall beat their swords into plowshares, and their spears into pruninghooks" (Isa. 2:4). In the poem the speaker inadvertently steps on the blade of a hoe, causing the handle to hit him on the head. He comments:

> You may call me a fool,
> But *was* there a rule
> The weapon should be
> Turned into a tool?
> And what do I see?
> The first tool I step on
> Turned into a weapon.
> (p. 450)

Other poems are more complex. The best known of Frost's exegesis, by virtue of its appearing in one of his most highly celebrated and thoroughly studied poems, is in "Directive," which is informed by three scriptural passages. "If you're lost enough to find yourself," the speaker says, and the reader presumably recalls Jesus' oft-recorded dictum, "He that findeth his life shall lose it; and he that loseth his life for my sake shall find it. (Matt. 10:39), The concluding lines, "Here are your waters and your watering place, / Drink and be whole again beyond confusion" (p. 379), are reminiscent of the episode recorded in the Book of John of Jesus's conversation with the woman at the well: "Whosoever drinketh of this water shall thirst again: But whosoever drinketh of the water that I shall give him shall never thirst" (John 4:13-14). Both of these references suggest a dichotomy between flesh and spirit, and as such are appropriate to the poem and are helpful as glosses. The other reference is both more puzzling and more comic. Mark 4:11-12 is an explanation for speaking in parables. Frost interprets it this way:

> A broken drinking goblet like the Grail
> Under a spell so the wrong ones can't find it,
> So can't get saved, as Saint Mark says they musn't.
> (p. 379)

Within the poem's context the lines are gratuitous. When Frost speaks them he does so in the guise of the gullible simpleton who cheerfully agrees with the most contradictory of arguments. Robert Francis has recorded a conversation with Frost in which they discussed those lines. Frost said, "I know why I brought that into the poem. I wanted to say that it was as good a passage as any other people wish were not in the Bible."[6] In a late speech Frost again bent his exegetical expertise on the passage in question: "St. Mark says that these things of Christ are said in parables so the wrong ones won't understand them and then get saved. It seems that people weren't meant to be saved if they didn't understand figures of speech."[7] This explanation is no clearer than his other two glosses, but the force of it seems to be directed to his own emphasis on poetry as metaphor. In "The Constant Symbol" he couches his definition in Biblical terms: "There are many other things I have found myself saying about poetry, but the chiefest of these is that it is metaphor, saying one thing and meaning another, . . . the pleasure of ulteriority."[8] Apparently Frost derived much pleasure from the relation to the Bibilcal source in this poem.

In a poem not so well known Frost also uses an obscure passage in a way central to the meaning of the poem. "The Gold Hesperidee" tells the story of one Square Matthew Hale, who worked diligently on developing a hybrid apple. After five years the tree bore three apples, which he took special care of all summer. One Sunday morning in autumn he went to pick them, only to discover them gone. Square Matthew was in such a rage that he

> . . . took off his Sunday hat
> And ceremoniously laid it on the ground,
> And leaping on it with a solemn bound,
> Danced slowly on it till he trod it flat.
>   (p. 284)

Soon, however, he realized what he was doing and repented:

> Then suddenly he saw the thing he did
> And looked around to see if he was seen.
> This was the sin that Ahaz was forbid
> (The meaning of the passage had been hid):
> To look upon the tree when it was green
> And worship apples. What else could it mean?
>   (p. 284)

Ahaz, one of the obscure kings of Judah, is remembered for defiling the temple. In both Kings and Chronicles it is also recorded that he "sacrificed and burnt incense in the high places, and on the hills, and under every green tree" (II Kings 16:4; II Chron. 28:4). Here Frost is deliberately misinterpreting the passage, for nowhere are apples mentioned. But he has the gist of it right: several times the Old Testament prohibits worshiping in places other than the temple, and idolatrous altars "under every green tree" are frequently proscribed. In the poem Matthew is out stomping on his hat when he should have been in church. The three apples, significantly named Gold Hesperidee, but become objects of worship for him; thus Frost combines the Hebrew myth with the pagan one. (Acquiring the gold apples was the eleventh labor of Hercules, and one of them, thrown by the goddess of discord, Eris, was the remote cause of the Trojan War.) Square Matthew was spared from the eyes of onlookers when he did his dance in the orchard; "And so the story wasn't told in Gath," the poet says. This is an allusion to David's lamentation when he heard of the death of Saul: "How are the might fallen! Tell it not to Gath . . . lest the daughters of the Philistines rejoice" (II Sam. 1:19–20). The last line of the poem, in which Hale vows "To walk a graver man restrained in wrath," is reminiscent of a line in Psalms (76:10). The technique of this poem anticipates that of *A Masque of Mercy* in that it draws allusions from a variety of Biblical sources which gloss an essentially frivolous incident. Nevertheless, while the manner is comic, the thrust of the poem is quite serious.

Frost's two masques are the most elaborate and most broadly comic treatments of the Bible, for in them versions of biblical stories provide the subject matter.[9] *A Masque of Mercy* places Cain, Jezebel, Jonah, and Paul in the modern setting of a New York book store after hours. Jonah has arrived ostensibly to look for a Bible but actually is seeking refuge so he won't have to prophesy. A conversation ensues and Paul, Bel's analyst and also the Exegete, is described as "the fellow who theologized / Christ almost out of Christianity" (p. 408). Jonah is warned to be wary of him. Paul tries to explain everyone's difficulties and tells Jonah, who "can't trust God to be unmerciful" (p. 497), that he has the wrong attitude:

> You should be an authority on Mercy.
> That book of yours in the Old Testament
> Is the first place in literature, I think
> Where Mercy is explicitly the subject.
> (p. 508)

Paul's pet theory is that the Sermon on the Mount presents man with such an "irresistible impossibility" that he is bound to fail and so must ask for mercy. When Jonah is convinced that mercy is more important than justice he expires, explaining that all he was was his sense of justice. Thus Frost embodies and dramatizes a metaphor. The comedy here is rather heavy-handed. One of the notable devices is the use of outrageous puns, usually delivered by My Brother's Keeper, as Cain is called. Once he calls Jonah an old-fashioned sapient, or "a poor old sape" (p. 518). When Jonah suggests that New York might be visited by an earthquake, he asks, "Have you any grounds / Or undergrounds, for confidence in earthquake?" (p. 502). Then there is the line "I'd rather be lost in the woods / Than found in church" (p. 513). But it is also Keeper who has the final, significant statement, "Nothing can make injustice just but mercy" (p. 521). The poem is not entirely successful because Frost does not sufficiently delineate his four disparate characters or provide a rationale for their being together. There is a lack of cohesiveness between the seriousness and complexity of the problem and the dramatic situation—or dramatic chaos—of the poem.

A Masque of Mercy suffers by comparison with A Masque of Reason, which is more successful and more comic. Since it purports to be an additional chapter to the Book of Job, it has considerably more artistic unity than the later poem, although it too ranges widely and wildly through the Bible. Within the framework of God's apology, in both senses of the word, to Job, there are references to the Burning Bush, the Deuteronomist, Judgment Day, the Witch of Endor, the Star of Bethlehem, and so on. The poem begins with God's "pitching throne," a prefabricated plywood affair that collapses shortly, and ends with Job's wife, a stereotypical shrew who has notions of being an emancipated woman, taking snapshots of God, Job, and Satan. God has returned to earth to give Job his often-asked-for reason for all that suffering, and is portrayed as a well-meaning bumbler who has trouble with words. After dithering about, he explains that what he had been doing was showing off to the Devil and hopes that Job will not mind the answer. Job's wife comes nearer to the mark when she says:

Of course, in the abstract high singular
There isn't any universal reason;
And no one but a man would think there was.
You don't catch women trying to be Plato.

(p. 478)

Even though this poem deals with a theological problem as paradoxical as that of mercy versus justice, it manages successfully to maintain a lightly burlesque tone.

Frost's comic use of the Bible results from two impulses, I believe. One was to show off. He knew the Bible so very well that biblical cadences came naturally to him, and by assuming the guise of the good-natured simpleton who explains profundities in the most simplistic terms, he was able to make good use of those allusions. This affectation of innocence allows the reader to see the joke and at the same time feel superior to the speaker; it is a time-honored humorous device. The jokes Frost makes about the Bible are aimed not so much at the Bible itself but at the received interpretation of it; thus he poses as the inept exegete for the very serious reason of exposing inconsistencies in people's attitudes towards the myth. More importantly, he treats the Bible humorously in order to achieve an aesthetic distance from his subject matter. In a letter he once said, "Belief is better than anything else, and it is best when rapt, above paying its respects to anybody's doubt whatsoever. At bottom the world isn't a joke. We only joke about it to avoid an issue with someone . . . Humor is the most engaging cowardice."[10] Johan Huizinga, in *Homo Ludens,* discusses the redaction of myth to a literary mythology. He says that "to the degree that belief in the literal truth of the myth diminishes, the play-element . . . will reassert itself with increasing force."[11] Harvey Cox, in *The Feast of Fools,* applies Huizinga's theories in a specifically modern Christian context. "Only by assuming a playful attitude toward our religious tradition," he says, "are we able to make any sense of it."[12] From this point of view Frost's Biblical games have anticipated a current attitude among theologians and helped to reinvest religion with a significance it might not otherwise have.

NANCY C. JOYNER

Western Carolina University

Notes

1. David S. J. Parsons, "Night of Dark Intent," *Papers in Language and Literature,* 6 (1970), 205–10.

2. Nitchie, *Human Values in the Poetry of Robert Frost* (Durham: Duke Univ. Press, 1960), pp. 68–109.

3. Jeffrey M. Heath and Richard Poirier exchange interpretations of this poem in "The Mail," *Atlantic Monthly,* July 1974, pp. 24, 26. Poirier's explication of "Never Again Would Birds' Song Be the Same" appeared in the April 1974 *Atlantic Monthly* (pp. 50–55) as well as in his *Robert Frost* (New York: Oxford Univ. Press, 1977), pp. 169–72.

4. *The Poetry of Robert Frost,* ed. Edward Connery Lathem (New York: Holt, Rinehart and Winston, 1969), p. 428. Further references to Frost's poetry will be to this edition.

5. For a fuller treatment of these two poems, see Stephen D. Warner, "Robert Frost in the Clearing: The Risk of Spirit in Substantiation," in *Frost: Centennial Essays,* ed. Jac Tharpe (Jackson: Univ. Press of Mississippi, 1974), pp. 398–411).

6. *Frost: A Time to Talk* (Amherst: Univ. of Massachusetts Press, 1972), p. 5.

7. P. C. Duvall, "Robert Frost's 'Directive' Out of Walden," *American Literature,* 31 (1960), 486.

8. "The Constant Symbol," *Atlantic Monthly,* Oct., 1946, p. 50. Frost's syntax here has a biblical overtone. Compare "the chiefest of these is that it is metaphor" to "the greatest of these is charity" (I. Cor. 13:13).

9. See Peter J. Stanlis, "Robert Frost's Masques and the Classic American Tradition," in *Frost: Centennial Essays* (pp. 441-68); and Thomas McClanahan, "Frost's Theodicy: 'Word I Had No One Left But God,' " in *Frost: Centennial Essays* II, ed. Jac Tharpe (Jackson: Univ. Press of Mississippi, 1976), pp. 121-24.

10. Quoted in Lawrance Thompson, *Robert Frost: The Years of Triumph* (New York: Holt, Rinehart and Winston, 1970), pp. 650-51.

11. *Homo Ludens: A Study of the Play-Element in Culture* (Boston: Beacon, 1950), p. 130.

12. *The Feast of Fools: A Theological Essay on Festivity and Fantasy* (New York: Harper and Row, 1969), p. 171.

The Greek World
and the Mystery of Being

Robert Frost had no use for the kind of modern painting in which a head may have three eyes. No supporter of the "extreme modernists," as he called them,[1] Frost defined himself by the language, the custom, and the landscape of his own New England. From William Faulkner to Charles Olson, of course, localism has been one aspect of the modern movement, and yet for most readers "modernism" in poetry has meant the cosmopolitan experiments of Ezra Pound or T. S. Eliot, not the plain style of chicken farm and country school. Beyond the stylistic innovations which Frost viewed as mostly self-indulgent, however, the modernist movement was characterized by a seemingly paradoxical concern with both tradition and revolution. Questioning the basic premises of modern industrial society, many of the poets sought to build a radically different future on a foundation salvaged from the distant past. In Frost's verse there is little of the overt allusiveness which creates such a learned (and forbidding) surface in poems like *The Waste Land* and *The Cantos*. But Frost, like Yeats or Eliot, was deeply interested in the past. Discussing Frost's newness, Richard Poirier has shown that his exploration of a distinctly American style by no means makes him another D. H. Lawrence, aiming to "help us slough off a European consciousness in order to allow the growth of a new one."[2] If Frost rejects many of the stylistic tenets of the modernist poets, he nevertheless shares their profound belief in the necessity to "make it new," to appropriate tradition to the needs of yet another age, and not simply to turn to the New World in the pretense that there had never been an Old. Unpromising as it might seem, there are few better ways to approach Frost's modernity than by looking to his use of a tradition which is very old indeed.

When Frost was asked in a *Paris Review* interview whether he had "read a lot in the classics," his reply was revealing: "Probably more Latin and Greek than Pound ever did."[3] Beyond the decades of rivalry behind this statement there is the simple truth that Frost's familiarity with classical literature began with his mother's storytelling and continued through years of study, both formal and informal. He began his study of Greek as a sophomore in high school, and by the time he finished his years at Dartmouth and then Harvard, he had received consistently high marks in a wide range of courses in Greek language, literature, history, and philosophy. Though his poems seldom display their learning in obvious ways, he made no effort to conceal his general interest in the classics, and critics very early found ways to relate the poetry to what seemed its earliest ancestry. Lascelles Abercrombie, for example, reviewing *North of Boston* in 1914, thought the volume exhibited "almost the identical desires and impulses we see in the 'bucolic' poems of Theocritus."[4] His review went on to suggest that Frost's poetry, written in a world comparable to that of third-century Alexandria, was an attempt to find new vigor by consciously turning back to "the minds and hearts of common folk." This assertion is interesting for a number of reasons, including what it reveals about the difficulty of attempting to establish the lines of literary influence in Frost's work. Typically, the poet responded to this review by denying that he had ever read Theocritus, that in fact he was "too lazy to bother with Greek."[5] Many years later, however, in a letter to Conrad Pendelton, he reversed himself completely: "I read Theocritus early and found here and there echoes of the real voice."[6] Given his rather thorough education in the classics, and his early defensiveness about being thought to "imitate" any other poet, the second position is probably closer to the truth.

Beyond the controversy, however, Abercrombie's view has been characteristic of most critical approaches to the question of Frost's debt to the Greeks. For obvious reasons, the rural substance of the verse has seemed most striking, and the similarity to ancient pastoral suggested itself early and has continued to occupy the critics. Some writers have attempted to select poems (e.g., "Mowing," "In Hardwood Groves," "Waiting") which might best be seen in light of the pastoral tradition. Others have argued that Frost is not a pastoral poet, in the classical sense,[7] or that his version of pastoral must be seen in its modern context as an attempt to create a new myth of rural life.[8] Clearly, there is much yet to be understood about how Frost learned to alter a pastoral tradition which had seemed exhausted to Dr. Johnson two hundred years earlier. And yet in exploring Frost's use of the Greek world there are paths far less travelled than this one.

When John F. Lynen argues that a pastoral poet must be "a man of sophistication writing for a sophisticated audience, and that the genre is primarily found in times like those of Virgil or of "the cultural ascendancy of Alexandria," he is thinking of a particular kind of "classicism" in relation to Frost.[9] Other commentators have held similar assumptions in viewing Frost as resembling Horace, "the Horace of 'the golden mean' between extremes,"[10] or in suggesting that there is a romantic yearning in Frost's work which cannot be reconciled with his classical side because it does not end in a "calm elevation of perfect beauty and symmetrical proportion."[11] Needless to say, there is another side to the classical world than this, and one which can accommodate romantic disorder very well indeed. In emphasizing Frost's interest in the balance and sophistication of late Greek and Roman writers, however, too little attention has been paid to the fact that his imagination was deeply rooted in the grand creative turmoil of the earlier centuries of antiquity.

Frost once admitted to Robert Newdick that he loved philosophy next to poetry, though he cautioned against the dangers of "taught wisdom."[12] His dislike for the constraints of institutional schooling was an old one, but he seemed to feel similar discontent for learning itself when it began to be too rigorously organized. In "Boeotian," for example, he plays with the idea that wisdom, long associated with Athens, may actually occur in so humble a district as Boeotia. Primarily agricultural and the butt of Athenian jokes about its provincial character, Boeotia was nevertheless the home of Hesiod. If there is the countryman's suspicion of big-city wisdom in this little poem, there may also be a turning away from the "systematic" wisdom of the Athenian shools in favor of Hesiod's older kind of wisdom—rural, unsystematic, mythic. Certainly Frost showed little enthusiasm for the fully developed institution of Greek philosophy, however much its subject matter fascinated him. "The Bear" is a poem about the pursuit of wisdom, and in describing this "peripatetic" animal he clearly alludes to the school of Aristotle. Unlike the bear that freely roams the universe, however, the caged philosopher-bear of Frost's metaphor seems to represent that tradition of dialectic which had channelled our instinctive desire to know the world into a pointless, frustrating game, an endless shifting back and forth "between two metaphysical extremes."

With regard to Plato, Frost was more direct. Discussing his lifelong philosophy in a letter, he chracterized it as "non-Platonic."[13] In another letter he was quite explicit in rejecting Plato's ideal realm: "Then again I am not the Platonist [E. A.] Robinson was. By Platonist I mean one who believes what we have is an imperfect copy of what is in heaven. The woman you have is an imperfect copy of some woman in heaven or in someone else's bed."[14] Unlike the Plato of *Symposium,* Frost affirms the wisdom of "Birches": "Earth's the right place for love." To climb *"toward* heaven," like the boy of that poem, is fine, but we must always ride the tree back down to the things of earth. In "Wild Grapes," which could be a companion piece to "Birches," Frost makes a very similar point. The speaker is a young girl pulled up to the top of a birch tree when her brother releases it, and there she is left suspended like the grapes she was trying to pick. Frost compares her to Eurydice, but he inverts the myth so that she is stolen away "into space," not down to the underworld, and when her brother comes after her she is "brought down safely from the upper regions." As in so many of Frost's poems, the mention of Eurydice could be taken as just a simple metaphor, and yet the poem and the myth are more closely related than that: both concern loss, loss of the earth to begin with, and beyond that the stubborn refusal to "learn to let go with the heart." Frost's girl is no Platonist seeking to escape her animal heart in the upper regions, but someone who needs "to weigh something next time," someone who needs to feel the ground under her feet.

To see the myth of Eurydice as signifying our human involvement with earth is not new (William of Conches read it so in the twelfth century), but it is entirely in keeping with one vital thread of Frost's vision. His most succinct statement of the position is probably the gloss to "Rose Pogonias" which was part of the table of contents of the original edition of *A Boy's Will*: "He is no dissenter from the ritualism of nature." The poem, about picking flowers in a beautiful meadow, is filled with words which establish a religious context: temple, prayer, grace, bowed, worship. The flowers to be picked, however, are "orchises," which in Greek means "testicles." Thus the religion in question is hardly a Christian one, but rather a pagan nature ritual focusing around the symbolic sexual sacrifice of the vegetation. Far removed from the rational discourse of Aristotle, the poem reaches back to an earlier age when the gods invested all of nature. For many of Frost's poems, this ancient vision is central. "Mowing," for example, has been discussed in terms of "Mediterranean agricultural mystery cults" by Helen H. Bacon. Though she does not mention the pun on "orchises" which is repeated in this poem (Pound was shortly to use the same pun in *Hugh Selwyn Mauberly*), she does point out other symbols of sexual fertility, such as the green snake.[15] Numerous critics have remarked on the highly sexual imagery of "Putting in the Seed," where the fertilized Earth in springtime is only partially personified—as it is in the most archaic myths of creation. Fully aware of the larger cyclical pattern which these rituals were intended to interrupt and facilitate, Frost is explicit in a poem like "In Hardwood Groves." There is a somber dignity in this poem which is appropriate to the tone of religious meditation with which he invests nearly all of the poems about nature's periodic death.

The motif of recurrent cycles in nature does appear in a somewhat lighter tone in "Hyla Brook." The little stream (on the Frost farm in Derry) disappears underground each summer, taking with it the frogs ("the Hyla breed") which had "shouted" like bells earlier in the spring; sought for, it is nowhere to be found. Frost himself identifies the Hylas as small frogs, and there is no need to go any further than this quite literal explanation.[16] Given the playful quality of Frost's mind, however, it is impossible not to wonder whether there might be an echo in this poem of that earlier Hylas of Greek myth. The friend of Herakles, Hylas went to fetch water at a spring, but the water nymphs found his beauty so appealing that they seized him, and when Herakles came searching for him he could not be found. The parallel is interesting (if impossible to prove) and it is reinforced by the fact that Hylas was a minor vegetation deity whose yearly disappearance and then rebirth in spring were marked by the people of Kios in a ritual search which they conducted each year.[17] In any case, "Hyla Brook" is concerned with that mysterious cycle of birth and death in which searching for a vanished stream can only be a ritual, or an act of wonder.

Nowhere is the animistic quality of Frost's world more apparent than in "Paul's Wife." Paul, like the legendary lumberman of American folklore, is defined in the poem as a "hero" in need of a herione, but as the poem progresses he and his mysterious lady seem less and less compatible with the rude workmen who ponder their case. Discovered in a hollow tree, magically revivified in the water of a lake, and shining with her own light in the dark, this wife seems to be the amalgam of countless mythic figures. She is associated with the pith of a tree and then with a snakeskin and seems to be some kind of tree or water nymph. Whatever her exact nature, she and her rescuer-lover represent still another instance of a sacred marriage celebrating the sexual regeneration of dead nature. Perhaps the most primitive example of animism to be found in Frost's poetry occurs in "Directive." One critic argues that this poem is about "the spring of the Muses and its attendant imagery of Dionysus and Apollo," and while her reading is very suggestive it does present some difficulty.[18] In asserting that "Apollo and Dionysus share the cult at the spring of the Muses on Panther Mountain, as they did on Mt. Parnassus," she collapses two distinct traditions into one. While there was a prophetic spring at Delphi, shared by Apollo and Dionysus, it was not the spring of the Muses—which was located on Mt. Helicon, or, alterantively, in Pieria. In fact, there is not literally a spring in the poem, but a brook—described as being "cold as a spring." Other critics have also read this poem as being about poetry itself, but whether that is the case or not, it is certainly a poem about seeking the past.[19] Speaking in a troubled time, the poet would lead us back through the imagined lives of our ancestors, as if we might renew ourselves through them. For the early Greeks rivers and springs were among the most primitive ancestors, and there seems to be some sense of that here, in this brook which is clearly sacred. Simpler and purer because it is "so near its source," the brook offers respite from the raging confusion of valley streams. just as the streams of human births must have possessed a wholeness near its beginning for which later generations, in the confusion of the present, can only yearn.

Like many writers who came to maturity in the early part of this century, Frost was interested in the primitive stuff of vegetation rituals and dying gods— though his contemporaries were often more ostentatious about it, and more likely to have received their information through secondary sources such as Frazer's *Golden Bough*. But Frost was attracted to the world of early Greece by more than water nymphs and tree sprites. When asked to choose ten books which should be in every public library, he had no difficulty beginning his list: "The *Odyssey* chooses itself, the first in time and rank of all romances."[20] Throughout his life Frost never hesitated to affirm his love for the *Odyssey*, which he had frequently read to his children when they were young.[21] In an interview with Morris P. Tilley he said that "in the *Odyssey* the swim of Ulysses from the raft has powerfully possessed my imagination. It is one of the things that has gripped me."[22] Simply on a superficial level it is not difficult to see why Odysseus "of many devices" should be admired by a poet who could reveal an important aspect of himself to Louis Untermeyer in one pithy question: "Ain't I wiley?"[23] Odysseus was preeminently the hero of craft and cunning, qualitites which appear often in Frost's writings. In *A Boy's Will* they may appear as the slightly willful self-withholding of the young lover, exactly caught by Frost's gloss: "He is in love with being misunderstood." The motif may appear as the purely private scorn for other men which the hero of "The Vantage Point" indulges, or it may take the form of a more complicated, ambivalent response, as it does in "Revelation," where the speaker agonizes over his game of "hide-and-seek." Later, in "A Drumlin Woodchuck," Frost creates a mock-heroic image of a small animal whose very survival in the face of a hostile world has been won through "guile," through his ability to make others believe "that he and the world are friends." Lawrance Thompson spends many pages in the biography discussing this aspect of Frost's character, and he ventures the explanation that Frost learned to create imaginative defenses to protect the "mythic ideals of heroic struggle" which he secretly treasured.[24] Be that as it may, Thompson's Frost is a rather crafty manipulator, too often reminiscent of the portrait of Odysseus which began to emerge in the later classical period as his reputation declined and he came to be seen as a kind of con man. But this reading is overly simple, and it obscures a greatness in Odysseus—and Frost—which is closely bound up with intellectual cunning.

Frost was particularly impressed by the scene in which Odysseus swims to shore at Scheria after his raft has been destroyed. Safely on land, the exhausted hero shelters for the night by covering himself with leaves, an act which Homer compares to a farmer's covering the embers of his fire with ashes to preserve it overnight, and Frost has written about this metaphor as a kind of touchstone: "There you have something that gives you character, something of Odysseus himself. 'Seeds of fire.' So Odysseus covered the seeds of fire in himself. You get the greatness of his nature."[25] Poets like Blake and Yeats knew that "fair and foul are near of kin," and so it is with Odysseus. The characteristic craftiness which could lead some readers to judge him harshly was, seen from a different perspective, only the darker side of that very quality of mind in which his greatness lay. Far from being a prudent self-protector, the hero of the *Odyssey* most often used his guile to extricate himself from dangers he need not have faced at all, had he not possessed a mind eager to venture after knowledge even to the gates of death. For Frost, it was just this bold seeking-to-know which constituted the seeds of fire in a hero he admired above all others. He puts it very clearly in "Misgiving," a poem about falling leaves which almost dare to fly off with the wind, but merely drift to sleep instead:

> I only hope that when I am free,
> As they are free, to go in quest
> Of the knowledge beyond the bounds of life
> It may not seem better to me to rest.[26]

Because Frost has sometimes been regarded as anti-intellectual (a view he did not always try to dispel), it is important to see that his distrust of "taught wisdom" by no means implies a lack of interest in wisdom gained beyond the constraints of schoolmen: the bold questing of Odysseus is one thing, the systematic questioning of Plato quite another.

To leave the familiar world and follow less-traveled ways is not an easy choice, and Frost is well aware of the ambiguities involved. The poem which opens *A Boy's Will* ("Into My Own") contains a note of adolescent solipcism, but it does initiate a journey into unknown parts in search of truth. "Flower-Gathering," later in the same sequence, presents an uncertain homecoming for the lover who has been gone so long ("the ages of a day") that he wonders whether, like Odysseus, he will go unrecognized. The tone is gently ironic about this youth who has grown "gaunt and dusty gray" as the result of a grueling day of picking flowers, but Frost's most playful images are often his most serious. Looking for flowers provides the focus for "An Encounter," a poem which is explicit in its depiction of the difficulties of Odyssean quest. Hiking away from road and trail through a cedar swamp, the poet is startled to find a telephone pole where he stops to rest, and the discovery leads him to think about the contrast between the civilization he has left and the wild country he now explores. Worn out with walking, he admits doubt about his present course ("sorry I ever left the road I knew"), and yet he clearly rejects the safe, responsible world of telephones and "news" which the wires on their "resurrected tree" represent. Unlike the messages which rush over the wires to specific destinations, the poet lets himself drift:

> Sometimes I wander out of beaten ways
> Half looking for the orchid Calypso.
> (*The Poetry*, p. 125)

Once again drawing on the very appropriate sexual connotations of "orchid," Frost sets against the modern industrial world an older, mythic time of irresponsible self-indulgence and sensuality, of magic rather than reason. One critic has rightly pointed out that in the case of "Stopping By Woods" the speaker is like Odysseus in honoring his worldly responsibilities.[27] But Odysseus, though ultimately bound homeward, did spend many years with the likes of Calypso and Circe, and while he often regretted bitterly ever leaving the road he knew, there was no other way to be Odysseus, no other way to see what he would see. Frost knew it too.

Odysseus left many companions dead as part of the price for his journey, and in poems like "An Encounter" and "There Are Roughly Zones" Frost considers the cost when "something comes over a man" and he can no longer remain within "limits and bounds." In the latter poem it is a peach tree that must die because a man wanted to see if it would grow too far north of its natural zone. But regret or no, the quest is irresistible, and for Frost it is finally joyful. "The

Generations of Men," a poem about journeying back in imagination to consult the ancestors, takes place in the cellar hole of a long-vanished house where many years earlier a family had begun. The young man and woman who meet there at a family reunion spoiled by rain are seeking the ghosts of their own ancestors, and when voices from the past speak to the man they tell him to

> Call her Nausicaä, the unafraid
> Of an acquaintance made adventurously.
> (*The Poetry*, p. 305)

This Yankee wanderer is instructed by the ghosts to build a new home out of the charred timbers of the past, and whether or not his Nasuicaä remains only an acquaintance, as she does in the epic, he has looked back beyond death, and like Odysseus found his past and future home.

Frost praised the *Odyssey* more warmly than any other work of literature, but there was a great deal more in the world of early Greece to catch his imagination as well. When Helen H. Bacon rejects the notion that Frost was a pastoral poet, she points out the "the shepherds of Vergil and Theocritus have griefs, but they hardly ever do any of the real work of the farm, which is the substance of so many of Frost's poems."[28] She suggests that Vergil's *Georgics* would be a more likely model, and yet we might as easily look back to the age of Homer as forward to Rome. One of the world's greatest poets of agriculture was Hesiod, whose *Works and Days* is filled with just the sort of nonsystematic wisdom of rural Boeotia which Frost seems to be calling for in "Boeotian." In both poets there is a deep sensitivity to the changing seasons with their attendant consequences for the kind of farm work that must be done, and both make us aware of the slow movement of constellations in the night sky which mark the year's progression. Few poets have written as vividly of winter, particularly, as have Hesiod and Frost, and both invest their descriptions with the sense that there are moral truths to be drawn from the smallest details. Frost could in fact have encountered the central metaphor of "The Road Not Taken" in a passage in which Hesiod advises Perses that he will encounter two roads in his life, and that it will make a great difference to him if he chooses the less traveled, but more difficult path which leads to Good, and not the easy, level path to Bad.[29] For all Frost's protestations that his poem is really an ironic spoof directed at Edward Thomas's melancholy, readers have always found a note of moral seriousness in the poem which is quite in the spirit of Hesiod's little sermon. Whether Frost was alluding to specific passages in Hesiod or not, however, the sensibility of the two poets is very similar, even down to some rather homely details. "The Ax-Helve," for example, is a poem in which one countryman sets up to offer farm lore and rural wisdom to another—the basic situation of *Works and Days*. In Frost's poem Baptiste, a French-Canadian neighbor, criticizes the store-bought ax which Frost is using because a proper ax handle should have a shape already "native to the grain," with "no false curves / Put on it from without." Hesiod (11. 424–29), discussing the various uses of wood, advises his brother that while gathering firewood he sould keep watch for a piece of oak which is naturally curved, because such a piece would make the strongest plough-beam.

There is a more general sense in both poets in which it is necessary to go with the grain of nature. For Hesiod that may mean respecting the sacredness of a stream:

> Never pass through, on foot, a lovely brook
> Of ever-flowing water, till you pray
> And look into the beauty of the stream.[30]

If one should show disrespect by crossing the brook without first cleansing oneself, literally and symbolically, the gods would later exact their punishment. Frost expresses a similar vision in "A Brook in the City," where he describes the destruction of a country stream by urban growth which literally buries it under cement. Frost views the brook as a living being, an "immortal force" which is being punished "for nothing it had ever done," but he concludes the poem by suggesting that even in our modern world, just as in the time of Hesiod, we cannot offer such disrespect to nature without suffering a kind of divine retribution:

> But I wonder
> If from its being kept forever under,
> The thoughts may not have risen that so keep
> This new-built city from both work and sleep.
> (*The Poetry*, p. 231)

There are other echoes of the *Works and Days* in Frost, such as his use of the myth of the golden age. In "Nothing Gold Can Stay," he links that archaic Greek myth of an original earthly paradise that passed away with its Judeo-Christian counterpart, the myth of Eden; while elsewhere ("It Is Almost the Year Two Thousand," "The Lost Follower") he uses Hesiod's myth ironically to criticize the modern millenialists who would recreate the golden age through social change. Fundamentally, however, Frost and Hesiod are kindred because they share a unique sensibility which combines the most practical concern for the details of farm life with a vision which is always aware of the mysterious grandeur of the universe. That vision is present in the *Odyssey*, and it is also present in the early Ionian philosophers who were learning to question the very nature of things, but who had not yet let their sense of awe yield to the sophistry which Frost deplored as sterile, "systematic" wisdom. Some of the apparent contradictions in Frost's attitudes toward philosophy (after poetry his avowed second love) can be resolved if we see him in relation to the pre-Socratic philosophers whose concerns were so like his own. Far from being merely one more subject to study while in school, their work provided concepts, problems, and metaphors which were a permanent part of Frost's attempt to know the world. In an essay written in 1931, for example, he alludes to various early theories of being, and then speaks of Pythagoras' "comparison of the universe to number," which had led on to the quantitative methods of modern science.[31] He goes on to compare Heisenberg's Uncertainty Principle to Zeno's metaphor of the arrow's flight, a comparison which not only points out that modern physics was reencountering very ancient problems about how we know the nature of being, but that Frost himself was using his knowledge of the past, in active and intellectually sophisticated ways, to understand the present.

Like Yeats, Frost was seeking metaphors for poetry (all knowledge for him being essentially metaphoric) and we cannot expect to find in his work a systematic account of the very complex issues raised by the pre-Socratic philosophers. The difficulties are quite apparent in one of Frost's most allusive, problematic poems. "Version" concerns an "Archer" who is engaged in a "New Departure" which turns out to be rather comic:

> For the game He hunted
> Was the non-existence
> Of the Phoenix pullet
> (The Mη ov of Plato)
> > (*The Poetry,* p. 427)

The poem refers to Plato's *Sophist,* where the attempt is made to distinguish between the sophist and the true philosopher, by means of a rigorous examination of some of the central tenets of the Eleatic school, particularly Parmenides' rejection of the notion of *not-being* (Mη ov). The central metaphor of the dialogue is that of a hunt, with Plato's spokesman, an Eleatic stranger, as the hunter chasing a highly elusive sophist who proves to be "difficult game" as he erects one defense after another in his denial of the existence of *not-being.*[32] For Plato the dialogue is a departure from his earlier dependence on Parmenides in defining the forms,[33] and Frost indulges one of his most elaborate puns in referring to the main point at issue: "pullet" is, of course, another word for *hen,* which just happens to be the Greek term for *one* as used by Parmenides to define Being. Thus the "non-existence" of this particular pullet (which like the phoenix is always One through all its seeming change) would indeed be the "Mη ov of Plato." The archer's shaft, however, is paradoxically blunted on the "non-resistance" of the Phoenix pullet, and Frost concludes with a line which is entirely characteristic of his attitude toward this kind of dialectical game: "That's how matter mattered."

Frost was not so much interested in following out all the intricacies of one or another philosophical position as he was in preserving metaphors which had served another kind of Odyssean quest into the heart of matter. He was a nature poet who wanted to see nature as "the Whole Goddam Machinery," not just "Pretty Scenery" ("Lucretius Versus the Lake Poets"), and in the early Greek philosophers he found a vital kind of poetry. Although very little notice has been taken of this aspect of Frost's thought, some critics have seen Heraclitean notions in "West-Running Brook."[34] The brook, which embodies "contraries" as it "runs counter to itself," does suggest an image out of Heraclitus. And in the strange "throwing back" which prevents its simply emptying into the void ("As if regret were in it and were sacred"), there almost seems to be a principle like that of Anaximander, who speaks, in the only existing fragment of his writings, of the compensation of the warring opposites: "for they make reparation to one another for their injustice according to the ordinance of time."[35] In the poem it is not the stream's falling to dissolution in which we see ourselves, but the "backward motion toward the source," the intricate compensation which leads not to death but to renewal.

Whether or not the sense of continually clashing opposites which so fascinated Frost may be traced to the stories his mother told him as a child, as Thompson suggests, the sense is there in poems as diverse as the early "To the Thawing Wind," and the little couplet of forty years later, "From Iron." In the latter poem the forces deep within nature which can make both "tools and weapons" out of iron and also force people to "take sides" suggest the Love and Strife of Empedocles, organizing and reorganizing the stuff of the universe through their eternal opposition. In "Any Size We Please" a man imagines his universe as infinitely extended and then as "space all curved," but when he contemplates this problem apparently out of modern relativity theory, he is also restating a dichotomy which was debated by Parmenides, Melissus, and Empedocles.

Another poem in which someone regards the heavens is "Skeptic," where the speaker begins by doubting that the evidence of his senses tells him anything real about the nature of a star, whether he is examining its faint image on a photographic plate or the red shift which is presumed to show how fast it is moving away from us: "I put no faith in the seeming facts of light." The passage could almost be a gloss on the skepticism of Democritus, who was also concerned with how we know the universe: "Sweet exists by convention, bitter by convention, color by convention; but in reality atoms and the void alone exist." And in another fragment: "It is necessary to realize that by this principle man is cut off from the real."[36] When Democritus comes to imagine the formation of our universe, he sees it as enveloped in a "caul," the membrane which sometimes covers the head of a baby at birth.[37] Frost, starting from a similar skepticism about the senses, also turns to metaphor—and to exactly the same, striking metaphor—as he explains that sometimes the universe feels "Like a caul in which I was born and still am wrapped (*The Poetry,* p. 390). Frost was a great collector of metaphors and he may well have been struck by this one in Democritus. But whether his allusion was a conscious one or not, he was thinking about the same problems which concerned the ancient scientist, and thinking about them in a similar way.

There is an obvious continuity in Frost's thought between his literacy about modern science, particularly physics and astronomy, and his interest in the ontological quest of the early Greek philosophers. One of the poems in which he brought the two together is "A Never Naught Song," which deals with the origin of everything that is. True to the terms of modern science, the beginning is in "atomic One," which Frost defines as the hydrogen atom, basis for successively complex levels of organization leading ultimately to men. But there is another pattern of language in the poem which does not seem to come from the physics lab, the tiny "gist" which is matter's beginning is "One and yet discrete / To conflict and pair," and it is shaped into the world we know by "the force of thought (*The Poetry*, p. 426)." Anaxagoras had offered a similar vision in the fifth century: "And when mind began to set things in motion, from all that was moved a separating off began; and all that mind set in motion was separated."[38] There are echoes of nearly all the major pre-Socratic philosophers through Frost's work, and no one of their formulations ever seems to be judged "right": to do so would be an anachronism in one as well versed in contemporary science as Frost was. But if all their theories are finally no more than metaphors, Frost still saw the deeper rightness in their bold decision to look to the stars and question the mystery of Being.

That was the beginning of Western philosophy. And yet for Frost this ancient speculation was strangely vital to his own modernity. One of Frost's contemporaries, Martin Heidegger, has written of the need for a philosophy which "heeds the call of Being"; he regarded Western history after Socrates as a long forgetting, an alienation from Being. With Heidegger, the existential philosophers who wrote in the early and middle decades of the century valued that sense of wonder in the pre-Socratics as a vital way back to what had been lost when our long obsession with technics—the mastery of things—began. In his celebration of nature Frost was part of the romantic reaction against that mastery, as it seemed to be culminating in the modern industrial city. But his love for the early Greek world was also a part of his struggle to seize life in a deadening time, and it was akin to the endeavor of Modernist thought in writers as different as Martin Heidegger and T. S. Eliot, Ezra Pound and D. H. Lawrence: to make some part of the distant past new, and so redeem the present. Sailing in imagination to an age when tree and stone and brook were alive and sacred, Frost could feel the primal sea with Odysseus, and play at understanding through the metaphors of men who lived before system had veiled the wonder of it.

JAMES F. KNAPP

University of Pittsburgh

Notes

1. *Interviews with Robert Frost,* ed. Edward Connery Latham (New York: Holt, Rinehart and Winston, 1966), pp. 80, 183.

2. *Robert Frost: The Work of Knowing* (New York: Oxford University Press, 1977), p. 13.

3. Reprinted in *Interviews,* p. 229.

4. Quoted in Lawrance Thompson, *Robert Frost: The Early Years,* 1874–1915 (New York: Holt, Rinehart and Winston, 1966), p. 451.

5. Interview in *The Boston Post* in 1916, reprinted in *Interviews,* p. 14.

6. Conrad Pendelton, "The Classic Dimension of Robert Frost," *Prairie Schooner,* 38 (Spring 1964), 78.

7. Helen H. Bacon, " 'In- and Outdoor Schooling': Robert Frost and the Classics," in *Robert Frost: Lectures on the Centennial of his Birth* (Washington, D. C.: Library of Congress, 1975), pp. 8f.

8. John F. Lynen, *The Pastoral Art of Robert Frost* (New Haven: Yale Univ. Press, 1960), pp. 9ff.

9. Lynen, p. 13.

10. Horace Gregory and Marya Zaturenska, *A History of American Poetry, 1900–1940* (New York: Harcourt, Brace, 1942), p. 160.

11. Pendelton, p. 83.

12. *Newdick's Season of Frost: An Interrupted Biography of Robert Frost,* ed. William A. Sutton (Albany: SUNY Press, 1976), p. 363.

13. *Selected Letters of Robert Frost,* ed. Lawrance Thompson (New York: Holt, Rinehart and Winston, 1964), p. 482.

14. *Selected Letters,* p. 462.

15. Bacon, p. 20.

16. *Selected Letters,* p. 171.

17. H. J. Rose, *A Handbook of Greek Mythology* (New York: Dutton, 1950), p. 200.

18. Bacon, pp. 14ff.

19. Reuben A. Brower, *The Poetry of Robert Frost: Constellations of Intention* (New York: Oxford Univ. Press, 1963), pp. 241f.

20. *Books We Like* (Boston: Mass. Library Assoc., 1936), p. 141.

21. Lawrance Thompson, *Robert Frost: The Years of Triumph,* 1915–1938 (New York: Holt, Rinehart and Winston, 1970), p. 81; Newdick, *Season of Frost,* p. 61.

22. *Interviews,* p. 24.

23. Thompson, *Years of Triumph,* p. 443.

24. Thompson, *Early Years,* pp. xiv ff.

25. *Selected Prose of Robert Frost,* ed. Hyde Cox and Edward Connery Lathem (New York: Holt, Rinehart and Winston, 1966), p. 42.

26. *The Poetry of Robert Frost,* ed. Edward Connery Lathem (New York: Holt, Rinehart and Winston, 1969), p. 236. Hereafter noted in the text as *The Poetry.*

27. Edward H. Rosenberry, "Toward Notes for 'Stopping by Woods': Some Classical Analogs," *College English,* 24 (April 1963), 527.

28. Bacon, p. 9.

29. Assuming that most readers of modern poetry would prefer to consult a translation of the Greek, I will refer here and in subsequent references in the text to an easily accessible modern version, that of Dorothea Wender, *Hesiod and Theognis* (Harmondsworth, England: Penguin, 1973), 11. 285-92.

30. Wender, 11. 740-43.

31. "Education by Poetry," in *Selected Prose*, p. 37.

32. *Plato: The Sophist and The Statesman*, trans. A. E. Taylor (London: Nelson, 1961), p. 171.

33. Paul Seligman, *Being and Not-Being: An Introduction to Plato's Sophist* (The Hague: Martinus Nijhoff, 1974), p. 29.

34. Patrick Morrow, "The Greek Nexus in Robert Frost's 'West-Running Brook,' " *Personalist*, 49 (Winter 1968), 24-33; Thompson, *Years of Triumph*, p. 303.

35. *An Introduction to Early Greek Philosophy*, trans. John Mansley Robinson (Boston: Houghton Mifflin, 1968), p. 34.

36. *Early Greek Philosophy*, pp. 202f.

37. *Early Greek Philosophy*, p. 213.

38. *Early Greek Philosophy*, p. 184.

Psychoanalytic Approaches to "Mending Wall"

We will eventually, we hope, have some extended psychoanlaytic studies of Frost and his work, possibly in the form of psychobiographies—books that study the psychological interrelations of an author's life and works. With intelligence and tact, such studies will avoid excessive blurring of the poems into mere products of the more hidden aspects of the poet's character and will help penetrate the total artistry of the poems and their experientially available content. Formally psychological treatments of Frost and his individual poems are now scarce. C. Barry Chabot has published a fine general essay on Frost's psychology and its manifestation in various poems.[1] Part of a theoretical essay by Norman Holland about reader response makes parallel judgments about Frost's character ("identity theme" is Holland's term).[2] Donald M. Jones has published an excellent psychological study of "A Servant to Servants."[3] Randall Jarrell has presented a brilliant piece on "Home Burial" that is full of psychological insights,[4] and I have published psychologically oriented essays on "Two Witches" and "The Death of the Hired Man."[5]

Norman Holland includes a long psychoanalytic discussion of "Mending Wall" in an essay on psychoanalytic critical method. It is his discussion and the poem it analyzes that will provide my main text in this essay.[6] Holland's treatment of "Mending Wall" has already provoked two critical replies, on which I will comment briefly. Doubtless there are psychological implications in numerous scattered discussions of individual Frost poems, though I suspect that few such discussions exist for the lyric poems. Chabot briefly cites a number of lyrics to support his general psychological interpretation. It remains to be seen if concentrated psychological interpretation can be extended out from Frost's narratives to his lyrics. In my view the most useful psychological readings of the lyrics are able to illuminate the poems independently of their relation to their author's life and works. An insistence on psychological readings within the full context of an author's life and work tends to limit understanding to the specialist and also to convince the general reader that interpretation of poetry either is only for experts or is extremely subjective. Perhaps "Mending Wall" can eventually serve as a link between poems with conspicuous characterization and interpersonal content and poems with single characters or the poet's persona confronting nature and experience generally. After considering Norman Holland's psychoanalytic reading of "Mending Wall" and offering my own as an alternative, I will very briefly propose two similarly oriented psychological readings of two Frost lyrics as an additional test of the strengths and weaknesses of these methods.

Norman Holland's effort to see "Mending Wall" not so much as the symbolic representation of an intellectual attitude but more as the dramatization of partially hidden inner tensions, apprehensions, and character traits seems to me a constructuve step, but I disagree with much of its method and many of its conclusions. Holland offers his treatment of "Mending Wall" as a major example of the psychoanalytic approach to literature. He describes a supposedly "regular way" to proceed in literary explication: "First, we go through the text noting particular words, images, phrasings, incidents, and the like . . . Second is to group these individual *apercus* into themes (p. 133)." The third step is to locate a central theme. In psychoanalytic explication, Holland says, one also moves through three steps: seeking evidence for a general level of fantasy, considering the psychoanalytic theory of such fantasies, and finally hypothesizing a nucleus of fantasy that unifies the material (136–39). He maintains that such explication looks for childhood fantasies under the headings of oral, anal, urethral, phallic, and oedipal (136). In his book *The Dynamics of Literary Response,* Holland explains that we cannot say much about postoedipal fantasies in our response to litearture because "fantasies at this level of maturity, and . . . in the adulthood beyond, are far too various to be generalized about."[7] Perhaps this variety and scope are precisely the basis of the rich psychological texture that I see as eluding Holland's method.

In "Mending Wall," according to Holland, supposedly oral material is gathered through "a nucleus of fantasy that brings together the separate themes and images of the poem with reference to the unconscious mind." Holland analyzes the poem around these definitions with little reference to its actual mimesis— the flow of events, feelings, and scene-creating images. These are fragmented and built into his own patterns. For Holland, "Mending Wall" is a series of oral fantasies about breaking down the wall between the separated self so it may return "to a state of closeness to some Other." Thus the poem is thick with oral images of speaking and eating. The speaker's regression causes his projection of his antipathy to walls into the "Something" of "Something there is that doesn't love a wall." The image of cows can be understood only when the poem's oral themes are recognized. The neighbor like "an old-stone savage armed" shows primitive regression to violence. The insistence that the speaker's apples will not eat the neighbor's pine cones shows concealed terror of being eaten and unconscious anger. The core fantasy then is fear that the lowering of walls between self and others will release primitive aggression and the self will be devoured by the new unit. The apparent tolerance of the speaker is a reversal of hidden rage into hidden humaneness. Later, Holland says that the two characters speak respectively for loving closeness and aggressive distancing but he sees this as a division between drive and defense. He, correctly I think, takes Frost's remark in conversation, "As if I weren't on *both* sides of that wall," to show recognition that the two characters represent different aspects of the poet. Holland offers a brief denial that he is reducing the poem to its nuclear fantasy, claiming that central fantasy and central theme transform each other, and he tries to relate his reading to several thematic interpretations—as if considering fantasy and/or theme were the only possible ways to read the poem. However, he regards this transformation as a disguise of the fantasy and a protection against its anxieties, for he sees activity of the ego not as the creation of the self and of creative adaptation to the world but merely as the control of defense mechanisms (140–45).

The idea that literary works are centered on nuclear fantasies raises huge theoretical problems. I am doubtful of the formulation, for it neglects the possibility that many literary works use and shape fantasy material as part of the process of self-clarification, no matter how limited. Surely most poems show a greater integration of the unconscious and the conscious than do most dreams. I would here cut through this massive problem by noting that for many literary works there lies between possible nuclear fantasy and intellectual theme or elaboration the entire realm of experience as described, felt, intuited, and analyzed by author (or author-protagonist) and within this operation doubtless lie all sorts of possiblities of authorial knowledge and self-knowledge. How much deeper a reductive psychoanalytic method goes than the knowledge and self-knowledge available to sensitive close reading—in the case of "Mending Wall," of a combined mimetic and expository structure—may be an open question. The essential question is whether such a method increases our grasp of the texture and depths of the experience. In Holland's analysis of "Mending Wall" I think the gains in insight are obscured by the reductive darkness.

In more literary terms, I would say that Holland's method of fragmentation violates the primary canon of all explication: looking in the work for the continuity, articulation, and wholeness of its action, experience, and feelings. Thus he tends to replace the reality of the poem and the complexities of its adult protagonist with an ordering of infantile fantasy urges and defenses, ignoring mimetic effects and thus employing what Holland elsewhere criticizes as "cookbook symbolic" interpretation. Holland doesn't trace the relationship of the narrator's consciousness to other consciousnesses, especially the neighbor's; he seems to regard creative and self-aware ambivalences as nothing but reaction formations; he contradicts himself in describing Frost's view of the mysterious "Something" as merely a projection (an unconscious defense mechanism), for Frost's pun on his own name (which Holland notes) shows him clearly and playfully aware of this "protection." Holland's method does make him sensitive to aspects of the confrontation and conflict around which the poem is organized but he slights the wholeness of the experience and especially of the narrator.

The selectivity of Holland's psychosexual concentration on oral material in "Mending Wall" has been criticized and satirized by Jeremy Hawthorn and by Edward Jayne, with results perhaps more amusing than instructive.[8] Can observation of anal, phallic, and oedipal as well as oral material in "Mending Wall" promote a reading better than Holland's? Both Hawthorn and Jayne recognize the arbitrary possibilities of such operations but that does not settle the issue. The crucial problem is whether such study can be connected to our experience. Most people, with or without formal psychological knowledge, have considerable sense of a wide range of human feelings about the self and others; a psychological vocabulary that increases this awareness must pursue general consent and not be merely part of a decoding process, but even if a blend of these two positions is possible, it may still result in such an elaboration of detail and rebuilding of pattern that the aesthetic whole and the imitated experience will get lost.

I propose to circumvent this problem by applying Erik H. Erikson's theory of eight developmental stages of human life to "Mending Wall." Erikson's theory is an elaboration of Freud's theory of psychosexual development, an elaboration that continues beyond the progress from oral to genital stages, that sees organ modes as highly generalized patterns of reaction, that stresses the interpersonal elements of each stage and the influence of the social context on these elements, and that stresses the forward and backward movement among all eight stages. Each stage of development is organized around a psychosocial nuclear conflict. These eight stages and their nuclear conflicts are: (1) Oral Sensory: Basic Trust vs. Mistrust; (2) Muscular-Anal: Autonomy vs. Shame and Doubt; (3) Locomotor-Genital: Initiative vs. Guilt; (4) Latency: Industry vs. Inferiority; (5) Puberty and Adolescense: Identity vs. Role Confusion; (6) Young Adulthood: Intimacy vs. Isolation; (7) Adulthood: Generativity vs. Stagnation; (8) Maturity: Ego Integrity vs. Despair.[9] Erikson's chart does not specify an oedipal phase, which Freudians see as appearing during the phallic (locomotor-genital) phase, to be repressed during latency, and to be overcome or reemerge during puberty. For literary purposes one must note that past the locomotor-genital phase, Erikson's stages are not clearly related to organ modes except for the sexual flowering of puberty. In Freud's scheme, everything that progresses normally past latency is maturely genital. One must also note that the content of Erikson's nuclear conflicts often blurs with the physical aspect of development insofar as identity, intimacy, and possibly even generativity and ego integrity strongly imply the infusion of certain qualitites into physical relationships. If one applies Erikson's chart to literature, the physical features should be chiefly related to the actual physical engagements and actions in the work rather than to organ modes suggested by descriptive and figurative terminology. Exceptions to this are notable when figurative or imaginative statements have a nonmimetic thrust. Thus it seems useless to find emotionally oral meaning in Frost's stones shaped like loaves, but reasonable—though not necessarily very revealing—to find it in apples threatening to devour pine cones.

This theory may be heavy artillery to apply to the situations and characters in "Mending Wall." Indeed, it will probably yield better results with extended works of fiction. Here the task must avoid overelaboration and diffusion. I will comment segmentally on the poem and then relate situation and detail to Erikson's theories, but since the poem does not show people in the process of development, it will not be possible to trace stages of development. My comments on oral material refer to proposals by Norman Holland. Those on other possible psychosexual material are intended as refutation of other possible views or as aids to understanding.

The poem opens with a strong response to the central fact of the dramatic situation: winter frost has partly dismantled an orchard wall, and though the speaker seems to have made some temporary repairs of damage caused by hunters, a springtime agreement requires a more formal repair. The opening line suggests identification between the speaker and the disordering force, yet the fact that he has made individual repairs shows respect for the ordering quality of the wall. Although it was a winter and not a spring force that made the gaps, the images of boulders spilled in the sun and two walking together suggest freedom, release, and comradeship. We have, then, images of disorder versus order and looseness versus tightness. On the psychosexual level the images suggest symbolic release of sexual tension and actual release through locomotion and comradeship. But the chief nuclear conflict, in very subdued form, would seem to be intimacy versus isolation. Ambivalence about intimacy with both man and nature seems marked, but the speaker scarcely seems infantile.

The mention of "another thing"—the damage made by hunters—switches the mood decidedly. The hunters cause irresponsible disorder. Their desire to please the yelping dogs shows them identifying their aggressions with the dogs' uninhibited behavior in order to lower their own inhibitions. The hunters' activity is a mode of release balancing the far more relaxed and ambivalent release of the poem's opening. Nevertheless, the narrator's vehement comment on the yelping dogs shows that he understands and perhaps partly shares the aggressive identification with the dogs. This prepares for the stronger ambivalences of poetntial aggression later in the poem. Holland declares that this passage shows the primitive rages of the oral phase but he does not note that the speaker is denouncing this rage, which may be why he misses the speaker's ambivalence. But why must it be oral just because the dogs are yelping after a rabbit? Would not the overthrow of stones and the implied scramble through a wooded area symbolize male sexual penetration as well? Better, I should think, since furious locomotion rather than oral-sensory qualities seems to mark the hunters (though in fact the oral and phallic seem decidedly fused). The pleasant ambivalence of locomotor and comradely activity in the opening lines here perhaps becomes the desperate ambivalence of a quasi-sexual thrust against the bonds of guilt, and a dramatic quality is maintained by the speaker's empathic grasp of behavior he condemns.

In terms of Erikson's conflicts, one might say that for the hunters initiative goes wild in its opposition to guilt and that the speaker is trying to reject this conflict.

Beginning readers often fail to notice the importance of the line "I let my neighbor know beyond the hill," and numerous critics insist that its revelation that the narrator initiates the tour of repair shows that he is the one who most desires it. Rather his act seems to me a combination of formal acquiescence, an ambivalent assent to the other's needs, and quite possibly a desire to control the situation. However, as the poem progresses we see that his attitude towards the task is playfully divided whereas his neighbor's is humorlessly rigid. But until the speaker mocks his neighbor, the neighbor's traits are not delineated. The description of the restoration of the wall is not promising material for psychosexual analysis. Boulders as loaves don't seem to relate to anyone's oral urges except on the purely lexical level and the possibility that placing stones resembles playing with feces (not Holland's idea) is helpful only if we feel that all physical activities derive their satisfactions from infantile psychosexual concomitants, and if this were true, one would still have to grant that adults simply do not think about their activities in this way and that telling them to do so doesn't put them in touch with whatever unconscious residues such behavior might have. The physical activity itself here is locomotor, kinesthetic, and tactile, and perhaps it does suggest some of the tension reduction of sensual satisfaction.

I do have an intellectual interpretation of this passage and though I am wary of its ingeniousness, I think it can be related to conflicts which in turn have some basis in body states. The task of restoring the wall resembles a life ritual. The two men walk a line, which may be said to symbolize life's formal requirements, and each picks up the stones on his own side, which may be said to symbolize fortuitous happenings and the necessity of bearing one's own burdens. Perhaps they are partly trying to restore their own balance. The wearing of their fingers suggest the painful joy of creative endeavor. The speaker experiences the line as a symbol of his ambivalent feelings about order vs. disorder, which would relate to Erikson's nuclear conflicts as they climb from trust vs. mistrust to intimacy vs. isolation. On the physical level intimacy vs. isolation (these are psychosocial terms but they describe the physical situation better than does "young adulthood") shows the way the men relate to each other and to the task. Perhaps the process of restoring the wall is an act of sublimation. My main point is that my interpretation creates general ideas for the necessity of formalizing or stabilizing ambivalences about social requirements and painful contingencies.

The sigh of "Oh, just another kind of outdoor game" expresses a bit of weariness, a bit of relief, and a bit of exhilaration. On the one hand, the task seems rather unnecessary, which means it must be tolerated with humor. On the other hand, it has a partly hidden necessity. The release of tension through exertions seems to help them—or at least the speaker—put up with and perhaps enjoy the ambivalence. We might find in this passage and the preceding one the conflict of industry vs. inferiority, the industry helping to overcome a sense of uselessness in the task, of doing what has to be done to others' requirements and done over and over, though the neighbor seems to have submerged his conflicts rather thoroughly under the pressure of the superego.

The passage on apples not eating pine cones shows such a marked identification between the speaker and the symbols that one must grant considerable oral force to the imagery. I agree with Holland that the passage expresses anger and a paranoidal defensiveness. I would even agree that it shows some regression to childhood and to conflict between trust and mistrust, but I would also claim that the speaker's mocking tone reveals some awareness of the sinister thrust of his aggressions, including an awareness that they may need to be walled in. I don't find Holland's discovery of oral themes in the cows to be sheer irrelevance, but the lines certainly are not mystifying without this explanation. The cows are completely natural mimesis, an observation appropriate to the speaker's point and to the New Englander's sense of propriety, and, more importantly, a thrust at the persisting childishness of the neighbor, the reiteration of "cows" underlining the stupid lowing nature of the creatures. Possibly the speaker associates the neighbor's need for external order with the cow's similar need, though the speaker has his own awareness of that need's validity. On the oral level I should grant a degree of mistrust like a child's mistrust of his own dependency, and it may be that this symbolic investigation adds a bit to our sense of the speaker's projected disgust. His mistrust, however, seems to be more part of an ambivalence than of the raging aggression Holland sees.

It is important to see that the six-and-a-half-line passage enclosed in quotation marks about putting "a notion in his head" is presented as thought, not as actual speech. Spoken, the lines would imply the expression of an anger that the speaker is in reality trying to keep to himself so he can understand and minimize it. This passage reveals that the speaker is proud of his own efforts to maintain inner order and sensitive to possible slights of this ability. He is proud of his own ability to live with more openness than his neighbor, proud of not following tradition and society's order. He puts up walls only when he himself clearly sees the need for them and has balanced for himself his need against the offense such walls give to other people—even though he is aware that the "Something there is that doesn't love a wall" operates in other people as well as in himself.

Although I do think that psychosexual material is present in or illuminates the concluding passage of the poem, I find little illumination in the idea that the wall in the passage just discussed is a barrier between infantile self and threat from mother or the desire to incorporate mother. And the Eriksonian nuclear conflicts don't cast too much light here unless one sees a whole group of positive trends such as trust, autonomy, identity, and intimacy trying to maximize themselves by taking down the compulsions and the limits of walls. Perhaps it is enough to see a free circulation of desires for integration and satisfaction struggling with barriers, compulsions, and ambivalences.

The picture of the neighbor "like an old-stone savage armed" moving in the darkness of his father's saying probably does receive some light from psychosexual interpretation. But what would be the point in seeing the stones as symbols of fixation at the phallic level (not Holland's idea)? The stones are mimetically accurate and one can see in them some repressed aggression without relating that aggression to the phallic level. If, however, the observation helps explain the neighbor, it may be useful. The darkness of his father's saying can be interpreted to refer to the superego repressing sexual knowledge and behavior and thereby, in Erikson's terms, limiting the neighbor's autonomy, identity, and intimacy. A logical concomitant of this view would be the suggestion that on the unconscious level one of the meanings for the neighbor of the phrase "Good fences make good neighbors" would be "Castration makes good children," which, of course, psychoanalysis would see as a pathological idea about oneself or others. This idea first occurred to me as an outrageous parody of psychoanalytic explication. I now suspect that it actually describes some of the psychodynamics of people in situations like the neighbor's. The question is whether this observation can contribute to our appreciation of the poem, or whether it can only be a special kind of decoding for a specially trained and sympathetic audience? I strongly suspect the latter to be true. In Erikson's terms, this passage shows the loss of autonomy and identity by means of the forbidding of trustful interchange. The protagonist is aware of this situation in his neighbor and he seems to be taking a stand against it in himself. Whether or not a psychosexual interpretation reinforces this view, the Eriksonian observation counterbalances Holland's idea that the poem stresses a terror of the self slipping away or being subjected to violent intrusions.

Erikson contrasts totalism and wholeness in the human personality, the first showing rigidity of attack and defense, the second showing a fluid interrelation within the self and between the self and the world.[10] I am not aware that Erikson says so, but I find the ideas of totalism and wholeness a kind of summary of the negative and positive poles of Erikson's nuclear conflicts. If Holland's view of "Mending Wall" were accurate, its narrator would be a tangle of psychopathology and would lean towards the negative poles of all eight conflicts. The opposite, I think is nearer the turth. Bearing in mind the skeletal presentation of this literary character, let me make a brief summary: (1) Trust vs. Mistrust. The speaker shows joy in nature and good-humored cooperation. His anger is controlled and his didacticism strives to be gentle and to limit self-righteousness. (2) Autonomy vs. Shame and Doubt. He doesn't criticize himself for acting decently in the face of his ambivalence. (3) Initiative vs. Guilt. He takes a specific initiative to help forestall an unnecessary guilt. (4) Industry vs. Inferiority. He takes an imaginative joy in his task. (5) Identity vs. Role Confusion. He accepts his own ambivalences and hence isn't torn by them. (6) Intimacy vs. Isolation. He desires to act gently and takes a ritualistic pleasure in cooperation. (7) Generativity vs. Stagnation. He has a fatherly feeling for his neighbor, recognizing and pitying his inner oppression or repression. (8) Ego Integrity vs. Despair. He achieves an overall feeling of balance and avoids the rigidity of past and present that confines his neighbor.

The relatively slight scope of character presentation in the poem has made this application of Erikson's scheme somewhat overlapping and repetitious. Also, unquestionably some elements of all the negative poles are present in the narrator and certainly some readers will register these contrasts quite differently. Applying the right conflicts to the even more slightly presented character of the neighbor, we find that the negative poles dominate and see much mistrust, isolation, and stagnation, and we suspect deeply repressed shame, guilt, and inferiority.

Let us now attempt a brief psychosexual fantasy interpretation and an Eriksonian developmental reading of two of Frost's best and most familiar lyrics, "After Apple-Picking" and "The Onset." If we follow Holland's method for locating nuclear fantasy, we must surely agree that the imagery and action of "After Apple-Picking" is overwhelmingly phallic. The poem is practially dominated by the image of a ladder and a man who has almost become one with it. The ladder is pointed and sticking. The speaker's foot aches from its pressure. The ladder and his body sway, partly under the influence (the weight, as it were) of abundant apples. The operation of hands receives almost equal emphasis. They have been busy picking apples, cherishing apples, half discarding spoiled apples. Even in sleep they will go on caring for apples. Also, his hands have been holding up an ice-sheet through which the world looks dully transformed.

But is this a fantasy of phallic penetration of the world of nature as female body, or does the curious insistence on the operation of hand suggest masturbation? Are the spoiled apples a sign of sexual guilt and, if so, is it connected to oedipal residues or merely to castration fears related to masturbatory guilt? Other images suggest scoptophiliac and oral longings or oral disappointments, but these fuse nicely with phallic longing. Does the speaker's dissatisfaction with his task relate to large-scale oedipal guilt or merely to that oedipal residue which Freud thought accounted for ultimate human dissatisfaction with sexual intercourse? Does the speaker desire a long sleep so he may recover from his guilt, seek deeper satisfaction in dreams, or wake refreshed for another try at sexual satisfaction? Of course there can be no question but that author and speaker think they are describing an experience primarily with an apple orchard, and the implied themes certainly seem to be generalizations about life and not about sexual matters. Does my not-entirely-serious psychosexual reading add anything to the poem? Well, maybe. The possible ambivalence about intercourse vs. masturbation may throw some light on Frost's and the speaker's narcissism but is this merely a transposition of vocabulary and hence a thrust into obscurantism? The sexual emphasis may relate to the poem's senuous intensity and may be intertwined with the kind of senuous pleasure it records.

This reading does not seem to me as effective as a consideration of a beautifully ambivalent approach to the phase of life Erikson sees built around generativity vs. stagnation. The poem shows, I think not so much the threat of stagnation as its ultimate residues. Reviewing Erikson's scale, I also see considerable trust, autonomy, initiative, industry, identity, intimacy, and ego integrity, all held in some tension with their opposites. To press these applications would create allegorical interpretations but none more farfetched than many that critics have offered about this poem. Surely sexual elements can be seen to feed into these other traits but more at the gential than the phallic level. With this in mind, one might even propose that the defects and incompletion of the task of apple picking show a blend of residual sexual dissatisfaction and a consciousness that not enough has been done for beloved others—both "sexual objects" and figures of generative care. However, the use of Erikson's vocabulary may merely provide a slightly artificial emphasis on aspects of life perceptible in the poem without its help. Still, just as for the psychoanalytic insider the psychosexual reading may locate interesting ambivalences, so the Eriksonian developmental view may reveal complexities of character or identity. But both of these readings (and I have found it a little hard to keep them separate) may well produce a kind of decoding of interest only to the initiate and provide a too-tempting example for many other possible kinds of decoding.

I will consider another Frost lyric, "The Onset," more briefly. I find this quite as good a poem as "After Apple-Picking" but less susceptible to useful psychoanalytic explication, partly because its body/sense associations are less clearly identified with the bodily presence and movement of the speaker and partly because seeing symbolic representations of people in the poem's natural images is a little more strained than in "After Apple-Picking." The most likely psychosexual fantasy for "The Onset" would seem to be the oedipal. The speaker's stumbling body appears to be wincing and crouching in a frightened retreat from the threat of a death-dealing (castrating) father embodied in the force of winter. One remembers that Freud saw the fear of death rooted in unconscious fear of castration. The speaker fears that all he is (or has accomplished) is threatened by a complete and retrospective negation. His personal and sexual identities are denied. The ambivalent appeal of the winter death which at first he cannot resist might represent the attractions of the prenatal womb as a substitute for the mother-womb that he is still denied.

But is this oedipal fantasy somehow continued in the marvelously hopeful and life-affirming second stanza or is the speaker breaking out of his oedipal bonds? Images of persisting trees, swift water, and revivified (though disappearing) snake suggest the possibility of resurrected sexuality. The womb of night and death is now replaced by the reborn and available body of earth and this rebirth is somehow sanctioned, protected, or even blessed by the human community symbolized by houses and church. Is the speaker breaking out of oedipal bonds in pursuit of a proper substitute sexual object? The human community doesn't bless oedipal attachments—at least consciously (there is always a wild card in this deck). If I must use this system, I prefer to see the ending of an oedipal fantasy and the beginning of a genital one. If so, isn't this development covered more sensibly by such Eriksonian categories as intimacy vs. isolation and generativity vs. stagnation? I think it certainly is, but as with "After Apple-Picking" I must ask again if these categories take us beyond a thematic death and rebirth interpretation of the poem? Do the psychosexual applications enrich the physicality of the poem? Does an Eriksonian terminology again invite wide allegorical speculations about the poem? Surely the idea of oedipal and even genital fantasies here can appeal only to some psychoanalytic initiates.

I began my proposal of an oedipal fantasy as pure parody. Having briefly rehearsed such an analysis, I now think that it provides some analogies for the deeper reaches of the kinds of experience the poem dramatizes or symbolizes. But since I feel no sense of enrichment as I try to feed these analogies into my experience of the poem, I see little point in asking anyone to take my psychosexual readings very seriously. In fact, my psychosexual readings of both lyrics seem very far removed from each poem's experiential base and only tangentially related to their universal human concerns. Whether readings like these could contribute to an overall psychoanalytic reading of Frost and his works that would deepen our understanding is more than I can at present tell. However, a comparison of these readings with the alternate readings (Holland's and mine) of "Mending Wall" suggests rather strongly that staying with fantasies that do not develop beyond the genital level blocks rather than contributes to our ability to connect psychosexual material with thematic material. My suggestion that both "After Apple-Picking" and "The Onset" move beyond pregenital levels helps to connect both poems to their apparent themes.

Norman Holland declares that "the psychoanalytic explications of poems ought to be grounded as much as possible in experience as visible and tactile as poetry itself" (p. 139). Although I find this a complicated matter, it doesn't seem to describe what Holland does with "Mending Wall." He selects only some of its tactile experience and transfers that into infantile terms. He neglects the redolence and physical engagement of the entire outdoor scene. He ignores the sense of flow between this engagement and the narrator's engagement with himself and with his neighbor. In the process, the whole human being is replaced by a quivering mass of aggression, defense, and reaction formation. Doubtless there is a degree of quivering in the articulation of the narrator's conflicts but it is held in strong balance with the struggle for integration, which accounts for the poem's psychological, thematic, and tonal unity.

While my speculative psychosexual readings of "After Apple-Picking" and "The Onset" are little more successful in grounding themselves in "visible and tactile experience," I see now that the chief problem here is what is meant by "grounded." If the grounding is the necessity to extend or plumb through the visible and tactile to the psychosexual, then the process becomes arbitrary unless the psychosexual adds to the reader's sense of the poem's sensuous and thematic resonances. I think that my reading of "Mending Wall" does do a better job of such extending or plumbing than does Holland's. But in my tentative readings of "After Apple-Picking" and "The Onset" once more the psychosexual and the sensual-dramatic can be better linked in the speculative imagination of the psychoanalytic initiate than in the experience of the moderately sophisticated general reader.

Certainly my attempt to blend the psychosexual with the Eriksonian developmental view has a danger that corresponds to the reductionism of Holland's method—the danger of seeking moral uplift, or replacing tough-mindedness with an applause-seeking assertion of one's own faith in man's moral self-awarenesses and abilities. Perhaps both of these potential weaknesses can be resisted by the tact of the critic, but the underlying problem must be related to varying psychoanalytic views of human motivation and character.

MORDECAI MARCUS

University of Nebraska, Lincoln

Notes

1. "The 'Melancholy Dualism' of Robert Frost," *Review of Existential Psychology and Psychiatry*, 13 (1974), 42–56.

2. "Unity Identity Text Self," *PMLA*, 90 (October 1975), 818–21.

3. "Kindred Entanglements in Frost's 'A Servant to Servants,' " *Papers in Language and Literature*, 2 (1966), 150–61.

4. *The Third Book of Criticism* (New York: Farrar, Straus and Giroux, 1965), pp. 191–231.

5. Marcus, "The Whole Pattern of Robert Frost's 'Two Witches': Contrasting Psychosexual Modes," *Literature and Psychology*, 24, No. 2 (1976), 69–78; "Motivation of Robert Frost's Hired Man," *College Literature*, 3 (Winter 1976), 63–68.

6. "The 'Unconscious' of Literature: The Psychoanalytic Approach," in *Contemporary Criticism*, Stratford-Upon-Avon—Studies 12, ed. Malcolm Bradbury and David Palmer (London: Edward Arnold, 1970), pp. 131–53.

7. *Dynamics of Literary Response,* (New York: Oxford Univ. Press, 1968), p. 33.

8. *Identity and Relationship* (London: Lawrence & Wishart, 1973), pp. 77–82. "Up Against the 'Mending Wall': The Psychoanalysis of a Poem by Frost," *College English*, 34 (April 1973), 934–51.

9. *Childhood and Society*, 2nd ed. (New York: W. W. Norton, 1963), pp. 247–74.

10. *Identity: Youth & Crisis* (New York: W. W. Norton, 1968), pp. 74–90.

Index